SOCRATIC QUESTIONS

SOCRATIC QUESTIONS

New essays on the philosophy of
Socrates and its significance

Edited by
Barry S. Gower and
Michael C. Stokes

London and New York

First published 1992
by Routledge
11 New Fetter Lane, London EC4P 4EE

Simultaneously published in the USA and Canada
by Routledge
a division of Routledge, Chapman and Hall, Inc.
29 West 35th Street, New York, NY 10001

© 1992 Barry S. Gower and Michael C. Stokes

Typeset in 10 on 12 point Garamond by
Falcon Typographic Art Ltd, Fife, Scotland
Printed and bound in Great Britain by
TJ Press (Padstow) Ltd, Padstow, Cornwall

British Library Cataloguing in Publication Data
Socratic questions: new essays on the philosophy
of Socrates and its significance.
I. Gower, Barry S. (Barry Stephen)
II. Stokes, Michael C. (Michael Christopher)
183.2

Library of Congress Cataloging-in-Publication Data
Socratic questions : new essays on the philosophy of Socrates
and its significance / edited by Barry S. Gower and
Michael C. Stokes.
p. cm.
Includes bibliographical references and index.
1. Socrates. I. Gower, Barry. II. Stokes, Michael C.
B317.S64 1992
183'.2 – dc20   91–3986 0   CIP

ISBN 0–415–06931–9

CONTENTS

NOTES ON CONTRIBUTORS

P. J. FITZPATRICK is Emeritus Reader in Philosophy at the University of Durham. He has written extensively on medieval philosophy, and is currently writing a book tracing ideas about transubstantiation.

BARRY GOWER is Senior Lecturer in the Philosophy of Science and Dean of the Faculty of Arts in the University of Durham.

IAN KIDD is Emeritus Professor of Greek at the University of St Andrews. He is the author of *Posidonius* (1972) and of the article 'Socrates' in the *Encyclopedia of Philosophy*.

SPIRO PANAGIOTOU is Associate Professor of Philosophy at McMaster University. He edited *Justice, Law and Method in Plato and Aristotle* (1987) and is the author of numerous articles on Greek philosophy, and especially Plato.

MALCOLM SCHOFIELD is a Fellow of St John's College and Reader in Ancient Philosophy at the University of Cambridge. He is the author of *An Essay on Anaxagoras* (1980), and co-editor of several collections of essays including *Science and Speculation* (1982) and *The Norms of Nature* (1986).

MICHAEL STOKES is Professor of Greek in the University of Durham. He is the author of *One and Many in Presocratic Philosophy* (1971) and of *Plato's Socratic Conversations* (1986). He is currently working on a new edition of Plato's *Apology*.

C.C.W. TAYLOR is a Fellow of Corpus Christi College, Oxford. He is the author of *Plato: Protagoras* (1976, rev. edn 1991), and co-author with J. C. B. Gosling of *The Greeks on Pleasure* (1982).

PREFACE

Socrates is a popular subject, and scholarly opinion about him moves very fast. A book of original studies on diverse aspects of his life, thought and influence accordingly needs no apology. The origin of this one may, however, be explained.

It originates from a series of General Lectures given in the University of Durham in the autumn of 1989, partly in celebration of the organisation of a Joint Honours BA Degree in Greek and Philosophy in the University. Two members of Durham's staff and five distinguished scholars from other universities contributed one lecture each. We arranged the series in the belief, in which we were not disappointed, that such a sequence would interest in the first instance a wide cross-section of the University's staff and students. It was hoped also that eventual publication would appeal to the very large number of people within and outside the universities who without necessarily knowing any Greek take a more than passing interest in the seminal and enigmatic figure of Socrates. With one exception, which we accepted with regret, the lecturers agreed to prepare their scripts for publication, and to our pleasure and gratitude Routledge agreed to consider the collection, furnished with a general introduction, for inclusion in their list.

We have left our contributors as free a hand as possible in the revision of their lectures. Some have kept to the scale of an hour-long oral delivery; others have expanded their presentations well beyond those limits in the interests of a full and fully supported argument or exposition. Any resulting unevenness should be laid at the editors' door; but we are unrepentant, thinking that the problems dealt with vary widely in nature, and that our readers will need and appreciate more extensive guidance on some of them than on others.

The planning and arrangement of the series of lectures was our joint responsibility. In the preparation of the book, B.S.G. did more of the editorial graft than M.C.S., who took the larger share of such critical discussion with some contributors as seemed necessary and possible in the time available; but we are content with joint responsibility also for such things as fall within an editor's purview.

Our References list, we would stress, does not aim at completeness at all. It merely gives details of works referred to compendiously in the body of the book. Those seeking a fuller bibliography are commended to T. C. Brickhouse and N. D. Smith, *Socrates on Trial*, which offers not only an extensive bibliography on Plato's *Apology*, but also a bibliography of relevant bibliographies on Socrates and Plato. Only one point of bibliography deserves mention here: those contributors who sent in their texts with extra-scrupulous punctuality were thereby deprived of an opportunity to consult Gregory Vlastos' 1991 book *Socrates: Ironist and Moral Philosopher*: reference to that book in the notes is accordingly a sign less of virtue than of vice.

It is a pleasure for M.C.S. to thank the Leverhulme Trust most warmly for a Research Grant which enabled him to spend some months of 1990 working with welcome continuity on Plato's *Apology of Socrates*, and for both of us heartily to thank the General Lectures Committee of the University of Durham for its sponsorship and financial support of the original series of lectures. We wish also to thank our contributors for their graceful lectures and their hard and remarkably punctual work.

Durham, August 1991   Barry S. Gower
                                                        Michael C. Stokes

INTRODUCTION[1]

Barry Gower

OPEN

In 399 BC, at the age of seventy, Socrates was accused of subverting
the religious and moral beliefs of his younger fellow citizens. The
precise terms of the accusation have been preserved for us by the
author of a compendium on the lives and doctrines of ancient philosophers, Diogenes Laertius: 'Socrates is a wrongdoer, inasmuch
as he does not believe in the Gods whom the city worships, but
introduces other strange deities; he is also a wrongdoer inasmuch
as he corrupts the young men, and the punishment he has incurred
is death' (Diogenes Laertius II.40). He was tried on this charge,
found guilty and condemned to death by a jury of Athenian
citizens; he was executed in the manner customary at that time
by being obliged to drink poison. Of the life that ended in this
way and of the character of the man who lived it, we know hardly
anything for certain. In itself, the extent of our ignorance is not at
all surprising, for such information as has come down to us about
the lives of people who lived at this or an earlier time is scanty
and unreliable. The art of biography had yet to be cultivated, and
it is very doubtful whether we should think of the descriptions
we possess as essays in that genre. Nevertheless, in the case of
Socrates, the poverty of our knowledge is particularly frustrating
in that he himself left no writings upon which we might hope to
base an impression, and we therefore have to rely upon the vivid
but conflicting versions of the sort of person he was which have
come down to us from people who knew, or knew of, him. These
accounts were not written as documentary records of Socrates' life;
rather they serve as representations of points of view on that life. As
such their purpose was not necessarily so much to inform us of the
facts as to persuade us of an opinion, which may very well not be
that of the historical Socrates. Of course, persuasion needs to have

CONCLUSION

1

some basis in the relevant facts if it is to be effective, but when it is difficult if not impossible to distinguish between fact and literary embellishment, the task of choosing between diverse versions is not at all easy. Thus, from Plato we have more than one flattering portrait of a complex and subtle intellectual; from Xenophon a dull portrait of a leisured worthy; and from Aristophanes a satiric portrait of a silly quibbler. And in the face of these differences, some modern scholars[2] have indeed despaired and drawn the pessimistic conclusion that no version is reliable; the real Socrates, they believe, remains inaccessible to us, and we must be content with a myth. Others, notably Gregory Vlastos,[3] claim that careful and judicious scrutiny of our sources is capable of revealing certain features of the man and of bringing to life a recognisable character with a coherent personal philosophy. No doubt we cannot believe everything we are told, but we are nevertheless able to identify a moral and philosophical personality even if it does reflect those ambiguities which, in any real life, are never entirely resolved.

The difficulty of knowing who, if any, among a variety of characters presented to us by ancient authors is most like the historical Socrates can be illustrated by reference to some of the important differences between those characters. On the one hand we have the fact that Socrates was judged by the majority of a large jury of his fellow citizens to be a criminal deserving death; on the other we have the judgement that he was 'of all those whom we knew in our time, the bravest and also the wisest and most upright man' (Plato, *Phaedo* 118). According to some he was first and foremost a patriotic Athenian committed to the city's democratic constitution and bound by its laws; to others he was above all else the friend, supporter and teacher of treacherous leaders of an anti-democratic faction which brought disaster on the city (the 'accuser' reported by Xenophon, *Memorabilia* I.2.12). He was presented as a sophist earning his living by teaching rhetorical tricks, and parodied as a 'scientific' cosmologist interested in the acquisition of useless trifling knowledge; but he was also portrayed as a worthy but pedestrian moralist, preaching glib sermons – 'the patron-saint of moral twaddle', as Hegel put it. To some he was an unscrupulous corrupter of the young men who witnessed, admired and enjoyed his demolition of traditional and commonplace sets of values and beliefs; to others he was the ideal educator of the young.

In seeking to appreciate how one man could be characterised in such very different ways, we will need to attend to the exceptional political, intellectual and cultural contexts in which Socrates lived. For in the case of each of these contexts we find a tension, a conflict, a dualism, which informs and animates thinking about how the business of life should be conducted. The Socrates we find portrayed, in such diverse terms, by his contemporaries can best be understood as a man sensitive to these tensions, and as trying to live his life in a way that responded creatively to the debates they engendered. Thus we may say that during his life he witnessed both the rise of Athenian political dominance and its subsequent eclipse in military defeat, and like his contemporaries he will have had to understand and come to terms with this phenomenon. How could it have happened that a state committed to democratic institutions came to be seen as tyrannical, not only and understandably by Athens' enemies but also by some Athenians themselves, as evidenced by the description attributed by Thucydides to Pericles of the empire as 'like a tyranny' (Thucydides II.65)? Moreover, partly because of its political and commercial prominence, Athens became in the fifth century BC an intellectual centre where ideas about physical and, especially, moral reality could be debated – ideas many of which have continued to command attention and respect to this day. Skill in devising arguments, which had been cultivated to a high standard by the Ionian natural philosophers and especially by their western Greek critics, as well as by sophists from various parts of the Greek world, made it seem that these ideas could be accepted or rejected, defended or attacked with more or less equal cogency. What was the ordinary citizen expected to think about such matters, especially when they had a bearing on the everyday business of living and working in a city where each person's judgement was supposed to be as good as any other person's? And finally we have the fact that some of these dilemmas, of individual versus community, of old-fashioned belief versus modern rationalism, of Greek versus barbarian, were presented in a particularly disturbing form by dramatists such as Aeschylus, Sophocles and Euripides, who created and sustained a rich literary culture for Athens. Their tragedies were moulded in part by the experience of war, and they saw all too clearly that the inhumanity and violence of war arose from, and was the inevitable consequence of, the exercise of free choice. Should we, people asked, place our faith in a divine order such as that described for us by the poets and seers, or should we turn to the purveyors of human reason – the intellectuals or, if you will, the sophists, and seek the guidance of experts?

3

Our account of Socrates had best begin, not least because it is relatively uncontentious, with his physical appearance. He was not, it seems, a handsome man: a flat nose, protruding eyes and thick sensual lips are mentioned; and in his later years he was, in all probability, both bald and bearded.[4] That, at least, is how he is portrayed in the statues and busts that have become associated with his name. Judged by the high aesthetic standards of late fifth-century BC Athens, he was an ugly man with features his contemporaries would have associated with those of the satyrs they had seen depicted in the theatre. In one of Xenophon's representations of a Socratic conversation (*Symposium* V.1–8), a mock beauty contest is described in which Socrates' clever argument in favour of his less than lovely features is pitted against the aesthetic qualities of the handsome young Critobulus, which have no need of verbal defence. Socrates loses the contest, though he wins the admiration of his fellows for his eloquence and wit. But although not handsome, he seems to have been physically robust, for he is said to have acquitted himself well in those gruelling military campaigns in which he participated. As for his customary clothing, that too was less than respectably conventional, for in a Platonic conversation he is depicted as barefoot and wearing 'the same cloak . . . that he usually wore' (*Symposium* 220a5–b7). He cared, it seems, nothing for his appearance. There are some early sculptures representing Socrates in which we can clearly discern these features, albeit in a softened form.[5]

Socrates was born in Athens and, apart from military service, seems to have spent the whole of his life in that city. His father, Sophroniscus, may have been a stonemason or sculptor; and if Plato's *Theaetetus* is to be believed, his mother, Phaenarete, was a midwife, though it is by no means clear that there was any such profession recognised in Athens at this time. Perhaps indeed this description of her was simply intended as a handy way of introducing the well-known analogy between the art of midwifery and Socrates' own efforts in bringing to light the ideas conceived by his interlocutors. We know nothing at all of Socrates' childhood and youth. He may well have learnt and, in his early years at least, have practised his father's craft, if any. Accounts tell that he was married, perhaps more than once, and at least once rather late in life, for his three sons were all still young at the time of his trial and execution.[6] Whatever financial advantages he may have had in his youth, and whatever effect the supposed aristocratic connections of his wife,

Xanthippe, may have had, Socrates appears to have spent a major part of his life in poverty. Whether deliberately chosen or not, this poverty contributed to the image he created and explains some of the hostility expressed towards him at his trial. For, as Pericles, the leader of the Athenian democrats, had declared, although there is no disgrace in poverty itself, there is real shame in a person not taking practical steps to escape from the clutches of poverty (Thucydides II. 40). There is an echo here of the standards and values of the elite in society, such as those of the Homeric heroes, according to which what really matters is the extent of a person's success in the eyes of his contemporaries and the consequences of this for his standing and reputation in society. Wealth was a significant measure of status, and inherited wealth was associated with a powerful Greek word of commendation – *arete*. To shun even a modicum of wealth seemed to be to court dependence on others, to risk defeat and humiliation and so become a person whose life counts for nothing.[7]

The Athens where Socrates was born and grew up was a free, independent, enterprising, and relatively prosperous city-state, or *polis*. It had recently emerged from a crucial war with Persia in which an alliance of Greek city-states – especially the Athenian fleet and the Spartan army – had triumphed. Much of Athens' growing political power in the middle decades of the fifth century BC derived from its newly developed naval supremacy, which enabled it not only to acquire and exercise some leadership in defence, especially in curbing the Persian threat to the Asiatic Greeks, but also to protect its commercial interests in the Aegean and Asia Minor. An early consequence of the initiative Athens seized after the defeat of the Persian forces in the sea battle of Salamis and the land battle of Plataea, some ten years before Socrates' birth, was its leadership of a league or alliance of Greek city-states. The Ionian cities of the west coast of Asia Minor, together with many of the Aegean islands, were among the prominent members of this league, and at the height of its power there were perhaps as many as two hundred city-states throughout the Greek world which had, with varying degrees of enthusiasm, joined. Its original purpose was to promote and enable aggressive campaigns against remaining centres of Persian power in the northern Aegean and in the eastern Mediterranean, and there can be no doubt that its success in this led to a significant consolidation of Greek power. But the alliance was even more successful in promoting the political ambitions and economic prosperity of Athens itself. For not only was the political hegemony of Athens in the relevant area unchallenged, but the economic control and management of the league was largely in the hands of Athenian officials. In the early years, each of the allies officially had an equal say in the determination of policy, but this equality was steadily eroded by treaties and other administrative measures drawn up in such a way that, collectively, they benefited Athens and undermined the independence of the allies.

One victim of the Athenian imperialism which this process promoted was the island of Samos, close to the western coast of present-day Turkey, and the birthplace of Pythagoras. In 440 BC this important Ionian ally attempted to secede from the league on account of unwanted Athenian intervention in a quarrel between Samos and Miletus, a city-state on the nearby mainland. The conflict that followed led to the suppression of Samian independence by the imposition of an Athenian garrison. There are some not altogether reliable indications that Socrates, then aged 30 or so, participated in the Samian campaign. If he did, then he would have been in illustrious company, for the dramatist Sophocles had been elected as one of the military commanders of the Athenian expeditionary force, and on the opposing side an important member of the Eleatic school of critics of natural philosophy, Melissus, was commanding the Samian navy – or so later sources tell us.

We have clearer evidence for Socrates' participation in a later campaign, of 432 BC, to subdue the revolt of another member of the Delian league, Potidaea – a city-state on the northern shores of the Aegean. The episode is described by the historian Thucydides, who counts it as an important incident leading to the outbreak of the Peloponnesian War. If, as Plato reports in his *Apology*, Socrates took part in this campaign, then it is very likely that he would have been present as a 'hoplite', i.e. as a heavily armed infantryman. Athenian citizens of moderate wealth were expected to serve when required in this capacity and would equip themselves with body-armour, a shield, an iron sword and a spear. He would have been in his late thirties at this time, and we have an account of Socrates' role which lays great stress on his powers of endurance (Plato, *Symposium* 219e5–220e7). But although Plato is our best witness on this matter, we cannot be altogether confident that Socrates took part in the campaign at all, for if he did, it is puzzling that the fact is not mentioned by Xenophon, who, as a soldier, would have wanted to draw attention to his hero's military exploits.

Whether direct or indirect, Socrates' experience of the effects of

Athens' aggressive foreign policy in these years before the outbreak of the Peloponnesian War will have made it plain to him that, as a result of exploitation of its controlling position, the allies had become little more than subjects whose dissent or discontent was ruthlessly suppressed. The alliance had become an empire; an arrangement created to foster the common objectives of free, equal and independent city-states had turned them into clients of a single imperial power. But while this had been taking place, the old rival, Sparta, leader of the Peloponnesian alliance of city-states, had been aware of Athenian power, and when those Spartan allies, such as Corinth, who saw themselves as victims of that power sought aid, it found the pressure to oppose the military aggression of Athens and to check its political ambition irresistible. Athens, for its part, had become committed to the new social and cultural ideals it had fostered. Defeat would entail abandoning those ideals; it would threaten, in particular, the autonomy and integrity of Athens itself, acting in accordance with decisions taken by free male adult citizens. Pericles, in his famous 'funeral oration' early in the war with Sparta, emphasised the differences between Athenians and other Greeks. What was common to the Greeks – their language, their history, their religion, their literature – was seen by him as less significant than what divided them. The democratic freedoms enjoyed by Athenian citizens, the success of the policies pursued by the elected leaders, and the cultural supremacy of the city were, he claimed, at risk. Athens could brook no challenge to its rightful position as the dominant city-state, since this position had been earned and sustained by the free actions of its citizens. In its view, the community of Greek city-states was a community of competitors. Power, influence and ability were what mattered in the dealings of the states with each other, as we can see from the terms in which the Athenians later addressed their rebellious opponents in the chilling Melian dialogue recorded by Thucydides: 'the standard of justice depends on the equality of power to compel and . . . in fact the strong do what they have the power to do and the weak accept what they have to accept' (Thucydides V. 89). It is as though the self-regarding tyrannical attitude adopted by Athens in its relations with neighbouring city-states, whether friend or foe, was a natural and inevitable, but contrasting, companion to the other-regarding democratic attitude cultivated, though not altogether successfully, within Athens itself.

The Peloponnesian War began directly after the start of the

campaign at Potidaea. It lasted, with varying degrees of intensity, for some twenty-seven years. Plato reports that Socrates fought in the war at Delium in 424 BC, and at Amphipolis two years later. By then he was in his middle to late forties and had acquired enough of a reputation as an intellectual to enable the playwright Aristophanes to satirise him in his comedy *The Clouds*, first produced at about this time. At Delium, near the borders of Attica and therefore quite close to Athens itself, the Athenian army was roundly defeated by Spartan allies. Socrates' tranquil bearing and fortitude during the subsequent retreat are described in flattering terms in two Platonic dialogues by characters representing the distinguished soldier, Laches and the scheming aristocrat, Alcibiades.[8] Amphipolis was a city of political and economic importance near the Thracian coast. Founded on the site of a former Thracian town as an Athenian colony earlier in the fifth century, it surrendered to a Spartan force in 424 BC, and Plato's Socrates says he was involved in the subsequent unsuccessful attempt to restore Athenian control.

Apart from some incidental references to him by the comic dramatists, we next learn of Socrates in 406 BC, some two years before the end of the Peloponnesian War. The Athenian navy had been victorious in a battle against Sparta and its allies at the Arginusae islands near the Ionian coast south of the island of Lesbos. Losses, though, were very heavy, partly because a storm prevented the rescue of many shipwrecked seamen. When news of the battle and its outcome reached Athens, it was these losses rather than the victory itself which were seen as the chief issue. Those held to be responsible – the commanders of the fleet – were accused of negligence. In the prosecution, under pressure from those insisting that action be taken against the commanders, the procedure adopted was a trial of the commanders as a group. Socrates, serving his turn as a member of the Presiding Committee of the Athenian Council at the time, objected on the grounds that it was illegal to prosecute groups of individuals. Feelings ran so high, particularly on the part of those bereaved, about the negligence of the commanders, that to express and maintain such an objection required considerable obstinacy and, indeed, courage. Socrates' stand in refusing to be intimidated was later seen to have been correct.[9]

At the close of the Peloponnesian War in 404 BC Athens was a defeated city, its inhabitants demoralised, its economy in disarray and its empire dismantled. Plague and famine, as well as military attrition, had taken their toll. The wisdom of democratic rule, with its reputation for indecision, fickleness and delay, was questioned, and for a period it was replaced, as it had been briefly during the war, by an oligarchic system of government after the model familiar to those city-states which had adopted something more like the Spartan way of managing political affairs. Some Athenians welcomed this change even though it abrogated the rights they had enjoyed under the democracy (Plato, *Seventh Letter* 324b-d), but the victorious Spartans obliged the Athenians to select thirty men to be responsible for the affairs of the city. In the chaos and confusion which followed the end of the war, their rule – of Thirty Tyrants, as they came to be called – became a reign of terror. With the help of a garrison from Sparta they imposed their brutal will on the city by sheer force of arms. Many democrats lost their lives; others fled to the countryside or to neighbouring cities, where they were able to regroup and gather reinforcements. Civil war erupted and eventually, in 403 BC, the authority of the Tyrants was broken and democracy restored. Some among the Thirty Tyrants had been acquaintances, at least, of Socrates – now in his sixties. And just as in the episode following the battle of Arginusae he displayed determination in repudiating illegalities perpetrated by a democratic Athens, so Plato's Socrates in the *Apology* reports – and the story is repeated in Plato's *Seventh Letter* – a similar determination to resist attempts on the part of the Thirty to implicate him in the unjust actions of a dictatorship. The Thirty had, it seems, ordered Socrates and others to arrest and return to Athens for execution a certain Leon of Salamis. Socrates refused to obey, thereby challenging the authority of the oligarchy in a very direct manner, and had the democracy not been restored so swiftly, he might well have paid for his disobedience with his life. Here again, though, there is a question about the historical authenticity of the report, for one can doubt whether Socrates' disobedience was followed sufficiently swiftly by the restored democracy to exempt him from any penalty.

How should we imagine Socrates using his time and energy when not serving the city in some official or military capacity? As a teacher, certainly, though a wholly unofficial one who in Plato's dialogues disowns the title. But it would be hard to say with confidence what he taught without presuming on the reliability of one or other of our sources of conflicting information. If the philosopher Plato is to be believed, his chief lesson was that in order to live and act rightly we must set aside the time-honoured teachings of tradition as unexamined and inconsistent, and acquire instead an education which brings together morality and rationality. If the comic playwright Aristophanes is to be relied on – and his characterisation, or rather caricature, does have the merit of being the earliest surviving record – then Socrates combined the attributes of a sophistic teacher of rhetoric with those of a natural philosopher, and in urging the claims of intellect and expertise was challenging the religious and some of the moral conventions which were embedded in, and which sustained, stable social relations in the *polis*. But however one describes the content of his teaching, he apparently acquired a group of followers, men – probably mostly young – intent on learning something useful from their association with him. No doubt some will have wanted to satisfy a natural curiosity, or simply to enjoy listening to an eloquent and forceful arguer. Others will have had a more direct practical motive, for they wanted to learn those tips, tricks and tactics which enabled an ambitious person to cultivate the art of speaking well in political debates and forensic enquiries. Effective speaking was the key to power in democratic Athens, and power was of increasing importance in the face of instability created by war and civil unrest. Socrates' own skills in persuading others that a certain view should, or should not, be accepted can hardly be doubted. It is not surprising, therefore, that he was thought of among many if not most of his fellow citizens as a sophist, i.e. as one who earned a living and a reputation by teaching others how to use reason and argument to secure success in private and public affairs.

For present purposes the justice of this reputation as a sophist, though as hotly disputed now as it was during and after Socrates' lifetime, matters less than its nature. Plato was indeed intent upon putting as much distance as he could between Socratic philosophy and the sophistry with which he thought it was confused, and historically he may well have been right to do so. But if we are to appreciate the ambiguities present in the intellectual as well as the political context of Socrates' life, we need to have some understanding of who the sophists were, of what they believed and, especially, of the ambivalent attitude of Athenians towards them and their influence.

The sophists as a group of intellectuals probably began to emerge during the middle years of the fifth century, when the Greek word describing these people – *sophistes* – was perhaps, though it is hard to find clear evidence, starting to acquire the unfavourable tone associated with the English 'sophistry'.[10] Previously, the word would simply have been used to describe an expert, and was applied in that sense to poets, rhapsodes and seers, because they were skilled in the craft of using words. The sophists whom Socrates would have heard of and probably met, men such as Protagoras, Gorgias, Prodicus, Hippias and Thrasymachus, were – in the absence of any regular education for the young men of the city – professional educators with a select group of pupils or followers paying for their instruction. They did not constitute a school of thought, for they were not bound by allegiances to common doctrines. They were, rather, exceptional individuals who were able, in the social and political circumstances prevailing in Athens in the second half of the fifth century, to exert a significant influence. For those circumstances created a demand for the service they were able to offer, which was, to put no finer point on it, instruction in how best to get one's way. Much of our information about them, their activities and their views comes to us from Plato, who presents them as characters in his Socratic dialogues. Their encounters with Socrates invariably end in defeat for them, though usually they are allowed to withdraw with some dignity and grace. In so far as we can identify a subject-matter for their teaching, it would be political skill, forensic eloquence and practical sagacity with respect to personal affairs – all of them valuable accomplishments for any ambitious young Athenian. Though most of the sophists were not citizens of Athens, that city became their intellectual home, for they found lucrative employment there for their talents, and it is there, too, that the effects of their teaching are most visible to us.

A number of moral and political ideas which have pervaded Western thought originated with the sophists, and history leaves us in no doubt that their impact has been both unsettling and powerful. Thus, the ideas that ethical values are relative to a particular time and place, that because virtue, or excellence – *arete* – can be taught, education will make us better people, and that what people call justice in society is what is in the best interests of those who are the strongest – these are ideas whose influence and effect on our lives can still be felt. Then as now, justice or fairness might seem to some to rest on desert – on their contribution to, and merit in, society; others might prefer to think of justice as equality. There is evidence of both views by the time of Socrates' maturity, and it may be that the manner in which Socrates invited individual Athenians to consider these views, in so far as it depended on reason rather than the authority of custom, was considered subversive of received beliefs. But at a time of social ferment and upheaval, when a consensus about values is hard to maintain, beliefs without *logoi* – or reason – are vulnerable. In a culture which prides itself on its intellectual as well as its artistic character, moral beliefs which lack rational justification will not command that allegiance which would enable them to survive social and political change of the kind that was overtaking Athens in the last quarter of the fifth century.

But although these foreigners enhanced the city's reputation for intellectual excellence, by no means all Athenians welcomed their presence in the city, for apart from the Athenians' suspicion of alien influence on the minds and characters of the young men who were the sophists' clients, they were alert to the fact that cleverness in speech and argument could be, and often was, used for bad rather than good ends. The ability of these professional pundits to manipulate people's attitudes and beliefs with words was widely distrusted; sophists were like conjurors performing tricks with words, or like poets, indeed, beguiling hearers and readers with verbal images. True, there were some who admired the skill with which the magic was performed, but there were many more who deplored the deception it could promote. The art of making the weaker argument appear the stronger has, no doubt, merit as well as use when the weaker argument delivers a true conclusion, but it can also be used, quite deliberately, to undermine or obscure the truth. At a time of political instability, a sophist's willingness to sell his skills to the highest bidder was seen by some as the cynical act of a corrupt intellectual, representing a real and immediate threat to the city.[11] No wonder, then, that some characters in Plato's dialogues are made to express vehement hostility to the activities and influence of sophists; none more so than Anytus in the *Meno*, who was a democratic politician and one of Socrates' accusers.

The fact that Socrates is represented, by Plato at least, as disagreeing with each of the sophists he meets does not, in itself, show that he himself was not one of them. Indeed, in so far as he sustains his disagreements by an appeal to the intellect of his interlocutors, rather than to tradition as an adequate guide to right conduct, he could well be said to count as a sophist. If there is no such thing as a coherent sophistic doctrine, then the reason for wishing to exclude Socrates from their number must lie deeper than his disagreement with them individually. And it seems clear that Plato's Socrates did hold that certain features of the sophists' method, style and approach were unacceptable. But from the point of view of his fellow citizens, what was distinctive about Socrates was his general view about the relationship between morality and culture – a view he can be said to have shared with the sophists and which was widely understood as threatening to the stability of society.[12] For whatever might be said about their coherence and rationality, the attitudes and values which had sustained Athens and promoted its political success prior to the influence of the sophists becoming established were those which had stood the test of time and had proved their worth in practice. Products of this traditional model of moral education may have been confused in their ethical suppositions, but nevertheless they were robust in body and mind, they were courageous and successful, and they were, moreover, intolerant of those who sought to overturn and replace the instinctive natural beliefs of patriotic Athenians. Some of the more conspicuous sophists had invited their pupils and followers to question this model – to dispute and to doubt the rationality of its unexamined assumptions. Clarity, they thought, must replace confusion in order that people may see what must be done to achieve their aims. But to right-minded Athenians, the sophists – including Socrates – were nothing but quibblers deceiving young and inexperienced people with a web of words in an attempt to persuade them to abandon sets of beliefs, ideals and values which had been so painstakingly built up over time. For them, the loss of these was an important cause of the decline, defeat and near destruction of a justifiably proud city.

Here too, then, we find a creative tension. Personal liberty and autonomy were prized attributes of the Athenian democratic culture. Yet beliefs and attitudes which were perceived as posing a threat to democracy could not be allowed to flourish. In particular, prejudice against the intellectualism of the sophists on account of its threat to familiar and trusted moral ideals became prominent. But this intolerance and anger, however understandable, itself represented a danger to the democracy. Socrates, far from being exempt from this conflict, was subject to it in a direct manner. In accusing him of corrupting the moral values of young men, his prosecutors were, in effect, objecting to the manner in which he, together with the sophists, had in their view abused and exploited the responsibilities of a citizen in order to undermine the very basis of the democracy. On the other hand, those prosecutors in their attempt to silence Socrates were themselves mounting an attack which was potentially at least as damaging to the democracy. Socrates, for his part, had long been aware of the serious and substantial nature of this kind of criticism, for it is clearly represented in Aristophanes' comedy *The Clouds*, written and performed during his lifetime. In Plato's *Apology* he refers to the allegation as an old slander which he must try to answer in order to deflect a long-standing prejudice against him and his activities. He would also have been aware of the damage to the fabric of a democracy which would result if that accusation, together with the official charges brought against him by his prosecutors, were to remain unchallenged. For Socrates, the freedom to pursue his mission and to engage in rational enquiry whomsoever he will, even including rational enquiry respecting the moral basis of society, cannot be curtailed without risk to the character of that society.

We come, then, to the final events in Socrates' life – his trial, imprisonment and execution. They overshadow all other events in his life, not just because they were at a personal level of the greatest moment, but also because their significance for our understanding of Socrates' life has remained controversial. Some have claimed that in these events we see simply a brutal but not especially remarkable response to a charismatic personality whose posturings had become too tiresome to be tolerated. The disaster of war had shown that lives are cheap, and this life, persistently irritating in its effect on others, was surely expendable. Others have discerned powerful political motives propelling Socrates to his death. His alleged oligarchic sympathies, and his association with leaders of the infamous tyranny, could be neither forgotten nor forgiven. The official charges are on this view no more than plausible but transparent substitutes for the banned charge of treason against the democracy. Still others see the events as a monstrous mistake engineered by Socrates himself in the belief that the time had come to make his claims about how a person should live more prominent in the city, even if this should mean that he would encounter overwhelming opposition and anger.

This is not the place to attempt a resolution of this controversy, depending as it does upon some nice judgements respecting the nature and reliability of the evidence available to us. For present purposes, we must rely on attested facts, even if that provides only a partial and sketchy account of the events in question.

By 399 BC, five years after the end of the Peloponnesian War and the subsequent tyranny, Athenian citizens were able to exercise their democratic rights and freedoms once more. The administration of the city was in the hands of an assembly of all its citizens, and the rule of law which was intended to secure justice for those citizens was restored. In the interests of a secure peace, new legislation had recently been introduced as a result of the decision that no one should be charged with offences alleged to have been committed before or during the dictatorship of the Thirty Tyrants. This amnesty, an attempt to provide a new beginning, was widely welcomed as a necessary first step towards reconciliation, but coming so soon after the calamities of defeat and tyranny, it could not altogether eliminate fear and suspicion. Anti-democratic sentiments, together with the practices thought to have encouraged their growth, were resented and distrusted. There would be many still grieving for family and friends who had become victims of civil strife, and many, too, anxiously facing an uncertain future. There were certainly some seeking redress for past wrongs, whether real or imaginary, and probably some determined to promote change in past attitudes in the hope of preventing a repetition of recent events.

We can do little more than guess at the reasons why charges of impiety and of corrupting young men were brought forward at the time they were. There is no firm evidence, or reason to believe, that Socrates had at this time begun to behave differently, which might justify a different and less tolerant attitude on the part of his fellow citizens. So far as we can tell, his questioning manner was still regarded by many as tiresomely persistent, and his severity with received but unexamined answers continued to be seen as destructively critical. It may be, indeed, that it was his failure to change his manner when so much else of significance for people's lives had changed that provoked the action taken by his prosecutors. For it is one thing to question and to criticise the values and assumptions of a previous generation, especially when the mistakes of that generation are plain for all to see and feel; but it is another and altogether more culpable matter to continue questioning and criticising as though nothing of importance had changed for the better.

The procedure that Socrates' prosecutors would have had to follow was to present their case in the first place to an elected magistrate with responsibility for dealing with the kind of charges mentioned in the indictment. In this case, because the overt basis of the charges was impiety and disrespect for acknowledged divinities, the initial enquiry would have been before the magistrate responsible for cases with a connection with religion – the *archon basileus* or King Archon, as he was called. In effect, this magistrate decided whether the crime with which Socrates was charged and the weight of the evidence that he was guilty of that crime were of sufficient substance to warrant a trial by jury. We know nothing of this aspect of the proceedings against Socrates, though it should be mentioned that Plato's *Euthyphro*, which is a dialogue about the nature of piety, opens with a scene in which Socrates is about to appear before the King Archon at the preliminary enquiry to answer charges brought by Meletus, here as elsewhere the principal prosecutor in law. Evidently, though, it was decided that the case should be heard by a jury which would determine the guilt or innocence of Socrates, and, since there was no fixed penalty for the crimes with which he was charged, also decide according to established procedure what punishment, if any, was appropriate. As in all cases decided by juries, there was no appeal against the decisions reached. In part, at least, this was because historically trial by jury was itself conceived as constituting an appeal against a magistrate's verdict.[13]

Athenian juries consisted of citizens who were expected to volunteer for this service. At the beginning of each year, several thousand volunteers of at least 30 years of age were chosen, and from this number juries to hear particular cases were formed as and when they were needed. The size of a jury could vary, depending on the nature and importance of the case to be considered, from several hundred to a few thousand. We do not know how jurors were allocated to courts; it may have been by lot, though such a procedure had not been formally adopted at the time of Socrates' trial. In order that poorer citizens should not be practically prevented from serving, each juror was given a small payment per day for his trouble. However, since the payment was less than could be earned by an able-bodied man, a substantial proportion of those who volunteered for the work were men who were too old for work. This circumstance may well have had some bearing on the outcome of the trial. Jurors were required to take an oath obliging them to determine guilt or innocence in accordance with the evidence presented and with the laws of the city; no such requirement was, it seems, imposed on the prosecutor or defendant.

Socrates' trial would have been held in public and would probably have been presided over by the King Archon. The role of the president was simply to keep order and allow prosecutor and defendant to be heard; unlike a modern judge he did not advise the jury on matters of interpretation or of law, nor did he provide any kind of summing up. He might, though, have been assisted by an official who would read out relevant laws or other public documents. Prosecutor and defendant would each be allowed an equal amount of time to present their cases *in propria persona*. They could, within these time-limits, call witnesses, or rather have their testimony read to the court, to support their cases. Since all jury trials had to be completed within the space of one day, the speeches of the litigants and their supporters cannot have been very long. Two or three hours for the presentation of the prosecution, and the same amount of time for the defence, is perhaps a reasonable estimate.[14]

In the case of the trial of Socrates, although we know what the charges were, we do not know what the prosecution said in support of its allegations. The chief prosecutor appears to have been Meletus, aided by two supporters – Anytus and Lycon. For different reasons, we know little or nothing reliable about either Meletus (who seems, however, from *Apology* 23e to have been a poet)[15] or Lycon, but Anytus seems to have been a man of some political influence. Anytus features as a character in Plato's dialogue *Meno*, and if his treatment by Socrates there is anything like any actual encounter between the two men, we can easily understand why he wanted to expose Socrates' activities to public scrutiny and criticism. On the other hand, two rather different versions from among several composed in the fourth century BC of what Socrates is alleged to have said in his defence have survived. The reliability of each is questionable, though Plato's version – the *Apology* – is often taken as a reasonably faithful reconstruction of what Socrates said, if not as a word-for-word transcript of the speeches he made in his defence. Xenophon's *Apology* is written in the form of a second-hand account, and such claims as it makes for authenticity are weak. Plato writes of himself as having been present at Socrates' trial, whereas Xenophon was in Asia at the time. Accordingly, scholars commonly suppose that Xenophon's version was written later than Plato's, and probably with knowledge of its contents. Neither writer tells of any testimonies being read to the court, so if there were any, we remain ignorant of their content. Unless we take our ignorance to imply that no testimony was provided, we should be wary of any inference we might draw from the omission of some relevant point in a representation of Socrates' defence, even supposing it to be accurate.

According to Plato's *Apology*, the vote taken at the end of Socrates' speech in his defence was close. He was found guilty of the charges by a narrow majority, though just how small it was is hard to judge in the confused state of our information about the total size of the jury.[16] Five hundred jurymen is commonly suggested on the basis of some slender evidence, and this would fit well with the claim of Plato's Socrates that had only thirty votes gone the other way, a majority of the jury would have judged him innocent of the charges. As it was, though, the jury now faced the task of determining a penalty. By law they could not, themselves, discuss alternative penalties and propose that which seemed the most appropriate. They could not even compromise; rather, they had to choose between the penalty proposed by the successful prosecutors and that proposed by the unsuccessful defendant. Meletus evidently suggested that death be the penalty, though again we lack any report of what he said in support of his proposal. Defendants in Socrates' position, facing the prospect of that penalty, were presented with a very difficult decision, for it would be vitally important that their counter-proposal should not be judged too lenient. Plato provides us with a version of the reasoning which eventually led Socrates to his counter-proposal of a financial penalty – much the commonest kind of penalty imposed upon unsuccessful defendants. It was, though, rejected as over-lenient, perhaps because of his evident reluctance to propose a penalty at all and indeed because of his provocative initial claim that what he deserved was reward rather than punishment. It could be that Socrates was expecting, reasonably enough, that none of the jury who voted for his acquittal would now vote for his death, and that a sufficient number of those who had voted for his condemnation would, especially in the light of a close vote, baulk at imposing the heavier sentence.[17]

As Plato describes it, the decision of the jury in favour of the death penalty is followed by a third and final speech from Socrates. There is no other example of such a final speech from this period of Greek history and we may, therefore, be reading no more than a Platonic fiction. It has, perhaps, the air of a considered and rehearsed conclusion, in that it addresses both those men of the jury who voted against him and those who voted for him, drawing attention to the consequences for them as well as for himself of their decision. On the other hand it conveys a vehemence and passion appropriate to the circumstances we are asked to imagine, as indeed one would expect from Plato, whatever our judgement respecting the authenticity of his version.

Normally, the sentence of the court would have been carried out directly after the jury's decision. However, according to Plato, the day before the trial marked the beginning of an important annual event for Athenians. For this was the time of the year when the city dispatched a ship to Delos in order to renew its thanks to Apollo for the safe return from Crete of the legendary hero Theseus together with his young companions. No public executions were permitted until this ship returned to Athens, and for this period of time Socrates was detained in prison. Two of Plato's dialogues, the *Crito* and the *Phaedo*, are set within the prison, and in the latter we are given the impression that a considerable amount of time elapsed before the sentence could be carried out. The final hours of Socrates' life are memorably described in the final pages of the *Phaedo*. It is not likely that we shall ever be in a position to judge the veracity of Plato's description, though there is some medical evidence that Plato improved on reality.[18] But in an important way, our uncertainty does not matter, for it is above all the literary qualities of that simple and straightforward description which have so successfully captured the imaginations of readers and remained in their memories. Plato's rare gift for conveying the life and vigour of philosophical ideas and for embodying them so vividly in the character as well as the words of his Socrates overshadows the doubts and debates among historians about the relationship between his Socrates and the real Socrates.

Each of the following chapters in this book takes the portrait of Socrates that Plato provided as its starting point. More particularly, there is a group of dialogues which scholars believe to have been composed early in Plato's career which display certain affinities with each other, and which are thought to portray at least some important aspects of the character and ideas of the historical Socrates. Among these early dialogues are listed *Apology, Charmides, Crito, Euthyphro, Gorgias, Laches, Protagoras, Republic* I and, probably, *Meno*. It is to these dialogues that the contributors have turned for their subject-matter. Certain other dialogues, of the so-called 'middle period' – including *Phaedo, Symposium, Theaetetus* and the other books of *Republic* – also feature a character called 'Socrates' and may well contain information which is authentic. But if Aristotle's views on the difference between Socrates and Plato are to count for anything, particularly with regard to the use of the theory of Forms, much of what 'Socrates' is made to say in these dialogues must be fabricated, and we should think of

'Socrates' at least there as no more than a mouthpiece for Plato's own ideas and arguments.

Michael Stokes' chapter focusses our attention on Socrates' declaration in the *Apology* that he has been charged by the god Apollo through his Oracle with a mission to the citizens of Athens. This 'mission' constitutes a dominant theme of Socrates' defence against the charge of impiety. Stokes subjects to critical scrutiny Plato's version of the reasoning which led Socrates to believe he had such a mission. Socrates makes out that his appointed task is to demonstrate to the Athenian citizenry the falsity of their claims to know truths of real value. Needless to say, Plato's picture of Socrates as undertaking this task is one of a deeply unpopular man; but short of a perverse courting of unpopularity, no immediately obvious reason connects it with Apollo's pronouncement that no man is wiser than Socrates. Curiosity may certainly have motivated Socrates' enquiries in part; but the nature of the obligation on Socrates to pursue them so steadfastly remains obscure. Stokes brings historical and literary, as well as philosophical and logical, considerations to bear in a sustained investigation of this and related questions which is intricate in its details and far-reaching in its implications. These are significant not only for Socrates' thinking but also for the general status, whether fact, fiction or 'faction', of the early Platonic dialogues.

Propounding a view of the dialogues as 'faction', the following chapter, by Ian Kidd, considers how Plato's Socrates used questions in order to further his mission. Opposed to a view of Socrates' questions as merely eliciting the respondent's opinions with a view to confounding them, Kidd argues that by appreciating the directive and guiding character of Socrates' questions we are enabled to see that something positive emerges from the apparently negative questioning process, or 'elenchus'. In the *Laches*, a dialogue which addresses the question 'What is courage?', two eminent and successful military leaders – Laches and Nicias – are quizzed; for they, if anyone, should be able to provide the right answer to such a question. Their attempts to answer lead under Socrates' questioning to the recognition that their answers are incompatible with other beliefs they hold. They do not, then, know about courage what they – and we – thought they knew. With this recognition of ignorance the dialogue comes to a seemingly negative end. Readers are, however, challenged to do better than Laches and Nicias, though it is clear from the form which the enquiry has taken in the dialogue that the difficulties they encountered were not simply the result of carelessness, or impatience, or lack of intelligence. But dramatic and literary structure here, as in some other dialogues of Plato's early period, provide the responsive reader with evidence of positive views being advanced by Plato's Socrates. For Plato has designed Socrates' questions not only to lead Socrates' interlocutors to the recognition that they are as ignorant as he, but to guide first the conversation within the dialogue and secondly the reader to an improved understanding, and ultimately perhaps knowledge, of positive answers to the fundamental questions with which Socrates starts.

Plato's Socrates evidently conceives of his mission to acquaint his fellow citizens with the extent of their ignorance as having a positive moral character. In the *Apology* he faces the prospect of punishment for persisting in his attempts to carry out his orders, to meet what he sees as his moral obligations. He tries, unsuccessfully, to persuade the jury that he of all people is not guilty of impiety and that he should be rewarded rather than punished. The jury decides that he *is* guilty and that his punishment is to be death. What, though, is to be said and done by those who think, with Socrates, that the jury's decision – in effect the majority decision of Athenian citizens – was wrong and unjust? This is the question that taxes Socrates and Crito in the conversation that Plato describes as taking place in prison near the end of the interval between Socrates' condemnation and his death. It is a practical, not this time a theoretical question, given urgency by the fact that Crito and his friends can arrange for Socrates to escape from prison and thus avoid the unjust penalty. The conversation occupies the dialogue *Crito*. Spiro Panagiotou's chapter examines the responses given there to the question about obedience to unjust laws and decisions. Once again the suggestion is that the direction in which the reader is led may not be immediately apparent. The dialogue contains a powerful argument to the effect that to disobey, after one has tried and failed to persuade the state, is always wrong. The fact that Plato makes Socrates put this argument in the mouth of the laws of Athens and direct it against Crito as well as himself has encouraged the attribution of the argument to Socrates himself, or at least to Plato's Socrates. There is, though, a well-known and much-discussed difficulty with this: the Socrates of the *Apology* says that if the jury were to order him to desist from his mission, he would disobey. Such an inconsistency cannot be tolerated if we hope to learn anything, however tentatively, from these sources. Panagiotou's proposals and arguments indicate a way in which inconsistency can be avoided. Plato's Socrates, on Panagiotou's view, is to be distinguished from the personified laws of Athens; the Socrates of the *Crito* does allow that civil disobedience on the part of a virtuous citizen is possible, and in the hypothetical circumstances described in the *Apology*, Socrates would be disobeying virtuously. On the other hand, virtue and civil disobedience cannot be so readily combined as Crito supposes; in particular, escape from prison for Socrates would not be a case of virtuous disobedience.

What, though, is it to be virtuous? Needless to say, that is not a question Plato's Socrates neglected to ask whenever the occasion warranted. One such occasion was that on which he encountered the famous sophist Protagoras. The dialogue in which the episode is recounted is named after the sophist; it displays a level of literary and philosophical sophistication appropriate not only to the intellectual calibre of its author but also to that of its principal protagonists. Malcolm Schofield's chapter draws attention to some significant but neglected aspects of the dialogue's literary character, especially those relating to the presentation of the encounter with Protagoras within the framework of an introductory conversation. This allows for some instructive contrasts between the cooperative character of what Schofield argues to be a genuine philosophical discourse, and the competitive nature of a sophistic debate. Hippocrates – not the doctor, but a young well-off Athenian – is led gently and helpfully by a paradigmatic Socratic elenchus to recognise his ignorance; the distinguished Protagoras is pushed and bullied by a questionable Socratic elenchus until he acknowledges his defeat. True philosophy, it seems, in so far as it depends on cooperative enquiry, cannot emerge from discourse with sophists. As Schofield indicates, however, there is one issue on which the sophists and Socrates can make common cause. For both agree that reason and argument rather than intuition and custom must inform our understanding of moral obligation. Protagoras and Socrates were both promoters of an unsettling intellectualism and can therefore undertake what sets out, at least, as a cooperative enquiry into the consequences of the view that virtue and knowledge are bound together.

C. C. W. Taylor's chapter, though focussed on the *Meno* rather than the *Protagoras*, is directly concerned with those consequences – the so-called 'Socratic paradoxes'. Can a person's knowledge of what is right really ensure that he or she will do what is right? And can it be correct to deny the possibility of akrasia or weakness of will, so that a person can never do wrong intentionally? To both of these questions Socrates' answer, 'Yes', has seemed puzzling and paradoxical, for it is not hard to think of examples which appear to demonstrate that he is mistaken. The clue to understanding these paradoxes, Taylor says, lies in a proper appreciation of their basis, namely Socratic definitions. We can say what virtue or excellence (*arete*) is, either by specifying what we take to be its component parts, if any, or by giving an account or theory of how a person comes, in practice, to possess virtue or excellence. The former – a conceptual elucidation – will say what kinds of actions or characteristics can be taken as indicative of excellence, but it need not entail any practical advice as to how excellence may be acquired. For such advice we do better to turn to the latter kind of definition – an explanatory account – for that will provide a theory of what it is that is manifested in any action or characteristic we can correctly call 'excellent', i.e. conducive to the best sort of life. In Socrates' view, according to Plato's representation of him in the *Meno* as well as other Socratic dialogues, an explanatory account of excellence is bound, for reasons of moral psychology, to link it with some cognitive state, so that whenever a person displays excellence, he or she manifests that cognitive state. Such an account will imply that there is some sense in which nothing more than the cognitive grasp of what is excellent is needed to motivate a person to do or to be what is excellent. And from this it is but a short step to the denial of weakness of will, i.e. to the view that a person's cognitive grasp of what is morally right is sufficient to ensure that that person will do what is morally right. It is accomplished with the aid of the claim, argued for so vigorously in the *Gorgias*, that what is genuinely excellent for a person and conducive to the best sort of life for him or her always coincides with what is morally right. In practical terms, then, Socrates' 'Cognitive Theory of Value' implies that we must strive to rid ourselves of our ignorance if we are to begin to live a life that is worth living.

In the final chapter in this volume P. J. FitzPatrick tells us something of the way in which philosophers, theologians, poets and artists have responded over the centuries to this Socrates, portrayed so subtly and effectively by Plato, who offers advice as startling, as important and as urgent as it is practical. To be sure, it is no easy task to distinguish between responses to Plato's Socrates and responses to Plato himself, particularly during that long period when so few of the relevant texts were available. It was, perhaps, inevitable that, at least to begin with, the main focus of attention was Socrates' trial and death, and thus that comparisons would be made and contrasts drawn between Socrates and the figure of Christ. Indeed, this study of Socrates' legacy is, in large part, a study of the complex interplay between pagan philosophy and Christian theology, an interplay which was affected by the texts available and by the wish to assimilate Socrates to what was regarded as the standard of goodness. Nevertheless, despite our dependence on Plato for our knowledge of Socrates, he has somehow resisted assimilation and incorporation into a creed more successfully than other philosophers, including Plato. Many theologians as well as philosophers can be happily and correctly described as Platonists or Aristotelians by virtue of the ideas or doctrines they adopt, whereas it would be sheer presumption to describe anyone as 'Socratic' unless one wished to use that term merely as a label for direct followers or disciples of Socrates. It is true that in one sense we are all 'Socratic' in so far as we think that reasoned discussion can bring enlightenment; but in another sense no one can be 'Socratic', for there are no conclusions we might adopt which could be so described. And history exemplifies this contrast: some have embraced and some have rejected Socratic method simply because of what it entails about the power of reason; but all have found it difficult to ignore the Socratic determination to challenge us with questions. His figure serves to indicate what changes of thought are occurring, and whether our concerns be theological, or political, or moral, that determination is a crucial part of Socrates' legacy, and the variety of responses to it cannot fail to impress. Often, as FitzPatrick shows, it is the forgotten writers of tracts, pamphlets and dissertations who provide the most reliable guide to this variety, for they exhibit a sensitivity to the characteristic concerns and debates of a particular age which is hard for us to recover. We may not share those concerns or wish to engage in those debates, but we can nevertheless learn something that is of value about Socrates by attending to the diverse ways these writers, as well as those more widely known, felt able to portray him. Today, what we say we know of the real Socrates is little enough, and what we really know may be a good deal less than we think. A study of the legacy of Socrates can serve to remind us of the extent of our ignorance and thus fulfil another part of the mission of Socrates.

NOTES

1 In preparing this general introduction, I was aided by Michael Stokes' wise advice. Dr Clemence Schultze also saved me from mistakes and infelicities. Naturally, neither is in any way responsible for the errors of commission or omission that remain.

2 For references see Lacey 1971: 24; and Brickhouse and Smith 1989: 5, n. 19.

3 Especially in his most recent study, Vlastos 1991.

4 See Plato's description, in *Theaetetus* 143e and 209c, and Xenophon's in *Symposium (The Banquet)* V.1–8. Vlastos has pointed out that none of the earlier Platonic dialogues tell of the physical appearance of Socrates; what little we know comes from dialogues such as the *Theaetetus* belonging to the middle or transitional period. See Vlastos 1991: 251.

5 An extensive collection of portraits of Socrates, with comments on their provenance, is to be found in Richter 1965.

6 For further information on this see Woodbury 1973.

7 See Adkins 1960: 77ff., 177, 159ff.; and esp. Dover 1974: 172ff.

8 See Rhodes 1985.

9 See MacDowell 1978: 186–9.

10 See Guthrie 1969: 27–34; or Guthrie 1971: 27–34.

11 See Kerferd 1981: 25–6.

12 For an eloquent expression of this view see Nussbaum 1980: 43–97.

13 See MacDowell 1978: 30–3.

14 See Rhodes 1986: 144–5.

15 See Brickhouse and Smith 1989: 27–9, with n. 94.

16 For the scholarly literature on this matter see ibid., 26, n. 86.

17 A useful recent discussion of the nature of Socrates' financial counter-penalty and of his reasons for proposing it is to be found in ibid., 214–34.

18 See Gill 1973: 25–9.

1

SOCRATES' MISSION

Michael Stokes

PRELUDE

Dickens once began a novel, 'What I want is facts!' In talking of
Socrates facts can be nothing *more* than a beginning, and they are
in short supply. Quite a number of them (his age at death, some
significant battlefields in Athenian history on which he fought, some
details of the charges against him at his trial) derive from, among
other places, the work of Plato's traditionally called the *Apology
of Socrates*; that means, in current English, *Socrates' Defence*.
Formally the *Apology* contains three speeches in Socrates' mouth:
one a defence proper against the charges brought at his trial; one
after the verdict of guilty suggesting (as defence and prosecution
each did in Athens) a possible penalty; and the third addressed
to the jury, uniquely in recorded Athenian practice, after sentence.
The work paints a portrait of a man who spent much of his life
questioning people, particularly (perhaps only) on ethical issues,
to their discomfiture, their edification or both – the discomfiting
questions being called 'elenctic' or (roughly) 'refutatory'; the verb
elencho, 'test' or 'refute', but not the noun *elenchos* or the adjective,
appears in the *Apology*'s text. That text portrays Socrates as insisting
(among other things) that he does not think he knows what he does
not know; whereas others do think they know things that in fact
they do not know. Much of what scholars say about Socrates'
mission also comes from this work. In proportion to its authenticity
as a record of Socrates' actual defence it offers a priceless source for
Socrates' view of himself and of his own activities.

In proportion, yes. But the Platonic Socrates' professions of
ignorance make it ironic that so many scholars argue for the

view, and some indeed appear to think they know, that Plato's *Apology* is essentially what Socrates said at his trial. In my view they do not and cannot know this. We should start, not from the assumption even that Socrates' general drift receives faithful reportage in Plato's *Apology*, but rather from the fact that the *Apology* is a work of Plato's. As such it should command no less and no more biographical credence than any other of Plato's earlier works. True, it could (but need not) have been the first Socratic writing from Plato's pen, but an early date does not seem to me a guarantee of biographical intention or historical authenticity in detail or even in significant argument. True, also, that Plato's text says he was there; and at first sight the *Apology* might appear to be on a different footing from, say, the *Crito*, which depicts a private conversation between Socrates and Crito alone. But authorial autopsy is sometimes in Xenophon a literary embellishment without substance, and may equally be so in Plato; to assume the contrary is risky. True, further, that if one accepts a parallel between Platonic writings and Thucydides' speeches, and emphasises the historian's words about keeping as close as possible to the general sense of what was actually said, one ends up attributing biographical intent to Plato; but to draw such a parallel is to assume that Plato and his readers saw his Socratic writings as examples of the same (or allied) genre as Thucydides' History – and thus to beg the question at issue.[1]

You are warned that when talking about Socrates I normally mean *Plato*'s Socrates. I commit myself to nothing about the real Socrates of history unless I expressly take on such a commitment; and most of the other contributors to this collection would probably echo this reservation. I personally would go further: I am prepared when speaking historically to deny to the real Socrates some important parts of Plato's version, in full consciousness that to do so is to go somewhat against the trend of recent major publications on the subject.[2] But in trying to make sense of Socrates' mission it is in the first instance *Plato*'s Socrates' mission I am trying to make sense of.

Making sense of it in context is not a wholly straightforward task. There have been scholarly doubts[3] whether even Plato's Socrates has any right to speak of a mission at all. There have also been those holding that he argues quite logically and clearly that he was acting, for much of his life, in obedience to instructions from Apollo, the god of, in particular, the Delphic Oracle.[4] This chapter argues for a sort of uneasy halfway house between these views concerning Plato's Socrates, while expressing serious doubts of Plato's biographical reliability. The truth is that Plato's text gets more difficult every time one looks at it; the difficulties are not those of following the meaning in the narrow sense, but of understanding exactly what is going on. Recent accounts have cleared up some points, but left others still obscure. But without the context one has no hope of grasping what is going on, so here, at some but I hope not excessive length, is the context.

The context mentioning the Oracle, at *Apology* 20e ff., has Socrates rebutting the first of two sets, as he puts it, of accusers. He *will* deal later with those who have accused him in court, and he *is* dealing at this juncture with the prejudice against him created by comic drama and by gossip (the 'first accusers', as he calls them). Gossip has it that Socrates belongs to one or both of two classes of intellectuals: those who produce grandiose theories of the universe and everything (with at most a minimal function for the traditional gods) and those who claim to teach young men goodness (where 'goodness' meant successfulness in personal and public life, and the values of success need not, but might, undermine traditional moral restraints). From both of these, from the so-called 'natural philosophers' and from the 'sophists', Socrates firmly dissociates himself. It is hardly coincidental that the two sorts of people he thus disowns correspond rather obviously and superficially to the two counts of the indictment – the charges respectively of impiety and of corrupting the young. The grounds of dissociation are those of ignorance. Socrates says he knows nothing of 'natural philosophy', and he disclaims knowledge of, and the ability to teach, whatever makes a personal success of a human being. But Socrates is sure the jury will suppose that there is no smoke without fire; and he sets out to answer the question what it was about himself that brought him a reputation for wisdom.

'Wisdom?' you may ask; 'wisdom' is a conventional rendering of long standing for a Greek word meaning 'intellectual qualities or achievements (real or supposed) setting a man apart from or above his fellows'. This word has a strong association in fifth-century Greek with knowing many things.[5] Socrates sets out then from a denial of two sorts of 'wisdom', two sorts of intellectual pretensions attributed to him, and seeks to explain how the false attribution arose. But his explanation would have startled a real-life jury, as it startles innocent first-time readers

28

of Plato. His false repute for 'wisdom' arose, he says, 'through nothing other than a sort of "wisdom"' (*Apology* 23d6). Of this paradox there will be more to say later; all that is needed now is that its resolution depends on there being two applications of the word 'wisdom', one human and one, if it be genuine, superhuman. Socrates lays claim only to a human 'wisdom'. This distinction does not appear at once to help explain his reputation; for his reputation was for something setting him apart from normal men, not from all human possibilities. Socrates' argument depends on his attribution of superhuman 'wisdom' to those he has just mentioned, presumably both the physical philosophers and the sophists – *if*, that is, their claims are true. It is hard to imagine anything more likely than this to induce restiveness in a sizeable popular audience. Socrates stands accused, he implies, of being a physical philosopher or sophist. He says (adducing little or no evidence) that he is neither; he says that his false repute for wisdom is due to his, well, sort of wisdom; and he adds that the highly suspect physicists and sophists, *if* genuine, are superhumanly wise. It should not surprise anyone that Plato gives Socrates here a sentence telling the audience, even if they think he is boasting, not to raise a clamour.

The paradoxes become not a whit less provocative as Socrates proceeds. That he is wise is no saying of his; he can produce a witness to his wisdom (to the questions, that is, whether he has any and of what sort); and his witness? the god Apollo of Delphi, the Oracle (*Apology* 20e7).[6] The respectable democrat Chaerephon, a man 'given to the excessive' or 'impetuous', asked the Oracle whether there was anyone wiser than Socrates; and he received the answer, 'No one is wiser than Socrates.' Nothing here, you will observe, dissociates Socrates from physics or sophistry; nothing here distinguishes human wisdom such as Socrates claims from superhuman wisdom, which he does not. All we have here is an oracle to say that there is none wiser than he; and Socrates produces Chaerephon as a human witness to it, though since Chaerephon is dead, his brother testifies from hearsay. Still nothing concrete explains Socrates' reputation, except an oracle nobody, apparently, knew about.

MISSION AND ORACLE: SOME MODERN VIEWS

Socrates now gets down to explaining why he came to be the victim of false gossip; and we may get down to his mission. Of course he

29

does not react to the oracle by saying 'The Oracle declares there is no one wiser than me; that gives me a mission to go around questioning people.' Socrates' logic, deeply though many readers suspect it, is not normally as bad as that. And yet, about two pages later, after explaining how he went around questioning people, we find Socrates describing this way of life as a 'help' and a 'service' to the god of Delphi, which are terms appropriate to a mission – and this though, as many have remarked,[7] there is nothing obviously jussive, no order, command, instruction or imperative, and no clear imposition of a task, visible to the naked eye in the actual oracle, nor any overt hint there that the god required of Socrates any help or service.

The puzzle thus set has a long history, and one cannot be confident of one's ability to end that history. But some solutions we can surely abandon. In the 1920s the great German scholar Wilamowitz could write of Socrates finding welcome confirmation from an external source of an inner vocation, without enquiring too closely how the logic of this external confirmation worked.[8] Theodor Gomperz earlier and Reginald Hackforth later[9] believed that Plato played up the oracle's significance in Socrates' life. Hackforth described Socrates' initial interpretation of the oracle as 'a typical example of Socrates' irony' and spoke of Plato *inventing* the connection between the oracle and Socrates' mission. There may be – and I suspect there are – elements of truth in these, but none seems properly to have faced the question why Plato, the master of creative argument, should suddenly become as incompetent as their views implied in the creation of a logical connection between oracle and mission.

More recently Guthrie[10] skated over the problem, saying, 'Having learned the lesson [of the oracle] himself he felt it to be the god's will that he should impart it to others.' '*Felt* it'? Socrates (and we) *ought* surely to be able to do better than that – though we shall have to see. More recently still, Brickhouse and Smith in their *Socrates on Trial*, finding no command in the oracle or Socrates' interpretation of it, take refuge in an analysis of Socratic piety (as discussed especially in Plato's *Euthyphro*); they argue[11] that this Socratic piety 'fits well with' Socrates' description of his mission in the *Apology*, and indeed required him 'to serve the gods by promoting what is good', as Socrates claims to do later in this same speech by urging Athenians to pursue virtue. This theory, you will not fail to observe, makes Plato not only have his readers read his *Socrates' Defence* backwards rather than normally but also assumes their knowledge of the contents of his *Euthyphro*. It leaves us with a fictional (I do not say fictitious) Socrates who confronts his mass audience at this point with a set of remarks likely to strike the more intelligent as thoroughly unconvincing and indeed irrational, who only later solves the conundrum he has thus set them, and in so doing does not stop to explain by even the briefest cross-reference that he has done so, or how he has done it. In this context one notices that Socrates' audience can certainly not have been supposed even in fiction to know the doctrines which emerge from the *Euthyphro*. Earlier theories made Plato an incompetent reasoner; this one makes him an unimaginative writer.

Yet more recently comes Reeve's stimulating and important essay *Socrates in the Apology*. Reeve[12] most helpfully identifies three separate problems. 'First, the oracle, even as he finally interprets it, is not an explicit command or imperative. Second, it does not mention elenctic examination. By the same token, and this is the third problem, it does not mention elenctic examination on ethical issues.' Reeve finds no explicit answers in the text, but believes that 'a plausible explanation is implicit in what [Socrates] tells [the jury]'. This explanation, boiled down, I hope, not misleadingly, runs like this: (a) Socrates was already devoted to Apollo, or he would not have spent the time and trouble he did over determining the oracle's meaning, or persisted as he did through unpopularity and poverty in the activity designed to find out that meaning. (b) The obvious people to go to for a counter-example were those with a repute for wisdom, and the obvious issues to discuss with them were ethical ones about which they were believed to be wise and he doubted his own wisdom. Building on this foundation, Reeve adds (c), Socrates' practice of refuting claimants to knowledge of the most important things will tend to show that things are as Apollo said, so that 'There is a sense in which Socrates is acting according to Apollo.'[13] This leaves open the question why Socrates should have persisted, as he says he did, after the truth of the oracle had been demonstrated to his satisfaction. (d) Socrates interpreted the oracle as making the value-judgement that the person is wisest who recognises that no human being knows the most important things. Delphi thus 'commended anti-hybristic awareness of human limitations in wisdom. And value-judgements and commendations . . . have – especially when uttered by a god to a religious person already devoted to him – strong action-guiding force.' Socrates' continuing activity brings about something which Apollo values.

31

This constitutes a 'much more full-blooded sense' in which Socrates aids or serves Apollo; and 'notice that Socrates speaks of coming "to the aid of the god" only at the stage at which he tries to get the interlocutor to recognise his own lack of wisdom (*Apology* 23b3–6)'.[14]

This reasoning is thoroughly grounded in the text. But it smacks of over-interpretation and at the same time of special pleading, inadequate to account fully for what Socrates says. For, in the first place, it is doubtful whether to ponder and take enormous trouble over an oracle was the mark of one already devoted to Apollo. The mythical Orestes and Oedipus, who took extreme measures or great pains to fulfil or avoid fulfilling respectively what Apollo's Oracle advised or foretold, were not made out by the poets to be devotees, and a personal oracle such as Socrates says he received through Chaerephon would have been a major event in anyone's life, provided that he believed in the genuinely divine nature of the pronouncement's source – and the whole story is predicated on that much by way of Socratic piety. In the second place, whatever one may think about 'acting in accordance with the god' and 'coming to the god's aid', this explanation hardly suggests an *order* from the god comparable, as Socrates later has it, with the orders of a military commander; and for Apollo to commend an acceptance of human limitations does not constitute an order, though it guarantees the god's approval, for the continual spread of that acceptance by refuting people – supposing, for the sake of argument, acceptance to be indeed the upshot of the refutation.[15] To claim that Socrates thought of himself as having *thus* been commanded in such a way as not merely to justify but to compel his lifelong practice of refutation and his persistence in it even at the risk of his life is to attribute to him a deduction much less clear than his normal arguments. We are back with a Plato whose Socrates reasons less than cogently and exaggerates what force his reasoning possesses; and that at a point where clarity and cool cogency are extra specially needed, at the very core of Socrates' whole life-story as Plato's *Apology* describes it.

If these views strike one as insufficient, there are others on the market, with which the scholars just mentioned fail to argue. These others[16] point to a statement by Socrates (*Apology* 23b1) that the Oracle probably meant that he was to be an example to humankind, and they notice that Socrates does not refer unambiguously to a mission from the god until after this statement about an example, but begins to do so *immediately* thereafter. It seems reasonable to associate the idea of a mission with the idea of an example to men. But one may have strong sympathy with these views stressing the notion of an example without thinking that they exhaust the topic, or that the argument is as simple and clear-cut as this theory would apparently presuppose. The precise nature of the example, of the mission itself, of the connection between the two, and indeed of Socrates' attitude all need closer attention, and Socrates' initial attitude may reasonably come first in this investigation.

SOCRATES' ATTITUDE TO THE ORACLE

Socrates' immediate reaction to the oracle, the one saying that no man was wiser than he, needs distinguishing from his later reaction to his own final interpretation of it. His immediate reaction was to wonder 'What does the god mean?' and 'What is he saying in riddles?' This, as we shall see, is interesting. Oracles in all probability did not actually deal at all extensively in riddles; Socrates is reacting as if they behaved in fact as they did in legend[17] or in Delphic propaganda. But Socrates, as we shall see, is also responding in a way he adopts elsewhere in dealing with human interlocutors who offer statements which seem to him counterfactual or illogical. At any rate, after prolonged puzzlement, he adopted a course he calls one of enquiry into the oracle. Others[18] have called it a criticism, and have doubted Socrates' profession of belief in the god's veracity or believed that Socrates changes his mind. Rather lengthy study of the relevant piece of Greek text leaves me in some doubt, but inclined to think Plato meant us (in so far as we believe anything in *Socrates' Defence*) to believe Socrates genuinely to have kept his faith in Apollo's truthfulness throughout. Since the question affects the origins of the Platonic Socrates' mission, it is necessary to explain both doubts and inclination.

But first, is *Apollo's* truthtelling relevant? There was always a problem with Greek oracles: granted that many people would have accepted that the god's message always spoke truth, and distinguished oracle-mongers as mentioned at *Apology* 22c2 from respectable Oracles such as Delphi,[19] what about the human messengers who transcribed or otherwise transmitted the message? Could one trust them? A famous example of mistrust is Oedipus' suspicion of his brother-in-law Creon after the latter brings home, in Sophocles' *Oedipus Tyrannus*, an oracle from Delphi. It was right not only to ask what the god meant, but who reported the message.

So, was Socrates *certain* that Chaerephon was a trustworthy and entirely credible reporter? In his speech he does his best to make him appear a credible witness for the jury in that he was a democrat, and to explain Chaerephon's credibility to himself by portraying him as a close friend from youth onwards.[20] No certainties are available; but Plato has seen to it that high probabilities abound, and that (as far as possible) it is indeed Apollo's truthtelling which is the focus of interest.

So, what does Socrates say? In what he clearly implies is an explanation of the nature of his process of enquiry, Socrates says at 21b7 that he visited a man with a repute for wisdom. The verb 'I visited' in his sentence is qualified by an adverbial phrase. That phrase says, literally, 'as there, if anywhere, being about to refute the prophecy and about to show the oracle "This man here is wiser than me, but you said I was [wiser]."' 'As being about to' renders a Greek conjunction and a future participle. The Greek future participle can have at least two meanings. It can be either 'prospective' or 'voluntative'. It can *either* view the future action concerned merely as a prospective future event, the future being regarded simply as a stretch of time within which the action will fall, *or* view the future action as part or whole of the *purposes or intentions* of the subject of the sentence. Accordingly, Socrates' visit to the man of reputed wisdom could, with voluntative participle, have been made *with the purpose* of disproving the oracle – which is the usual interpretation, *or*, with prospective participle, have been made *in the expectation* that he would, there if anywhere, refute the oracle by counter-example.[21]

If it was Socrates' *purpose* to refute the oracle, that argues a certain scepticism on Socrates' part, if not downright disbelief; if he merely thought that with this man if *anywhere* he would (prospective) refute the oracle, then he need not have been nearly so sceptical. With this prospective sense of the participle the conditional 'if anywhere' can have its full conditional meaning, and the sentence does not commit Socrates to the belief that there is actually any case which would refute the oracle. With the voluntative, or purposive, sense, it is hard to give any acceptable force to 'if anywhere'. It is difficult to see why his purpose should be hedged with a conditional; why should his purpose be to refute the god here just *if* it was his *purpose* anywhere? One can see why Socrates should want to cast doubt on his ability to disprove the oracle, but not why he should state his own intentions only to cast doubt on them. If, still with the purposive participle, we adopt the interpretation 'here above all', then Socrates' intention to refute the oracle is not so far hedged with any condition; it thus makes a break of the sharpest kind in his faith in Apollo's truthtelling. Further, it is difficult to see why Socrates' purpose should be to refute the oracle in this one case above all; that might necessitate the assumption that the man in question was *extra* specially distinguished, an assumption not warranted by the text (which says merely 'one of those thought to be wise') or by the context; but if the phrase 'if anywhere' is not truly conditional but means simply 'here above all', then we are faced with a Socrates who wants to refute the oracle in particular with a man reputed wise. Now to refute the oracle with the counter-example of a man not reputed wise would be much more spectacular and effective, so that on this interpretation 'above all' is difficult to follow. Indeed, 'above all' must refer to the possibility, not the desirability, of refuting the oracle with a man reputed wise.

Could one perhaps hedge one's bets, and render: 'intending there if he was able anywhere . . . '? That makes the verb to be supplied in the 'if anywhere' clause different from the verb going with 'there' – which may be possible, but would hardly make for good clear writing. It really seems best in this context to take the clause as giving not the purpose of, but the grounds for, i.e. the expectations involved in, Socrates' choice of person to visit.

Thus far runs my inclination to take the sentence as offering Socrates' grounds for and expectations in choosing this person as a possible counter-example against the god. What about my residual doubts? These are based on two things: first, some rather technical matters of Greek syntax; certainly in general the future participle can be prospective in force, but it is standard doctrine that if the grammatical subject of the participle is the same as in the main clause, and the particle 'as' is present, and the main verb is, like Socrates' 'I went' here, an active verb of motion, then the future participle is voluntative or purposive in meaning. It is uncommonly hard to find clear examples of prospective future participles in just this particular kind of context. One *can* find examples where the prospective force is possible, or where it seems subjectively to be marginally more appropriate.[22] I am unable to see any special reason for forbidding the prospective participle in such contexts, and no doubt, if Dr Strangelove in the film can learn to love the Bomb, I can learn to love a 'prospective' future participle in precisely this kind of context. But a clear example would help.

Second there is the matter of a seemingly parallel passage at 22a8 later in the text; just how far it is parallel is part of the point at issue. The passage, still from Socrates' explanatory narrative of how he came by his repute for wisdom, says: 'I must exhibit my wanderings to you, wanderings as of a man performing certain labours so that the oracle might be unrefuted' (*Apology* 22a8). Note, in the text I am following at present (in company with virtually all modern editors), the word '*un*refuted'; this has caused a good deal of disquiet since many have thought that the passage we have just left said that Socrates' purpose was to refute the oracle, not to leave it unrefuted. Certainly the upshot was that the oracle was unrefuted; certainly if we abandon the purposive interpretation of the earlier passage, we are left without the contradiction between the two passages which has bothered readers. But we are left with the rather obvious difficulty that if your purpose holds to leave something unrefuted, you don't have to perform any labours at all: you can just sit back and let it go unrefuted. On the whole it seems best to accept that the word rendered 'so that', though normally introducing a purpose, can on occasion, and does here, introduce a result presented ironically as a purpose. Editors supply examples, of which one from a fine rhetorical passage of Homer is specially convincing.[23] But I have to confess that part of the manuscript tradition has an additional negative in the relevant clause, giving the superficially easier 'so that the oracle might not be unrefuted'. On this reading we have most naturally, given a normal writer's symmetry, to suppose both of our passages to offer Socrates' purpose to refute the oracle. One is tempted to ask whether the appearance of such a pair could possibly, let alone probably, be mere coincidence due to scribal error. The answer is that it could, and that for two reasons: first that negatives are very frequently wrong either by insertion or by omission in medieval manuscripts;[24] and secondly that the temptation for a scribe to insert a negative in the second passage, given its slightly unusual syntax and a possible symmetry, would be extreme.[25]

But the matter is not *just* one of syntax and narrowly based textual criticism; it concerns Socrates' possible change of mind on something he purports on the surface of this passage and of the whole *Defence* to hold dear: the veracity of the god. To say this is not to allude to other passages in the dialogues, such as *Republic*

II–III, in which Socrates seems to think the gods incapable of deceit. It arises rather from the whole drift of this part of his Platonic defence: Socrates has only just said that Apollo could not possibly, could not by divine law, tell an untruth.[26] Did Socrates abandon that principle merely because of one oracle concerning himself that he found hard to understand? Even granting the long hesitation to which the text bears witness, that seems wrong; it seems much more likely that Plato envisaged Socrates as thinking of a process of enquiry which would *if possible*, if anywhere then here, find a counter-example. The upshot ought, then, to be that the context, and the impression of religious constancy the *Apology* conveys here as elsewhere, outweigh residual grammatical doubts.

SOME PARALLELS FOR SOCRATES' REACTIONS TO THE ORACLE

In the context of Socrates' 'attempted refutation' of the oracle it is essential to recall that Plato's Socrates attempts to refute, and attempts to find the meaning of, sundry human pronouncements in the course of discussions taking place in the dialogues, and that the two attempts, at refutation and clarification, are often linked. There is a case in the *Apology* itself. In refuting Meletus Socrates asks 'How do you say . . . ?' at 26b2 and seeks clarification at 26b9, *and* Meletus is said at 27a1 to resemble someone propounding a riddle in the form of a frivolous self-contradiction, a notion repeated at 27d4–7. The frivolity of Meletus' riddle stands in strong contrast with the serious view Socrates takes of the oracle.

A further example is *Republic* 331d ff., which offers points of particular similarity with Socrates' handling of the oracle. There Polemarchus refers to Simonides the poet as holding a certain view; Socrates avers at 331e5 ff. that it is difficult to disbelieve a *wise and divine* man such as Simonides, but the poet cannot mean what a counter-example has just scuppered. Polemarchus does accept the counter-example? Yes. Then Simonides' reputed view cannot bear the meaning attached to it so far; Simonides must mean something else, and Polemarchus obligingly reinterprets him. Here we have a poet, 'wise' presumably as the poets were thought to be wise in the *Apology* and doubtless 'divine' in the sense 'divinely inspired' as at *Apology* 22b–c; but at any rate, being 'wise and divine', he cannot (it is presupposed) be telling an obvious falsehood, so his words are to be given a new sense. Further, Simonides' behaviour is described, at 332b9, just like the Delphic Oracle's, as 'speaking in riddles' on the nature of justice. Without mentioning riddles, Socrates behaves somewhat similarly at 338c ff. of the same book: he first expresses the expectation that Thrasymachus will speak well; when Thrasymachus speaks and asks for approval, Socrates offers it conditionally, 'If I first understand what you are saying, for at present I don't yet know.' He extracts clarification by offering possible but ridiculous meanings. The resultant exposition, at 339a5, he can, now that Thrasymachus has said what he means, examine for truth or falsehood. Both here and in the Polemarchus episode understanding what is meant precedes thorough examination; in the *Apology*, examination precedes understanding. But with both Polemarchus and Thrasymachus it is after questioning that a sense is discarded in which a lauded proposition (or one from a lauded source) is clearly false; and this is parallel to the *Apology* in that there too a sense of the oracle which Socrates thinks obviously false, and therefore not in accord with the Oracle's likely intentions, is discarded after questioning.

Again, at *Theaetetus* 151e ff., Socrates expresses cautious approval of Theaetetus' proposition that perception is knowledge, and says it coincides with Protagoras' 'Man is the measure of all things'. Socrates then asks if Theaetetus knows Protagoras' saying, questions him about its meaning, describes Protagoras, at 152b1, as 'wise' and suggests following him. At 152c8 Socrates (how playfully or seriously is, as often, unclear) suggests that Protagoras is 'all-wise', and speaking in riddles to the general public while speaking the plain truth to his disciples, and again Socrates expresses cautious approval at 152d of the 'secret doctrine'. Here again someone is supposed to mean something not obviously identical with what he says, and the expression 'riddle' is used as of the Delphic Oracle in the *Apology*. Further, the 'real' sense is examined; at first it is found good and with it Theaetetus' original pronouncement (160d5 f.), and Protagoras is called 'very wise'. But the discussants have still to examine related propositions; after a suggestion attributed to Protagoras in passing at 161c7 f., that they admire his wisdom like a god's, his theory is demolished, and with it his special claim to wisdom (161d–e); demolition in the immediate, but not the wider, context takes the form of a counter-example: frogs and other animals perceive but cannot be said to know or be wise as men do/are. The point of comparison with the *Apology* here is Socrates' readiness before embarking on an elenchus to investigate the sense of someone else's 'riddling' proposition and his willingness to disprove – or to accept if it survives – the 'real' sense.

In the *Charmides* we find a further parallel. At 161c9, the definition of *sophrosyne* as 'doing one's own thing' is 'like a sort of riddle', which makes it difficult to discover its truth or falsehood. It resembles a riddle, Socrates explains, in that the intention or meaning does not coincide with the words. Socrates then takes the locution 'doing one's own thing' far more concretely than its author meant, and shows that such a reading of the expression produces absurd results as an account of *sophrosyne* (as Charmides agrees). The locution was therefore not meant in that sense, and as it stands will not do. So, at 162a10, its author must have been speaking in riddles; he cannot have been so foolish, and indeed Charmides thought the definition's author 'wise'. In that case, says Socrates with redoubled assurance, it *must* have been a riddle, the expression 'doing one's own thing' being hard to understand. Since the author is human, the possibility arises (as it does not with Apollo in the *Apology*) that the author himself did not know what he meant; so 162b9 ff., answered indignantly by Critias d4–6. Critias solves the problem, at least temporarily, by distinguishing 'doing' from 'making', as Charmides had not. Socrates accepts whatever vocabulary-stipulations Critias wants, but insists on his speaking more clearly.

In all this it is clear that to call what somebody says a 'riddle' is a way either of ridiculing it or, more often, a way of rescuing the speaker when what he says turns out to be wrong, foolish or otherwise out of keeping with his wisdom. It was indeed a *procedure of Socratic elenchus* to put what somebody said in that light. The procedure is closely related to that of enquiring what a refutand means. This same passage of the *Charmides* supplies another parallel to our *Apology* passage: for Socrates says at 165b8, 'I enquire [or seek, *zeto*] always with you into what is suggested, because I myself don't know'; and at *Apology* 21b4–5 he does not know, or is not conscious, that he is wise, and turns to enquiry (*zetesis*). Further, in the *Charmides*, on finding out that a certain line of enquiry is wrong, he amends it slightly: this at 165e–166a. 'Enquiry' using this verbal root and with this degree of flexibility is a regular phenomenon of the elenchus; Socrates is again, in the *Apology*, treating the oracle as he would (supposedly later: see below) treat anyone else who ventured on a pronouncement Socrates had reason either to doubt or to suspect he had not fully understood.

In the case of the god, as he says, doubt is impossible, *so* the god must be riddling.[27] This way of enquiry into the meaning of what is said obscurely is one method of Socratic elenchus. Before he understands the oracle, Socrates is deploying a procedure which he calls elench-ing, and which shares prominent features with some elenchuses as later practised, and one of these procedures was the production[28] of counter-examples. Socrates is trying to produce a counter-example to the oracle.

It is hard to tell what the significance of this is. If the *Apology* is relatively late, some readers well versed in Plato might understand what was going on; if Plato's 'early' Socrates was essentially the historical Socrates, then Socrates' friends will have known what was going on whether in the speech at this point or in Plato's composition. But on other plausible hypotheses even fewer people will have taken the point; the riddle-resemblance between this passage and the refutation of Meletus is not glaringly obvious, and Socrates does not use the word or root 'elench-' in the Meletus passage. Yet it is hard, if not impossible, to believe that *Plato* was unconscious of the fact that Socrates was treating the Oracle as he treated others when later, and supposedly under the Oracle's influence, he launched an assault on their pronouncements. There is of course no inconsistency in this; Socrates could have devised the technique first for use on the Oracle and then deployed it against seeming-wise human beings. But it seems odd that a technique for exploring the truth or falsehood of a proposition should first be deployed on a proposition which must be true. Did Plato perhaps want to display two very different elenchuses, a successful one of Meletus and an unsuccessful one of the Oracle, before Socrates' account of his later general pursuit of elenchus? Did he want to show the elenchus thus both in hostile form (against Meletus) and in friendly form (against Apollo)? Plato is hereabouts displaying all his remarkable capacity to keep the reader guessing, to distance himself from the reader and leave him or her wondering how profound is the writer's irony and just how far his writings undercut, undermine or even deconstruct themselves.

One difference between the seeking of Apollo's meaning and the other elenchuses is evident. Socrates is reluctant to turn the technique on the god, but displays no reluctance (unless that engendered by growing unpopularity) in examining any human being who offers him a statement worth testing. The god could not be wrong, so that the elenchus could not be used against him for its otherwise universal initial purpose, to prove somebody wrong as being inconsistent with himself or with the facts. Socrates presumably dared so audaciously, and in spite of his reluctance, to turn the elenchus on a god precisely because the god's surface meaning actually appeared to be at variance with the fact of Socrates' non-awareness of knowing anything.

SOCRATES' MOTIVES FOR HIS REFUTATIONS

Socrates, anyhow, if I am right, goes to his first apparently wise man with the expectation and on the grounds that here if anywhere (but not, probably, anywhere) he will refute the oracle. What happened to him when, still with no explicit orders or mission, but engaged in investigating Apollo's meaning, he visited a prominent politician and, as he says, conversed with him? First, Socrates tells of his own private internal reaction: he thought the man seemed 'wise' to many other people and especially to the man himself, but was not wise in fact. Secondly Socrates explains his more public response. 'And then', he says, 'I tried to prove to the man that though he thought he was wise, he was not.' Why did Socrates react in this way? He offers no reason or motive for trying to prove this to the man himself, and it would, as usual, be a mistake to read back into this passage motives or reasons for Socrates' mission which appear later in the text. It is tempting for first-time readers to suppose Socrates' motive and reason to have been sheer devilment: Plato's Socrates has a puckish sense of humour and a love of argumentative mischief.

But there is a lot more to be said. The detection of the unfortunate politician's ignorance and its demonstration to him both arise in a single conversation. Are they the same event under different descriptions? The words 'And then' (21c7) linking the two turn up in different kinds of Platonic context. In some they clearly denote temporal sequence; in some they may denote temporal sequence, but the important point is not that, but the combination of irreconcilables; in one place, *Cratylus* 411b, temporal sequence is at least extremely attenuated: 'They become giddy and then things seem to be going round them': the second half of this simply explains or amplifies the first. So in our *Apology* passage, did Plato's Socrates in fact distinguish between detection and demonstration, or was the process of demonstrating the victim's ignorance part or even the whole of the process of detection? Plato's connecting words 'And then' are ambiguous in this respect.

41

This ambiguity raises a question, and indeed a suspicion. Plato is suspect of deliberately having Socrates paper over a crack in the argument here. *We* know, as the first readers of the *Apology* may not have known, that Plato's Socrates distinguishes the detection of inconsistency from its demonstration to the inconsistent person at *Gorgias* 457e. Later in the *Apology* too (26e–27a), Socrates observes the contradiction inherent, in his view, in Meletus' combination of charges before he demonstrates it to the jury through a question-and-answer bout with Meletus extending to 27d. It looks indeed as if he knew himself that detection and demonstration are two different things, but has endeavoured at 21c to bury the difference in order to stop awkward questions arising. That is not to say that Plato's Socrates does not have an explanation to hand of his habit of publicly exposing ignorance. He does, and another passage in the *Gorgias*, at 470c,[29] reveals it: he himself thinks being refuted, and thus having one's ignorance revealed, is a great benefit. He could have pleaded at this point in his *Defence* that his questioning exposure was a benefit to his victim. But Plato has chosen to skate over the issue at this point of his narrative. It is a reasonable conjecture that in accordance with what seems to have been the best practice of the day in forensic speech-making, he did not want to distract from the narrative by what might be a lengthy piece of justifying argument. That did not have to prevent him from making the necessary points later, though he could hardly refer back to a difficulty he had done his utmost by a linguistic sleight-of-hand to conceal. From our vantage-point we should observe that there is now a major question-mark hanging over Socrates' mission. *Why* does he refute people, and, if he does think refutation is a service to them, why does he hold that opinion when some victims clearly take a contrary view (though not, for example, Nicias at *Laches* 188a–b)?

But for the moment Socrates has covered that crack; in the next paragraph he offers a somewhat different justification for going about *detecting* unrealised ignorance. He concluded, he tells us, that he was himself wiser than the politician – in a sense I shall discuss shortly. But one example, just that of the politician, does not settle such a matter, nor would similar conclusions from other politicians Socrates says he visited. Socrates went from one reputed 'wise' man to another, refuting them. Perceiving his thus steadily widening unpopularity, he nevertheless thought it necessary, he says, to set the greatest store by the affair of the god; and he thought that therefore in studying its meaning he ought to visit *all* those with pretensions to significant knowledge. And this is logical; before he could be *sure* of the Oracle's meaning when it said that *no* man was wiser than he, Socrates needed to investigate *all* apparent counter-examples. Socrates calls this search at 22a an enquiry 'in accordance with the god' – and a great editor[30] commented that this was equivalent to 'as the God commanded'. But that is to go too far: 'in accordance with' is in Greek a preposition of many possible English renderings, such as, in particular, 'concerning' or 'in relation to'. 'In relation to the god' or perhaps 'concerning the god' need imply no command yet. It is here that Socrates speaks of himself as performing labours 'so that the oracle might actually be unrefuted': and that is no command either, or even, as we saw, a purpose.

Socrates visited next, in succession, the poets and the handcraftsmen. The point is not of great significance, but it is hard to believe in the strict historicity of this succession. Socrates will hardly have exhausted systematically all the statesmen before going to a single poet, or all the poets before meeting up with a single craftsman; and it needs to be observed that Socrates' procedure in Plato's dialogues and in Xenophon is not normally to go deliberately to one particular person or type of person, but rather to take advantage of meetings in public or semi-public places. He 'went', however, to the poets in the expectation of catching himself red-handed knowing less than they, and to the craftsmen (rather differently) in the *knowledge* that they knew many fine things. His trouble with both groups was that because each man was skilled in his art, each thought he was also very wise in other matters, namely the most important ones; and that mistake masked his other 'wisdom'. Here (22e1) the Oracle crops up again; Socrates asked himself 'on the Oracle's behalf' or 'in its defence' whether he was better off in respect of wisdom than these people, and gave, he says, 'to myself and to the Oracle' the answer that he was indeed better off as he was. Now to ask himself a question in the Oracle's *defence* has been regarded as inconsistent with a continuing attempt to refute the oracle and rejected on that ground; but having doubted the intention to refute the oracle, we are not now obliged to reject this rendering. Indeed, the words 'to myself and to the Oracle' strongly suggest that the question comes from the Oracle, and that the relevant Greek preposition is intended, meaning 'on behalf of', simply to signal this point. But whether the Oracle's implied question tends to the defence or to the elucidation of what it had said is not very important; from the Oracle's point of view elucidation and defence are obviously closely linked. Nevertheless, Socrates' next remark about the oracle is his conclusion about its meaning.

MOTIVATION: SOCRATES AS AN EXAMPLE

'Probably', Socrates says (23a5) – note that 'probably' – 'the god himself is truly wise and is saying in this oracle that "human wisdom is worth little or nothing".' It 'seemed' – another modest expression – to be saying to humankind that 'he who like Socrates recognises that he is in truth worth nothing in respect of wisdom is the wisest, O mortals, among you'. Socrates says also that in speaking of Socrates the Oracle was additionally using his name as an example. Now, 'example' is a tricky word. An example may be simply one of a class, singled out for no particular reason, or it can be a paradigm, one selected to show something. It is fairly clear both from the context and from general literary considerations that in Socrates' understanding the god meant him in some sense as a paradigm, not just a mere instance. In the context he says to mankind at large that the wisest is like Socrates. If a man wants to be wise, he must emulate Socrates. Socrates therefore is an example held up, in a sense, to show something, and in his own view, a divinely chosen example to show something to humankind in general.

This impression of an 'example' in a paradigmatic rather than merely an instantiating sense finds support in the general Greek literary treatment of remarkable events associated with direct divine intervention. Divine manifestations of foreknowledge, of righteous vengeance, or simply of power[31] are traditionally accompanied by some reference to mankind in general in the context of an exemplary event or other divine communication. The reference to an example and to 'mankind' in the context of the *Apology* shows the literary tradition in which Plato's Socrates' narrative stands. In this typical passage it would be remarkable indeed if the speaker were using the word 'example' in a merely instantiating sense.

Now, I am not the first to suggest[32] that this idea of an example is extremely important for Plato's account of Socrates' mission. For down to Socrates' mention of himself as an example there are no unambiguous statements of Socrates' mission, of his serving or help-ing the god. After the term 'example' appears, we find immediately that Socrates describes himself not only (as before) as questioning 'in accordance with' or 'in the matter of' the god, but actually, in his demonstration of a man's unwisdom, as serving and helping Apollo. Furthermore, there is a clear logical link between being an example to show the particular point at issue and having a mission to do so. For, again, the god means Socrates, he thinks, to show mankind that men like Socrates, who are aware of their own ignorance, are the wisest of men, and to show this it is now, as it was not before, clearly relevant to convince other people who think they are wise that they are not; and it is equally relevant to do so in the presence of bystanders as numerous and potentially influential as possible; all this while acknowledging with due humility that one does not know any of the answers oneself. In fact it is not easy to see how Socrates could function as an example of the god's particular point otherwise; perhaps by pirouetting in the marketplace of Athens, ignorantly? Or, more seriously, by preaching his own ignorance and others' as well of the things that he deems the most important? But why should anyone in the false conceit of knowledge, for example, of what is right or wrong, believe Socrates when he preaches such a message? How would you, the reader, take to it if I told you you knew nothing that mattered? And would you take to it any better if, in response to the obvious kind of question, I said 'Oh no, I don't have the answer to that any more than you do'?

So here, then, is the answer in the text to the question why Socrates thinks he has a mission to pursue people and convince them that they are less wise than they think. But there is another question, and it is not easy to answer. The question is, 'Why should Socrates so construe the oracle's meaning? Does the run-up to that construal justify it?' Before answering that, it is necessary to say a few dogmatic words on a question I intend to discuss elsewhere. That concerns the content of Socrates' wisdom, or if you like, of his ignorance.

There is a popular understanding, once surprisingly popular among scholars as well as laymen, that Socrates says that he is wiser than other men because, whereas they think they know, he knows that he knows nothing. That this is a logically difficult, paradoxical, if not impossible thing to know has not always escaped notice, and Vlastos, for example,[33] suggested that Socrates was using two senses of 'know': Socrates knows, in one sense, that he knows, in another sense, nothing. But all such expedients depend on the finding in the text of an unambiguous statement to the effect that

Socrates knows he knows nothing. No one to my knowledge has found such a statement outside the pages of Plato's *Defence of Socrates*; and such apparent statements of this paradox as have been observed within its pages dissolve on closer inspection. Of these perhaps the most often cited is at 21b, at the very beginning of Socrates' discussion of the oracle. Usually rendered something like[34] 'For I know myself to be wise in neither a great nor a small way', the sentence need mean nothing of the kind. It could, and probably does, mean 'There is nothing, great or small, such that I know myself to be wise in it'[35] – which is very different and is not logically, though it may be factually, odd. To take another specimen I have quoted already, when the oracle is interpreted at 23b as meaning that the wisest man is he who, like Socrates, has recognised that he is worthless with respect to knowledge, one might be tempted to suppose that the oracle is saying that the wisest is he who like Socrates knows that he knows nothing; but one should restrain oneself in the face of this temptation. First, there is a loophole: perhaps Socrates and other men know a whole lot of other things, but none of them is of any value. Second, the text bears witness to Socrates having seen and shot neatly through that loophole: for one recalls that Socrates was not disappointed in his expectation, for which he uses at 22d1 the expression 'I knew', of finding the handcraftsmen knowing many fine things; their defect was that they did not know the really important things which they thought they knew in addition. The message from Socrates' experiences was not that men knew nothing; it was that what they knew was of no real importance, that the technical knowledge men had was no good to them; there were other more important things to know, which the apparently wise men he met did not know, and which he could not, and did not, claim to know himself.

But there is still a problem in Socrates' mission. It is one thing to speak of Socrates' message; it is quite another to speak of the god telling him, or giving him a mission, to spread that message. So let us return to that problem. Apropos of his first move beyond the circle of politicians with whom he started, Socrates says that, though pained and scared at the perception of the growing dislike of his attentions, he nevertheless thought it necessary to attach very great importance to, or to take extremely seriously (both possible senses of a vague Greek expression), the affair of the god – that is, clearly, the oracle. That, so far, is impeccable reasoning, in the Greek milieu; in the face of an oracle with personal reference to oneself, one was well advised to take it seriously. In particular, it was well to understand any such oracle: remember Croesus and Oedipus.[36] It is not in any way surprising that Socrates thought himself obliged – at least prudentially – to investigate the meaning of that to him strange pronouncement, or that it was necessary for him to make sure what it meant.

We have seen that to be sure what the oracle meant, Socrates had to visit everybody with any pretensions to wisdom, and that that meant a rather wide search. Of course Socrates could not carry out a universal search. It must, however, have extended in fact beyond the circle of acknowledged experts, since Socrates is at pains to point out at 22a that those of especially high repute seemed to him in his search most lacking, but *those of lesser esteem* (surely the majority, though Socrates does not say so) were better men with respect to prudence. But after visiting the politicians, the poets and the artisans, Socrates had not visited everybody who might be relevant. Admittedly our modern professions – lawyers, accountants, surveyors, estate agents (realtors to American readers) – were unknown to the Athens of Socrates' day; and he might have included doctors among the artisans; but he had still not addressed quite everybody who could claim an intellectual gift or skill that set him to some degree apart. What about, for instance, rhapsodes such as Ion? Or accomplished soldiers such as Nicias and Laches? Furthermore, over Socrates' long life statesmen rose and fell, poets came and went, and craftsmen trained, worked and passed on: there would never have been a lack of new subjects for the Socratic treatment. Just so long as there was anyone with a repute for 'wisdom' uninvestigated, Socrates had not completed his investigation of the oracle's meaning. His pursuit of the god's true meaning was necessarily a lifelong pursuit; he could never be *sure* that a genuine counter-example – one he could take in puzzlement to Delphi – was not just round the next corner. He himself mentions in Plato's version (21e6 f.) the need to investigate *all* with reputations for 'wisdom'. And this last point blocks a way out which might otherwise present itself. According to *Phaedo* 101d, Socrates' method included accepting as true what he could not show to be in discord with other propositions in some way following after; and the suggestion of a time-limit for the refutation of a hypothesis has met with some scholarly favour; and after years of trying, Socrates could reasonably have thought the oracle's case established by his failure to locate any counter-example. But there

47

it stands: he says he was obliged to visit *all* with an apparent claim to wisdom.

One naturally asks how Socrates could bring out a meaning for the oracle at all in these circumstances. But without making the obviously false claim to have achieved a universal search, he nevertheless comes up with his interpretation of the oracle. If he ever said that he knew, was certain, or even had discovered what the oracle meant, one could pounce on him. But he says none of these things. He does not even say, at least in this portion of the *Defence*, simply 'The oracle means such-and-such.' What he says at 23a–b is: '*Probably* the god is truly wise and means this by the oracle . . .,' and 'He *seems* to have used my name, making me an example. . . .' Now, by the time Socrates ventures in his *Defence* on this 'Probably' and 'seems', he is certainly to be thought of as having been pursuing his investigation for a good few years. Exactly how long is not a question on which it is wise to be dogmatic, but the chronological evidence, such as it is, suggests that Plato had in mind more than thirty years.[37] Whether the audience knew how long is more than doubtful, but the fictional audience are given no reason to regard Socrates' investigation as a recent phenomenon. So a goodly number of people have in Plato's version succumbed to Socrates' dialectic between the oracle and the trial. It would be on the whole surprising for Socrates to have arrived at no tentative conclusions by this time; but it would be wrong for him to represent those conclusions as certainties. Hence that 'Probably' and that 'seems'. Socrates' conclusion in this form does not detract from the necessity of envisaging his investigation as lasting the whole of his life. If it was advisable for Socrates to pursue the interpretation of the oracle logically if impractically with an attempted universal search, then it was advisable for him to continue after he had worked out what seemed to him the most probable meaning. Socrates' 'feelings' in favour of continuing[38] are as much reasons as feelings: the unspoken premise, that it was advisable to understand a personal oracle, would be unspoken because assumed obvious to religious people at the time.

The gap in Socrates' reasoning does not seem to fall between his starting to investigate the oracle's meaning and his continuing to do so; the gap, if it is one, seems to lie between the oracle and his starting to prove to the ignorant that they were indeed ignorant. Socrates offers his audience no reason why he should have started to do this; the idea of himself as an example cannot then have been in his mind. He has left them, if they so wish, to suppose wrongly that discovery and proof of ignorance were the same thing for practical purposes, or were inseparable parts of a single process. Can we do any better for Socrates than that? Could we, for instance, suppose that, although the two things are logically distinct, and open proof of someone's inconsistency does not always and inevitably follow on its discovery, nevertheless in a certain number of cases Socrates could only find out his respondent's ignorance by continuing his questions until not only Socrates but also the respondent was convinced of the respondent's ignorance? And that Socrates accepted this frequent concurrence of proof with discovery as sufficient to show that the apparent necessity of investigation entailed, for practical purposes, the necessity of showing some people that they were ignorant? One could perhaps argue thus, but the argument needs completing with another step or two, to connect those 'practical purposes' with the Oracle. One would have to add that Socrates, seeing what the Oracle's statement had in fact led to, namely the demonstration to many people of their own ignorance, had concluded that that result was intended by the Oracle. Since the god knows the future as a god of prophecy, he knew the consequences of making a pronouncement which Socrates was bound in prudence to investigate. If he knew the consequences, then *in effect* he was enjoining upon Socrates the task of proving to people that they were ignorant.

But if Socrates was prepared to accept that somewhat dubious line of argument, might he also accept a simpler one? If the Oracle was all-knowing, then it knew what sort of man Socrates was. If it knew what sort of man Socrates was, it would know that given implied advice to investigate people's ignorance, Socrates would be quite unable to resist making the results of the search known to the people concerned. But that would be a precarious kind of argument, since it would open the door, I think, to too many excuses for disreputable conduct. One doubts, on the whole, if this argument would appeal to Socrates.

Both these attempts to justify this crucial part of Socrates' mission, the demonstration of others' ignorance, suffer from the absence of any clear statement of the necessary connections in the text. This need not be conclusive against them; Socrates in Plato does not always spell out all his reasons. But it is undeniably a drawback. It grows in dubiety when one concedes the complexity of the premises involved, and the unlikelihood that an Athenian

49

audience whether actual or imagined would be able or, indeed, willing to supply them. They are worth exploring, and may be part of the answer to our question about the justification of Socrates' mission in full; but one doubts if they are the whole truth.

THE MORALITY OF SOCRATES' MISSION

Let us try again. Towards the end of Socrates' account of his wanderings from person to person, he tells us that he asked on behalf of himself and the Oracle whether he would prefer to combine in his own person the craftsmen's knowledge and their ignorance or to combine a lack of their wisdom with a lack of their ignorance; the answer he gave himself and the Oracle was not simply one of preference, but rather that it *profited* him to be as he was, that is without the craftsmen's special skill or wisdom, but also without their false opinion of their own knowledge of other things. If Socrates thought that it was actually good for him to be aware of his own ignorance, and certainly better for him than to be ignorant without being aware of it, then obviously he thought he was conferring a benefit on those whom he caused to be aware of their own ignorance. In normal Greek thinking he was behaving justly towards those he treated in this way, by doing them a good turn when it lay in his power to do so. At the same time Socrates did of course make them, if he had read the oracle's meaning right, wiser than before. But that in itself might or might not actually be a benefit to them; the important fact is that Socrates was convinced that he was conferring a benefit, and hence, presumably, that he was behaving in accord with the dictates of justice.

If we now suggest that Greeks in general thought one had an obligation to behave in accordance with justice, that Socrates was certainly no exception (see *Crito* 49), and his jurors (historical or fictional) were certainly no mass exception either, then our way lies open to a further suggestion: not directly that we have already justified Socrates' notion that he had a mission from Apollo, but that *if* the gods were normally held to enjoin just behaviour, then, once Socrates had perceived where just behaviour lay in his particular circumstances, he could maintain that such behaviour was enjoined by the gods. If we ask the further questions, why Apollo in particular, and why not simply expound the benefit and mention the gods in general, then the answer could conceivably be that Socrates would not have recognised the benefit as a benefit or even as a phenomenon if it had not been for the insight conveyed to him by the oracle.

But this is again a thin line of argument. It leaves too much to the audience's or readers' imagination. There is no obvious reason why Socrates could not have spelt out directly either in court or in Plato's pages that it was the oracle which convinced him that refutation was a benefit he was morally obliged to confer. And the oracle does not say that Socrates' special wisdom is more valuable to men than their normal technical knowledge; Socrates may be wiser, but does his wisdom profit him? That is in the last analysis Socrates' opinion and judgement, not a direct implication of what the Oracle said. Special intellectual endowments are not unambiguously beneficial to their possessor; many distrusted *sophia* or wisdom, and could continue to do so whether it was labelled as 'wisdom' by god or by man.

TRUTH OR FICTION?

General

It begins to look, though it will need confirmation by analysis later, as if Socrates' own values might offer a better, easier and safer road to the justification of his life's work than the oracle Plato's Socrates reports from Delphi. And with that prospect, however distantly, in view, it is well to put to ourselves, in full awareness that we are not the first to put it, the question, Was Plato being truthful when he portrayed Socrates as invoking the testimony of Delphi's Oracle? Was there any such oracle as Plato's Socrates recounts? Did it take the form it has in Plato's *Apology*? These questions continue to disturb a minority of scholars. The majority of those writing on the subject today seem satisfied with affirmative answers to them all. Socrates, they argue for the most part, was (as Plato portrays him) a teller of truth and not of lies: he seeks to persuade the jury by rational means, not by emotional appeals and certainly not by fraud or deceit. So indeed does Plato portray Socrates, and it is indeed hard to conceive of 'Socrates' as telling a deliberate falsehood. But we do not have the original words or necessarily the arguments of Socrates. We have only what Plato, perhaps for purposes of literature or of propaganda rather than those of biography, chose to put in his mouth. The oracle which occupies so prominent a position in Socrates' argument could in principle be Plato's creation. A distinction is necessary here: what was false in objective fact could be true within Plato's fiction; Plato's fictional Socrates could within the fiction be telling the truth even if the experiences he represents were not had by the historical Socrates. To accuse the fictional Socrates of lying would in that case be to confuse fiction with biography.

Obviously this kind of approach rests on the assumption that Plato's *Apology* might be a literary fiction. That is a large question, not to be dispatched in a single paragraph, but deserving a separate paper or chapter. I shall be tackling the general question elsewhere; I hope readers of this book will bear with the assumption for now of the theoretical possibility that Plato was as much creative writer as biographer, and be prepared to leave its defence against the current majority opinion to another occasion.[39] The general defence of such an approach to Plato's *Apology* would take up too much time and space in this present context, which concentrates on the sense of mission which Plato's Socrates in this work appears to say he owes to the Oracle. If in the end the story of the oracle for Socrates turns out to be fictitious, that would in itself settle the issue whether the *Apology* is a fiction, and precisely for that reason I expect fierce resistance to doubts of the oracle's historicity. But the reader should not run away with the notion that this is the first broaching of the question in recent times: scholars such as Montuori, Armleder, Toole and Fontenrose (the last very hesitantly)[40] have ventured to express doubts. But their arguments (most of them Montuori's) have not in general found acceptance and do need careful attention.

Chronology

One set of arguments in Montuori's writings[41] depends on the date of the oracle or, more precisely, on the difficulty of determining its exact date. Scholars accepting the oracle as historical generally place it in one of the periods of peace, either before the outbreak of the Peloponnesian War in the late 430s or between the Archidamian War and the campaign of Mantinea, around, say, 420. It is a question, on the usual assumptions, whether it is better dated before or after the spate of comic uses of and references to Socrates in the late 420s. The late 430s are the most popular dating, since (among other pieces of evidence) the opening scene of Plato's *Charmides* suggests that Socrates' dialectical activity dates from before the siege of Potidaea at that time. Specific difficulties in dating the oracle precisely with reference to that opening scene, raised by Montuori, carry no weight: it is not the oracle which that scene mentions with reference to Socrates' delay before finally approaching Alcibiades, but rather Socrates' 'divine sign', pretty certainly to be regarded as quite distinct from the Oracle's response. But the whole line of argument from chronological difficulties is dubious. Whatever the difficulties of dating the oracle to Chaerephon, chronological difficulties are a familiar feature of events in the fifth century BC, and Plato in particular was not a careful chronologer. Moreover, if we are going to pay attention to things in Plato with chronological import, we should consider a passage in the *Laches*.

In the *Laches*' opening scene, the general Nicias has heard the elderly Lysimachus agree to him and Laches answering Socrates' questions. Nicias replies: 'Lysimachus, I think you really and truly know Socrates only from [your acquaintance with] his father, and have not met him except as a boy, if in his father's company somewhere among his demesmen he came near to you at a rite or some other occasion for the demesmen to congregate; but obviously you haven't met him up to now since he has grown older.' When Lysimachus replies: 'Why in particular, Nicias?' the general adds: 'I don't think you realise that anyone coming very close to Socrates and approaching him in conversation must necessarily not, even if after all he starts the conversation on some other subject, stop being dragged around in his talk by this man until he falls into giving an account of himself, of the manner of life he is leading at the time and has led in the past; and when he does fall into that, that Socrates will not let him go before subjecting that to a good and proper test – all of it' (*Laches* 187d6–188a3).

On this passage we may start from Reeve's brief discussion,[42] which says: 'Socrates began his elenctic mission sometime after the oracle to Chaerephon . . . [This] passage from the *Laches* suggests that he was then in early adulthood'; after quoting, Reeve adds: 'This would date the oracle in the 430s or some thirty years prior to Socrates' trial in 399. And most scholars now accept that rough date.' But this date is *not* what the *Laches* text points to. As the 430s neared their end, so Socrates approached the age of 40 (perhaps 39, if one wishes to be pedantic). What the *Laches* indicates is that Socrates was engaged in elenctic practice soon after he *ceased to be a boy*. 'Older' here means 'older than he was in the preceding sentence'. The word 'older' cannot be taken out of its context, given some absolute meaning and then be put back into the context. If Nicias had been thinking of Socrates developing his dialectic in the 430s, he would have had to say 'You obviously haven't met Socrates since he was a young(ish) man', not '. . . since he was a boy', for otherwise Lysimachus' friend Melesias could in certain circumstances have interjected in surprise: 'But I met him when he was [say] 28 and he wasn't known then for any such practice as you mention.' In no context would an Athenian of the Classical period have been called a 'boy' into his thirties – to say nothing of his *late* thirties, nor would he have had to be in his father's company at deme ceremonies after the age of 18 or (at the latest) 20. *This* passage certainly does not date the oracle in the 430s; if it dates it at all, it dates it around 450, but it mentions neither Oracle nor mission, referring only to Socrates' elenctic practice, for whose date of origin we have no good separate evidence. If the Oracle was, as some suppose, closely linked with Socrates' 'divine sign', then as *Apology* 31d dates the sign from Socrates' boyhood, the oracle must also have been early; but the link is unconvincing.

Nor is the other evidence still convincing which was produced by A. E. Taylor in the 1917 *Proceedings of the British Academy* in favour of a date as late as the 430s. Taylor's passages[43] offer, apart from the evidence of the *Charmides*, which gives no *terminus post quem*, an allowance of time for Socrates to develop through a 'scientific' phase (doubted now by, for instance, Reeve[44]) and for him to have gathered a devoted circle (when all we need is the 'impetuous' Chaerephon) and to have acquired a reputation for 'wisdom' (of which Chaerephon may have had an exaggerated notion, and see further below on whether a reputation would have been a *desideratum*). I doubt if many people would now accept Taylor's portrait of Socrates as a famous head of a scientific school suddenly converted by the oracle.[45] Altogether the dating of the oracle may seem curiously vague, but that is not in itself a good reason for doubting its historicity.

Ancient scholarship

Nor, come to that, should we be weighed down by the evidence of disbelief in the story of the oracle about Socrates by certain ancient scholars cited by Montuori, such as Athenaeus or Colotes as quoted by Plutarch.[46] These are no better for our purposes than the arguments they present, which amount in Colotes' case as cited by Plutarch to nothing but abuse, and in Athenaeus' to a sustained piece of tendentiousness suggesting a limited knowledge of and/or a careless approach to Plato's *Apology*. Most ancient scholarship on this theme is suspect of derivation from Plato's and/or Xenophon's *Apologies*, apart from the occasional citation of a spurious metrical version of the oracle.

The argument from silence

A much more significant group of arguments centres on the absence of references elsewhere to the oracle, except for the probably derivative Xenophontine *Apology of Socrates*. Montuori instances the *Gorgias* and Plato's *Seventh Letter* as places where one might have expected a historical oracle to be mentioned.[47] One could add such places as *Meno* 71b–c, where Meno expresses great surprise at Socrates' claim to total ignorance of what goodness is, or even *Republic* I (337a), where Thrasymachus attacks Socrates for his unwillingness to answer questions. On both occasions the oracle of the *Apology* would have supplied a devastating answer to implied or actual criticism. The Oracle is not said or implied to have enjoined silence. Nor is it reported even to have suggested that the *only* method of spreading its message was by elenchus. One could argue that in maintaining silence Socrates and his close friends, if, as one presumes, they would have been in the know, were failing in their duty to promote the spread of the true message to all men which they believed the oracle to convey. And was the 'impetuous' or 'over the top' Chaerephon silent all his life about the remarkable response he received from Apollo, except for telling his brother Chaerecrates conveniently so that Socrates could cite the latter as witness (*Apology* 21a)? If not, then, granted the majority dating of the oracle before the Peloponnesian War, how could the oracle fail to become known to the comic poets who made Socrates the butt of so many jokes? Was there no material for comedy in the man who was wiser than others with Socrates' strange 'wisdom'? Plato's dialogues do, it is true, display certain reticences hard to explain, but the absence of the oracle from the whole extant literature of Socrates' lifetime and from all but two related works of the next generation is, humanly speaking, extraordinary. Was it really the best-kept secret of a lifetime? And that with no obvious reason for keeping it? It seems to me improbable.

A discrepancy between Plato and Xenophon

A passage of Xenophon's *Apology of Socrates* falls to be considered next. This is not the place for a full discussion of the exact nature of the relation between the two *Apologies*. Adopted here is the rather widespread view that Xenophon's was written by him after, and in the knowledge of, Plato's. This does not exhaust the problems. The difficulty that particularly concerns us now arises from the very different accounts they give of the oracle they have in common.

Plato's oracle says, in response to the question 'Is any man wiser than Socrates?', that no man is wiser than Socrates. Xenophon's account does not specify the question, but gives the Oracle an answer different enough to suggest a different question – and if the Oracle in such contexts gave merely a yes-or-no answer, as some have supposed, then Xenophon's Chaerephon's question was *certainly* different. The Oracle's response in Xenophon is that no man is more generous or more just or more *sophron* than Socrates. That word *sophron* presents many difficulties to the interpreter: in some contexts it is clearly a term of moral evaluation, commending moderation or temperance; in others it has a much more prudential colouring, referring to good sense and meaning something like 'sensible' or indeed 'prudent'. One further complication: the Greeks in general, and Plato in particular, were aware that there are many occasions when the temperate or moderate is sensible and prudent. Doubts about the text of the Xenophontine account do nothing to simplify matters: in Xenophon (according to the manuscripts) the Oracle does not use the word 'wise' but does say that nobody is more *sophron* than Socrates; Socrates himself, in detailing with insufferable boastfulness how right the Oracle was, does not use the word *sophron* but declares by rhetorical questions that nobody is more in control of his desires than he, more generous, more just or more wise. It is possible that for Xenophon's Oracle being *sophron* included wisdom; possibly von Arnim[48] was right to insert in the text of the oracle the words 'or wiser'. But it is clear that Xenophon's Oracle either spoke with different words from Plato altogether or at least added much. One could argue that Plato included the other virtues under 'wisdom' because he thought all virtues were the same, namely 'wisdom'; and/or that Xenophon separated out the different virtues because he disbelieved in the paradox of the unity of the virtues. But this seems unsatisfactory. Socrates' wisdom in Plato's *Apology* is an awareness of ignorance;

the ignorance has for its subject-matter the answers to moral questions, but is not itself a moral quality for praise or blame – rather a
universal property of human beings; and it was not the awareness
of ignorance which for Plato constituted the possession of virtue or
goodness. If the Oracle in historical fact gave the response we find
in Xenophon, then Plato has missed half the strength of his case –
for how could a man divinely so described be guilty of corrupting
the young? And if the Oracle actually gave the Platonic response,
then Xenophon's account is largely fictitious – for *Xenophon* did
not so much take for granted the unity of the virtues in wisdom
as to have that particular excuse for rewriting in terms of the other
virtues an original response mentioning 'wisdom'.

How should we now respond to the differences between the
Platonic and Xenophontine oracles? One way is to suppose simply
that Plato correctly put into his Socrates' mouth the plain truth,
whereas Xenophon was an arrant and apparently unblushing liar.
Those who do not quite like this sometimes suppose the *Apology*
in the Xenophontine corpus to be not the work of Xenophon.
But no less easy a solution is to stop talking about 'truth' and
'lies' in this black-and-white fashion and start thinking in terms of
fiction. Suppose that Xenophon read Plato's *Apology* not as faithful
reportage from which to differ was to lie but rather as a piece of
creative writing. That would mean, in Greek literary terms, that
it was there to be drawn upon, imitated, over-trumped, just like
any other piece of literary fiction.[49] Xenophon's procedure would
on this hypothesis be perfectly natural – and so would Plato's, for
that matter. If Plato's early readers, as is often supposed, checked
the Platonic 'account' of Socrates' defence against their own or
others' recollections of the trial, and thus guaranteed that Plato
could not produce a substantially false 'report', then this would
naturally have been fairly widely known: 'Plato got it right' would
have been the established view. To attempt to overthrow it with
an 'account' which invited the response 'Well, if *that* was how
it went, why on earth didn't Plato say so, and why should we
believe this Johnny-come-lately?' would have been more than
usually insensitive and unwary a proceeding for Xenophon. It
would have been specially awkward for Xenophon to assert in
the face of Plato's account guaranteed by people's recollection that
his version of the oracle was given 'in the presence of many people'
(Xenophon, *Apology* 14). To respond to these points by declaring
the Xenophontine *Apology* spurious would be (in what I believe to

be the absence of independent and cogent arguments for that view) a counsel of despair. There are of course many other questions to be settled and arguments to be met before one can have confidence in scholarly acceptance of an understanding of Plato's *Apology*, let alone the Socratic literature in general, as fictional to an important degree; but the evidence concerning the oracle by no means tells against it.

Questions concerning oracular practice

The rest of the arguments about the oracle's historicity concern the uniqueness, the motivation, the method, and the occasion of the Oracle's declaration of Socrates' 'wisdom' as pictured by Plato. This too is a complex matter, depending in part on one's view of the general probabilities of the Oracle's history and practice. Of these there are very varied estimates on the market, from the painstaking and valuable amassing of evidence by P. Amandry and by H. W. Parke and D. E. W. Wormell to the equally valuable and no less wide-ranging sceptical scholarship of J. Fontenrose.[50] This, again, is not the right moment for the renewed comprehensive re-examination of the material which my studies suggest would serve scholarship well, but rather for a cautious treatment of the evidence as it concerns Socrates.

How was the Socratic oracle given? A. E. Taylor[51] suggested that the response was merely what those running the Oracle thought the questioner wanted. There may be some truth in this; but, as we shall see, the Oracle did not always respond as the questioner desired, and some examples exist to show that responses at least were thought to show an exactly opposite tendency, to *avoid* the clearly expected and wanted answer.

A suggestion which has found more favour is the use at Delphi of divination by drawing lots in some way under the auspices of Apollo. If this is the right account of the oracle about Socrates, then the answer Chaerephon received was the result of pure chance; it might just as easily have been 'Yes, there is somebody wiser than Socrates' – at which point the response would have sunk into oblivion. On this interpretation, to its credit, two things need no further explanation: first and most obviously the Oracle's priests' motivation for singling out Socrates, since on this hypothesis they did no such thing; second Xenophon's point cited above that the oracle about Socrates was dispensed 'in the presence of many people', since lots could have been drawn in a place more public than that where the Pythian priestess normally offered the supposed divine wisdom. But Xenophon's remark may have been meant more loosely, for example of Chaerephon's telling many people as he rushed out from the room where the consultant listened to the Pythia; and to abolish the problem of motivation in this way may not be the only way to solve it.

Further, the actual evidence for the use of the lot in Classical Delphi is less than cogent. It consists of (1) a disputable inscription;[52] (2) sundry special cases where the Oracle was asked to choose from a list of names with or without a choice of lots supplied by the consultant(s); (3) the expression 'you bestow speech by lot', addressed to Delphian Apollo by Euripides' Creusa, *Ion* 908; (4) the use of the word *anheilen* ('took up'?) for '[the Oracle] said'; and (5) various vases usefully pictured and analysed by Amandry. The first two of these are less than secure; the third is ambiguous, referable *either* to the Oracle itself *or* to the ballot for a place in the queue to consult it.[53] We may helpfully take the last two together. Item (4) has been popular evidence ever since Lobeck[54] in 1829 conjectured, adducing no evidence whatever, that the special use of this word for an oracle's pronouncing referred to the 'taking up' or drawing of lots. The conjecture would be more convincing if examples occurred of this verb being used in non-oracular or otherwise clear contexts of lot-drawing; but Amandry cited in this context only oracular ones where the verb has its normal sense for such surroundings, and I have seen no others. *Iliad* III. 316 and similar Homeric lines have the simple verb *heilen*, 'took', in a context to do with lots and not oracles, but the verb clearly describes an action that takes place *before* the lots are shaken up or shuffled and does not denote the 'drawing'. Further, the Oracle, i.e. the god, is said to 'take up' – or whatever the verb means in such contexts – but Amandry's vases do not show the god but rather the consultant doing something Amandry interprets as drawing lots. This inherent contradiction in the evidence adduced leaves one wondering whether Amandry's interpretation of the vases is correct *and* whether we have yet got to the bottom of the semantic issue concerning the verb 'take up'. K. Latte's very different explanation of the verb deserves more respect than Amandry gave it, but any explanation can only be conjectural.[55] The use of the lot at Delphi in the Classical period cannot be taken as established, and Fontenrose[56] brings arguments against it based on the lack of negative answers. We should not abandon the search for a proper motive for the particular oracle about Socrates in misplaced confidence that it was the result of chance.

Possible literary motives

Genuine motivation is best found in the context of a group of oracles noticed by R. Herzog and further analysed by Montuori and especially by Parke and Wormell.[57] These concern the type of question 'Who is the most x man?' where x may be replaced with 'pious', 'happy', 'wise' or 'prudent', or indeed 'fortunate'. The pattern of answer is no less easily discernible than that of the questions. The enquirer has what he thinks is a good reason to think himself the most x of men: Theopompus' anonymous Magnesian the wealthiest, Gyges of Lydia the most fortunate, Chilon or Anacharsis most wise, and perhaps most fortunate, an unknown figure in the story Pliny tells of Pedius; and one compares[58] Herodotus' story of Croesus and Solon, in which Croesus seeks the title of 'most fortunate' and Solon plays as it were the part of an Oracle, and that in a story replete with Delphic themes. In this chain of stories the Oracle disappoints the conceited enquirer: it does *not*, contrary to A. E. Taylor's view mentioned above, give the answer the consultant expects. Instead the Oracle names an insignificant person who is surely intended as typical of a range of undistinguished worthies who are none the less worthy for their lack of apparent distinction – Clearchus in the Magnesian story, Aglaus of Psophis for Gyges, and Myson of Oeta for Chilon or Anacharsis. Again Pedius may be a similar case. One may compare Tellus and also Cleobis and Biton in the Croesus–Solon legend. The enquirer expresses surprise, implicitly in Theopompus' story of the Magnesian, explicitly[59] in the similar tale of Croesus. After the oracle, two enquirers, the Magnesian and Anacharsis, each visit the man deemed by the god more x than they, and in the story of Gyges there follows a description of the preferred Aglaus, a visit being in this case, one imagines, ruled out by Gyges' Lydian remoteness and kingly preoccupations. In two of the three stories this visit elicits an explanation, direct (Aglaus) or indirect (Myson) of the oracle, which was at first not understood by the enquirer.

Now all the obvious points laboured above about this group of oracles are highly relevant to the oracle in Plato's *Apology*. For it presents a very sharp and consistent contrast to them.

(1) The enquirer is not enquiring in conceited expectation of receiving the answer 'himself'; Socrates is not the enquirer, but the 'impetuous' Chaerephon, who, however, on this occasion lays no claim to wisdom of his own. (2) The oracle does not disappoint the enquirer; it gives the 'expected' answer. (3) The person named is accordingly not a figure remote from and unknown to the enquirer. (4) It is not the enquirer who visits the person named and receives there an explanation of the oracle. It is rather the person named who visits numerous other people and thus ultimately receives an indirect explanation of the oracle's naming of himself. (5) The surprise one would expect is that of the enquirer; but in Plato it is not Chaerephon who is amazed – he has received the expected answer; rather, the named person, Socrates, is amazed. (6) The story is told not by some third party but by the actual person named. Furthermore, in most cases of riddling oracles, the straightforward sense is the one accepted by the person most nearly concerned; it mostly makes a better story that way. One compares Oedipus and Macbeth, and recalls Croesus, who interpreted the Oracle's doubtless legendary pronouncement that on invading Persia he would destroy a mighty empire as a prophecy of success, and protesting on his defeat was told – too late – that the mighty empire destined for destruction was his own. But Socrates in Plato's *Apology* doubts at once the literal truth of the oracle, is not deceived by it, and eventually works out for himself what it means and how it is true.

One might argue, but the argument would hardly be cogent by itself, that the case of Socrates is so untypical that it could not be genuine;[60] to this by itself the counter-argument is too obvious: 'I believe just because it is absurd', as St Augustine is popularly quoted as having said of the Crucifixion of the Son of God. What impresses is the neatness and comprehensiveness with which Plato's story reverses every single major feature of the story-pattern. Truth can be stranger than fiction; but it does not normally exhibit an attention to the detail of the fiction. Plainly put, the exactitude with which Socrates' story reverses, turns upside-down, a standard Delphian story presents evidence of a *design* to turn the pattern upside-down. Such inversion of known patterns is a standing feature of Greek literature, as generic studies in our time have shown. Those of us who believe that Socrates himself was no literary creator of fiction, and certainly not on so solemn an occasion a liar and perjurer, may, and in my judgement should, conclude that the story of the oracle in Plato's *Apology* is likely to be Plato's fiction, executed with a master's hand. The motivation we should look for is not that of the Oracle, but that of Plato. We should look for *literary* motives.

Literary effectiveness

What literary motives, apart from sheer delight in creative ingenuity, offer themselves? That depends in part on the motives other than the religious one which one can attribute to the Socrates, if not of history, then of Plato's *Apology*. We must see if there are any ways, other than by his account of a mission from Apollo, by which Socrates could justify his sense of a duty to spend, and ultimately to lay down, his life in the cause of dialectical philosophy; and we must take a good look at what Plato might reasonably think of their likely effectiveness. True, these enquiries presuppose the possibility of Plato's willingness to put rhetorical effectiveness above truth – and perhaps even above plausibility to his more intelligent and better-educated readers, for it is hard to tell how many would have believed in the writer's own time a story of this kind crafted thus. The issue here is not so much Plato's credibility or integrity or honesty or anything of that sort; the question is rather what type of literature was Plato writing, and what were the canons of the genre? Was it biographical, in a quasi-modern sense? Was it 'historical'? What did Plato's contemporaries expect of a 'Socratic *logos*' (here 'tale' or 'discussion'), a genre mentioned apparently as such by Aristotle in his *Poetics* and elsewhere perhaps a couple of generations later? I hope to study these questions in another publication, and admit that no answer to them is likely to achieve finality. My concern here is that a literary origin for the Apolline oracle of Plato's *Apology* be not ruled out by a priori judgements such as the one cautiously framed by Fontenrose: 'Or could this response be a pious fiction of the Socratic circle? That is not impossible, though perhaps incredible.'[61] On the present view the oracle may have found a place in a literary work because it was effective as literature. It can hardly be denied that it *is* effective literature, and none the less so for being a neat inversion of a probably well-known type of story.

But what alternative defence could the Platonic Socrates have offered? What explanation is there other than the dubiously historical oracle for his way of life, and for his persistence in it to the end? We may start[62] with Socrates' opinion that his practice of refutation confers a benefit on those he refutes. *Gorgias* 470c offers the following exchange: '*Polus*. It is hard to refute you, Socrates; but wouldn't even a child be able to refute you for not telling the truth? *Socrates*. Then I shall be grateful to the child, and equally to you, if you will refute me and rid me of nonsense. But don't weary of benefiting a friend, but refute me.' At least on the moral issue between Polus and himself, and presumably on other moral issues, Socrates regards as a benefactor anyone refuting him. The Platonic Socrates must therefore think his refutation a benefit to the person refuted.

Socrates also makes clear that he regards his services to individual Athenians as a service also to 'the Athenians' collectively. This much comes out clearly, in a context whose relationship to refutation in particular stands admittedly in need of further discussion, at *Apology* 29d–30b. It emerges also from the *Gorgias* (502d10 ff.) that the politician's proper public function is to better the characters of individual citizens. If Socrates viewed his refutations as a benefit to the individuals concerned, he will almost certainly have seen them as improving the individuals' moral standing, and a life spent in thus improving them as a life spent not merely in the service of individuals but in the service of the state. Plato's *Apology* 30b finds him, we note, treating goodness of the soul as the source of the goodness of everything else to man *both individually and publicly*. Socrates might, then, have pursued his way of life with determination to the end for the benefit of individual Athenians and of their state.

But this leads naturally to a further question: why should Socrates be so determined to benefit his fellow citizens in their individual and corporate capacities? What obligation weighed so heavily upon him? Now one may or may not think Socrates lay under any obligation to individual Athenians he had perhaps never met before; but there should be no doubt whatever of his own patriotic and well-founded belief in his deep indebtedness to the Athenian state. In the *Apology* he does not spell this out in detail, but he does give the very broadest of hints: he tells the jury at 29d, 'Men of Athens, I salute you and *am your friend.* . . .' The Greek word for 'friend' here is a notoriously complex one; but standing in a relationship of 'friendship' might, and here beyond doubt does, include standing in a relationship of mutual benefit and obligation. But the nature of the state's benefits to Socrates emerges in detail only in the *Crito*. There 'the common of the city' or 'the city as a community' (50a) joins with the city's laws, which (51c–d) in effect 'gave [him] birth, educated [him], and gave [him] a share with every other citizen of all the fine things they could'. The reader may want to argue that Socrates in *Republic* I refutes the notion from Cephalus that it is always just, that there is always a moral obligation, to repay a debt. To be sure, one may reply; but that refutation consists of a counter-example where the repayment would do harm, or what the repaying agent would think a harm. This in no way affects the *general* (not universal) truth that it is just to repay a debt; and there is no reason to doubt that Socrates would have regarded it as just to return benefit to the city which had benefited him. Indeed it would be *unjust* not to repay such a debt. We can hardly suppose that Socrates' standards in the matter of justice and injustice were *lower* than those of his contemporaries.

One can go a step further, I think, though here a priori argument is easier to find than evidence from the texts. If Socrates were to stop doing to his fellow citizens individually and collectively what he thinks is a good, he would in effect be depriving them wilfully of that good. And to deprive someone wilfully of a good is to do him harm. One can show that Socrates would have regarded his cessation of activity as depriving the Athenians of a benefit: at *Apology* 31d6–e1 he says that political activity on his part would have led to his early demise 'and I would not have been any benefit to you or to myself'. This notion is repeated at 36c2–3. It is a plausible view that Socrates regarded this deprivation of these people of this benefit as wrong: not so much because he says at 30c that the Athenians will be doing themselves no less harm than they do him if they kill him, being the kind of man he is – since that could be the harm that their own injustice will do to their souls – as because he goes on at 30d to warn them not to make a mistake concerning the god's gift to them. He is the god's gift to the city in its need (30e5), and if the god sent them such another, it would be in his care for them (31a6–7); if it would be a mistake, wrong, for the Athenians to deprive themselves of him, it would be a damage to them if *he* were to deprive them of himself, and he could not plead that he was doing such damage other than deliberately. Then again: if in exile (37e3 ff.) Socrates were to remain silent, that would be disobedient to the god, and, leaving that on one side, to discuss in this way goodness and allied topics is the greatest good to human beings, and, especially, 'The unexamined life is not liveable for a human being.' To remain silent in Athens would, it follows, deprive the Athenians of the greatest good, and so far as Socrates is concerned, would condemn them to a life not worth living. And Socrates does not need to give any other reason for not living on in silence; it is clear that he regards it as wrong thus to leave his fellow men in the lurch. Socrates, it is entirely reasonable to suppose, thought that voluntarily not to pursue his practice of dialectic was deliberately to injure and to wrong his fellow Athenians. It would be deliberately to wrong those who – at least in the overwhelming majority of cases – had done him no wrong, except perhaps to repeat slanders against him of whose falsehood the majority were presumably unaware. To wrong those who had done one no wrong was certainly 'unjust', *adikos*, in Socrates' Greek.

So it was just, in Socrates' belief, to pursue dialectic and go about refuting Athenians on ethical matters, and it would have been unjust for him to have stopped. But the questions do not quite stop there. Did Socrates feel an overwhelming obligation to behave justly and to refrain from intentional injustice? To this the answer is a resounding and obvious 'Yes!' Death, he says at 28d6–10, is preferable to the shameful – and that for Socrates certainly includes, if indeed it is not coterminous with, the unjust. To attempt an unjust killing, he says at 30d5, is a great harm, a great *kakon*. At 32c8–d3 he insists, having just previously cited actions of his that tend to prove the point, that he is not concerned about dying, but is wholly concerned with doing nothing unjust or impious. He refuses to plead irrationally for the jury's favour partly on the ground that it would not be just (35b9–d1). The Platonic *Apology* itself makes pretty clear just how important, how *all*-important, just behaviour was to the Platonic Socrates. It certainly makes it clear that on his scale of values death paled into insignificance beside injustice, and it also explains why (29a–b). For the Platonic Socrates in general there is clearer evidence elsewhere, notably in the *Crito* (49a–c); but the *Apology* is clear enough for our present purposes.

We set out to find a plausible explanation other than the oracle for Socrates' sense of mission, for his determination to die rather than abandon the elenchus of Athenians at large. We have found one, in Socrates' firm belief that his elenchus conferred a genuine benefit on his victims and his probable judgement that to refrain deliberately from offering that benefit would be wrong and unjust, and his absolute and iron conviction that wrongdoing and injustice were evils and indeed harms to be avoided at all earthly costs. What is more, there is more than a suspicion that a reasonable proportion of his audience in the actual or fictional jury would have been convinced by the argument that there are divine ordinances supporting and enjoining just behaviour on mankind. Classical Athenians of an unsophisticated stamp were likely to believe that the gods approved of and duly rewarded justice and had their sanctions against injustice.[63] In brief, passages in late fifth-century BC literature of a thoughtful kind suggest that a belief in the gods went with and supported a belief in moral imperatives (including, of course, justice); that a disbelief in the gods of tradition was worrying in part because it suggested the undermining of moral imperatives; and that it can hardly be coincidental that the indictment on which Socrates was before the court was that he did not believe in the city's – i.e. the traditional – gods and that he corrupted the young. The combination of irreligion (or new-fangled religion) and dubious moral teaching is a significant feature of the indictment, and one which we may be sure Socrates' accusers thought rhetorically and politically useful. Socrates could therefore assume, and Plato could legitimately have him assume, that his audience would suppose him to be under a divinely supported obligation not to behave unjustly in omission or commission. Assuredly not many people on the jury would have felt like rising to their feet and proclaiming their doubts whether Socrates, given the chance, ought to have benefited his fellow men.

They would, however, have been much more inclined to react by doubting that Socratic refutation was really a benefit. Socrates' reasons for believing that would take us too far afield, but it is worth the trouble to point out that Socrates suggests in the *Apology* that they would have taken him also too far afield. Not only does he complain that he has but a short time to deal with slanders that have been going the rounds for many years (19a1–2 and 37b1–2); at 38a he declares pretty roundly that though the pursuit of dialectic is the greatest human good, and life unexamined is not liveable, the jury will not believe him if he says so. 'That is how things are, as I say, gentlemen; but it is not easy to persuade [you of this].' Accordingly he offers it simply as his own judgement that he is better off with his awareness of ignorance than those who know more but are unaware of their ignorance (22e); and at 29b he merely suggests, in a rhetorical question, that to be unaware of one's own ignorance is culpable; the only semblance of an argument that appears in the *Apology* for the benefits of his refutations is at 31a7 ff. There he argues on grounds other than the oracle-story that he is the sort of man to be given to the city by a presumably benevolent deity.

The argument runs that it looks like something divinely sponsored that he has so neglected his own affairs for so long in the service of the Athenians, and at that without even the humanly understandable reason that he was being paid for it – witness his poverty. Socrates was doubtless right: it is not *this* easy to persuade a sceptical jury. Socrates, they will have said at this point, always was an odd man. To convince people that Socrates' refutations were beneficial to the victims would have meant convincing them that their souls were what mattered, that goodness (the quality or group of qualities required for success) was knowledge, and that refutation was a necessary step on the way to the relevant knowledge. This is quite a task for a single day in court or for a correspondingly brief work of literature; and nobody would have found it easy to construct a persuasive defence on these lines.

How much less philosophically difficult it would have been, or was, to construct the speech as we have it. That is not meant to belittle Plato's artistry; on the contrary, it is meant in praise of the unerring literary skill of his youth and middle age. If indeed the oracle is a fiction, it is one designed to persuade Plato's readers of Socrates' fundamental innocence of the charges – or Plato's own innocence of corrupting the young and propagating irreligion – without stating and arguing the whole Socratic or Platonic case in consecutive detail. In this, over the centuries, it has been remarkably successful. At least on the surface of the text it offers the backing of Apollo's Oracle for Socrates' practice. It thus supports the elenchus which so vexed the victims, and which could well have impressed others as essentially subversive of ordinary people's ordinary moral beliefs, inconsistencies and all. It gives Socrates an arguable case, without going into too much philosophical detail, for his good faith if (in sceptical eyes) for little else. It backs up and gives substance to the Platonic Socrates' habitual annoying disclaimer of knowledge; and it manages to do so without diminishing, and even while enhancing (at least for the more credulous of conventional religion), Socrates' stature as a sage. It serves to explain, in the context in which Plato introduces it, that what Socrates was about was different from what other would-be sages were about; and in the process it lends to his proceedings not only an air of appealing innocence but, more significantly in the presence of Meletus' charges, an appearance of wholly conventional but unusually persistent piety. If it is not true, it is *très bien trouvé*. As a fiction, or perhaps one should say as a deliberately constructed myth, it is brilliant. But brilliant fictions – or even, come to that, factual truths – deserve plausible presentation; and we have not yet finished examining Plato's version of Socrates' mission for plausibility.

PROBLEMS IN PLAUSIBILITY

Why Chaerephon's question?

From this point of view there are still problems about the start of the whole process. The first problem is, why should Chaerephon have asked the original question? A few have supposed that before he can reasonably have asked Apollo this particular question, Socrates' repute must already have been widespread and formidable, and hence that as an account of Socrates' beginning on his life's work, the whole is incoherent. It is indeed possible, whether Plato's *Apology* is a true or a fictitious story, that Plato hoped his readers would not think of asking the relevant questions. To suppose Socrates to have acquired a reputation for *knowledge* before the incident at Delphi would be to demolish the defence rather effectively. The way out of this by supposing that Socrates had had extensive knowledge but had not thought it of any value leads to further difficulty. For in that case either Socrates' immediate response to the Oracle, that in nothing, great or small, was he aware of being wise, was disingenuous or he had already concluded that what was normally called wisdom was of no value (an estimate he appears in the *Apology* to owe to Apollo). Perhaps he already thought ordinary human knowledge of little or no account, and the oracle as finally interpreted was simply making an example of him in a perspective he came to by the light of nature? That would make only a rather difficult sense of his long and roundabout quest for the oracle's meaning. These difficulties are not to be lightly dismissed. To suppose Socrates, on the other hand, to have gained already a reputation for skill in argument would argue either skill in attaining positive conclusions (which would have the same effect on the story as the first supposition above) or skill in refutation (which would involve his having practised it before the oracle). The question will not go away; but Socrates has answered the basic problem here after a fashion in the text, in a way I have not seen noticed, though it appears obvious enough: he expressly mentions

Chaerephon's character as one of a man liable to go over the top in everything he did. The reason why this is mentioned is presumably not because the supposed or real jury are interested in Chaerephon; it is rather, one may suppose, that Plato's Socrates is excusing what would otherwise have been an absurd question to put to Apollo. We may reasonably view the picture Plato thus offers as a plausible one, of a Socrates known perhaps to a few close friends as clever and full of good advice, and of one friend whose over-enthusiasm took him to Delphi.

Why start with public refutations?

Why, to broach the second problem, did Socrates *start* refuting people? We have seen that interpretation of the oracle required discovery of people's inconsistencies, but not their demonstration to the individual concerned. Once Socrates had understood the oracle and found that it meant him as a paradigm for the transmission of a general message, it made sense for him to promote the message by showing people in detail how inconsistent, and hence ignorant, they were. The purposes attributed to the god could be furthered also by such demonstration in public. On this basis the Socratic procedure as pictured in Plato's earlier dialogues is perfectly intelligible. But it remains hard to see why Socrates should have *begun* the practice of *public* refutation before reading, as it were, the god's message. Yet Plato's *Apology* is quite clear: Socrates' refutations were conducted in public from the start – witness the references to bystanders at 21d1 and 22b7, with reference to the politicians and the poets respectively. (It is perhaps curious that Socrates mentions nobody else present at his examination of the handcraftsmen.) If the *Apology* were straightforward biography it would be possible to believe he was that sort of argumentative, not to say simply cussed man, but that can hardly have been the sort of impression Plato wished to create. If Plato's Socrates did feel that the best way to discover people's real thoughts is to try and refute them, one would be entitled to expect some justification for that belief. Justification could be required to start by defending his decision to attempt discovery of the oracle's meaning by finding a counter-example to its surface statement. In sum, Socrates in Plato's version seems to start on his life's work before understanding the oracle which gives it meaning. That is exactly the sort of thing one might expect if the oracle were an adventitious short cut to justification of a career for which the full genuine motivation was quite different. It is worth adding that such a gap in the argument is perhaps the best support for Guthrie's mention of Socrates' feelings (see p.30 above), as opposed to his reasoning. But to fall back on feelings remains unsatisfying.

Socrates' knowledge of his mission

Does Socrates have anything more to say about his mission? Yes, and indeed not the least problematic things about it are to be found in other pages of Plato's version of his *Defence*. The question being considered at 29c–d is whether Socrates would be willing to give up what he calls philosophizing in return for the sparing of his life. I do not now delve into the wider problem of the consistency of the *Apology* and the *Crito* on this point;[64] there is another difficulty demanding attention. Socrates here compares his orders from the god to the orders of the Athenian generals who set him in the ranks in battle. It would be dreadful if he obeyed the generals, but did not obey the god, who, as he 'thought and understood', ordered him to live a life of philosophy examining himself and others, but rather in fear of death or anything else forsook his ordered place. Notice in that sentence the words 'thought and understood'. Socrates does not say he knew that the god had given him his marching orders for a life of dialectic and philosophy; he says only that he thought he had. What then are we to make of the next few lines? In these Socrates says that if he disobeyed the Oracle for fear of death, he would indeed be proving his atheism and his opinion that he was wise when in fact he was not. For, he says, the fear of death is a case of thinking one is wise when one is not. No man knows whether death is a boon or a bane. Socrates, unlike other men, does not think he knows this. But he does know that to do wrong (*or* act unjustly) and to disobey a better than oneself, whether god or man, is bad and shameful. He will not choose what he knows to be bad in preference to that of which he does not know whether it is good or bad. Hence, if offered his life on condition of ceasing to philosophize or conduct his search, he will not accept. 'I will obey the god rather than you', he says. Now it is very tempting to read this argument as advancing from the quite legitimate *opinion* that Apollo had given him marching orders to the much more dubious claim that he *knew* the oracle had done so. Indeed, if we are to reason strictly about this, in order to know that to desist from philosophizing would be wrong, and for his argument to take effect, Socrates must know that desisting from philosophizing would be in disobedience to a superior; and to know that desisting from philosophy would be disobedience he has to *know* that he has received orders not to desist from philosophizing, or, if you like, positively to continue philosophizing all his life. But we have seen that the proposition that the god has made him an example to men is modestly labelled by Socrates himself – and with good reason – as probable, rather than certain or known. There is a major discrepancy here.

The first possible solution to this discrepancy deserves inspection, even though inspection may lead us to cast it aside: it has a certain intrinsic interest. Socrates speaks at 29b6–7 of what it is he knows, as opposed to the goodness or badness of death for men, which he does not know. What is it he knows? He knows in that context that it is bad and shameful to 'act unjustly and disobey somebody better'. Most readers assume that the words 'act unjustly and' are there because in general to disobey one's betters is unjust; that is to say that one's betters have a just right to issue commands which will be obeyed. On this reading Plato's Socrates is emphasising disobedience to a better, saying that he can't give up his enquiries, because to do so is thus disobedient, and because he knows such disobedience is unjust. But there is another way of taking the phrase. If we could suppose that to give up philosophizing would be unjust in itself, and is only secondarily also a case of disobedience to the god, the discrepancy between Socrates' judgement of the oracle's probable meaning and his certain knowledge here would dwindle, if not vanish. But in order to fit this idea to the text we have to suppose Plato and his Socrates guilty of more than one rhetorical sleight-of-hand. The first is in the injustice-and-disobedience passage itself, where in context the audience ought to be expecting more emphasis on the oracle than on morality – in view especially of Socrates' specification eleven lines earlier of disobedience to the oracle. Second, Socrates says very soon (29d1–3) apropos of the hypothetical bargain of his life for ceasing his investigations, 'Athenians, . . . I will obey the god rather than you'; the Oracle and not justice is verbally the prime interest here too. If the usual reading is to be wrong, Socrates is twice suppressing 'justice' and pushing forward the Oracle alone when what he is actually saying concerns justice more than the Oracle. Symmetry and rhetorical continuity are against these implied rhetorical tricks. And they would constitute this whole section of Socrates' argument a rather

71

too crude use of the Oracle as a cover for his reference to the dictates of morality and of its divine sanction.

'Oracles and dreams'

The difficulty remains solid, that Socrates' defence of his refusal hypothetically to drive a bargain with the Athenians has a hole in it: it makes Socrates imply that he knows something for which he elsewhere rightly claims no more than probability. The hole gapes especially wide in the context of a man desperate not to claim knowledge he does not possess. Further, uncharitable solutions such as a simple mistake by Plato or by his Socrates are unlikely in so highly wrought a work by so careful and fastidious an artist.

People might want to resolve our original discrepancy by an appeal to a later section of the speech; for Socrates later says (34c4 ff.) that 'I claim that I have been ordered [to investigate those thinking themselves wise] by the god both from oracles and from dreams and in every way in which any other divine dispensation ever ordered a mortal to do anything'; and this, if true, would perhaps, in the Classical Athenian climate of thought, have more readily entitled Socrates to claim knowledge of his orders from Apollo. But there are difficulties about this.

First, as we have seen before, it is intolerable to be compelled to read a speech backwards, and it is hard to think of a competent writer causing his readers to imagine an audience listening to a speech backwards. It is necessary rather to think of a way out of the discrepancy which makes sense in the immediate context, if we are to do justice to Socrates' speech as a developing argument addressed in its fictional context to a not especially sophisticated jury likely to have been much more numerous than our juries are.

Second, the passage is difficult in itself. Socrates in fact takes the argument an unexpected route. This time he is explaining the tendency of young men to spend time in his company; they gather round and listen when he refutes people – as he says, a not unpleasant experience for them. He says then that he has been ordered by the god to do this; ordered by oracles and dreams and every means by which a divine providence ever ordered a mortal to do anything. Perhaps he has, whether in fiction or in fact. But, if so, why did he not tell us and the jury before? We required hard evidence for Socrates' sense of having been *ordered* by the god to refute people he met; we saw room for doubt whether the

Oracle had provided Socrates with hard evidence; and instead of mentioning the evidence he has, and spelling out in detail how it convinced him, Plato's Socrates passed over chunks of it, left us with a mere probability which he needed for his argument to know, and brought out those chunks only later and only in passing. One might legitimately wonder how Socrates could produce convincing evidence of dreams he had had; but he could at least suggest that he had mentioned them to his friends at the time. If true, such a suggestion would have come in handy several pages earlier in the *Defence*. As for 'oracles' in the plural, are we or a jury supposed to take seriously the proposition that the gist of the oracle Chaerephon received was repeated, or that Oracles on other occasions gave responses which in different and perhaps more direct terms gave Socrates his marching orders? If neither of these is the case, did Socrates here speak loosely of 'oracles' when in fact only the one was given? And, if so, what becomes of Socrates' recent reputation for strict veracity and rejection of an advocate's tricks? Furthermore, Socrates backed up the earlier account of the Delphic oracle for Chaerephon by the hearsay evidence of Chaerecrates; why not produce more evidence of the same kind? Socrates does declare these hard sayings true and easy to test, and appears ('For if . . .' at 33c8) to foreshadow an explanation; but none is forthcoming: all that comes forth is a challenge to produce anyone he has corrupted. That is not, and could not be, evidence for the divine command. Socrates' certainty of mission remains without a plausible explanation, and indeed I have none to offer. Plato and his Socrates seem merely to cover up the difficulty with rhetoric. This passage, rather than supplying a solution, leaves Socrates' certainty yet more problematic.[65]

THE RHETORIC OF PLATO'S VERSION

What this passage does is to demote the oracle from its position as chief evidence for Socrates' mission and make it just one among many occurrences or deductions pointing in the same direction. One of the deductions might be the argument mentioned above, that Socrates' life *must* be a gift from the god. Why does Plato's Socrates want at the same time to demote the oracle and lend added evidence – if one can call it that – to the mission? The suggestion lies ready to hand that the oracle was sufficient for the speech's purposes at that earlier point in its development to give the mission a dramatic start, and one not requiring too much by way of philosophical argument. The oracle helps at that stage to account for the mission's continuance even better than it accounts in detail for its start. At no moment earlier in his defence did Socrates need, rhetorically, the dreams and other oracles or divine commands; he has a highly dramatic narrative and reasonably forceful argument without. But he is now approaching the rhetorical climax of his defence: this is the last paragraph of actual argument in his favour before he makes the final very effective point of his reluctance to produce what he labels unjust and impious sob-stuff. He wishes to argue that the only reason the young flock around him – and that not to their detriment – is the pleasantness of hearing those with a conceit of wisdom examined. In awareness, one supposes, that this leaves him open to suspicion of mere impish enjoyment himself, he reminds his audience or Plato's readers that he has another and better reason for his refutations. And so he deploys all the evidence he can, and indeed some that he only very doubtfully can. Plato doubtless hoped that reader or putative audience would not ask the question why the dreams and plural oracles appear only at this point in the speech; and certainly many readers have not asked it, as they have been swept on by the rhetoric of a past master in both style and literary construction.

SOCRATES' MORAL MISSION

One final problem seems to me to be less problematic than it has appeared to some other critics.[66] Socrates launches at 29d into an account of what he would be giving up if he were to bargain his philosophy for his life, an account which differs at least on the surface from our previous impressions. 'I will not stop', he says

> exhorting you and showing each of you that I meet, saying as usual 'My very good man, you who are an Athenian, from the greatest and most famous city for wisdom and strength, you are not ashamed of yourself for making an effort to get as much money as possible, and reputation and honour, but making no effort and taking no thought for prudence and truth and for the soul's greatest possible improvement?' And if one of you disputes this and claims to make an effort [for his soul], I will not at once let him go ... but will question and investigate and refute him and if I

think he has not goodness, but claims it, I will reproach him with taking things of the greatest value with little seriousness, and things of lesser value more seriously . . . This, you should know, is the god's command, and in my opinion no greater benefit has been conferred on you in the city than my service to the god. I simply go around persuading young and old not to make more effort for their bodies or their money than they do for the greatest possible improvement of their souls.

This sounds indeed a rather different note from Socrates' previous account of what he actually did. The reference to enquiry and refutation echoes previous narrative, but there is far more positive content here. In particular the paragraph quoted refers to Socrates actively reproaching the Athenians for getting their values wrong. This in turn implies his own belief that his values are right, that he is right in regarding moral values as paramount over what may broadly speaking be termed material ones. Does this make Socrates or his story inconsistent?

The view is clearly tenable that it does not. Socrates, one recalls, did not say that he knew that he knew nothing; he said he did not think he knew what he did not know. He went about demonstrating other people's false conceit of knowledge. Now they certainly claimed or appeared to claim to know that their values were sound, and it was no doubt mostly about these that Socrates questioned them. These were, it makes sense to assume, the 'most important things' of which the poets and craftsmen proved to be ignorant despite their technical knowledge. But then if other people did not know that their values were sound, how did Socrates know that his were? If he can accuse them of not knowing values, then how is it he can be so positive about his own? This problem presents perhaps a special difficulty for our time, which tends to distinguish fact sharply from value and then say that facts are knowable but values are not, or are subjective. Clearly Socrates cannot have been making the point that values are subjective; on the contrary, he is strongly associated with the idea that goodness *is* knowledge. What he would claim, I think, is that his values are, so far as he has been able to discover, of an iron consistency, whereas other people's are inconsistent. His values, as he makes clear both on and beneath the surface of the *Apology* (to say nothing here of other works of Plato's), are those of justice, of helping and certainly not of harming others. He is not like others who pay lip-service to moral values of that sort but in fact pursue pleasure or wealth or honour or power or technical expertise or whatever. He is not like yet others whose values alter according to the convenience of the moment. These people are the people he keeps reproaching, and will continue, if released, to reproach. And he is not like other species of the inconsistent who make their unfortunate appearances in Plato's dialogues to have their self-contradictions shown up: one thinks, for example, of Callicles in the *Gorgias*, who cannot in the last analysis maintain a consistent hedonism. And Socrates knows, as he says, that to commit injustice, to do something wrong, is bad and shameful. He knows it, one may suspect on reading the *Apology*, because nobody can refute or prove him inconsistent in this belief and (on reading other Platonic works) because that is, in his view, what the gods wish and enjoin. And it is legitimate for Socrates to represent his practice of refuting other people's values as tending to establish his own; that is all that is required to explain his report that he goes around exhorting people to follow his own anti-materialistic values. Many will have been found in his own time to agree in principle, some of the time, with some or much of what he says; but fewer will have been consistent, and fewer still of the moral stature to continue courting a finally fatal unpopularity in the cause of any beliefs they shared with Socrates.

Plato's *Apology* paints a brilliant picture. It is a portrait which might indeed have convinced a jury. It has convinced many critics since. But the fact had to be faced: Socrates did, historically, fail to convince the jury. It is by no means clear that the speech Plato put into his mouth would have convinced the jury either. It might not even have found favour with the historical Socrates. But that is not because Plato failed to lavish upon it all the resources of his literary art.

Others besides the young men of his time have found it a 'not unpleasant' experience to follow in Plato's pages Socrates' refutations of the conceited. Others besides the young men of his time have failed to see or to pay attention to the moral point. In an age largely, in this country, godless and, it seems, increasingly materialistic in its values, we could profitably learn from a Socrates who is concerned to show how difficult it is to sustain, humanly rather than philosophically, a consistent set of materialistic values, and to show us by the example of his courage and his stubborn faith the strength of his own values. True, Plato's Socrates is not quite the guileless, unpractised speaker Plato has him suggest he is at the outset of his defence; but the subtle nuances of language and rhetoric he uses, in Plato's version, should not be allowed to obscure either the essential moral force of his position or its continuing relevance to normal human concerns.[67]

NOTES

1 The Thucydides passage, I. 22, is quoted by Gregory Vlastos in his 1991: 49f., n. 15, and 253. It would be presumptuous of me even to pretend to discuss this book thoroughly here, having received it only shortly before completing this chapter: but it would equally be discourteous to ignore it (a judgement I have not abandoned despite receiving while this book was in the press the very sad news of Gregory Vlastos' death).

Vlastos teases out with impressive detail the extensive differences between the Socrates of the early and of the middle dialogues, Soc_E and Soc_M. Vlastos (especially 91ff.) reminds us that Aristotle's evidence favours Soc_E as, in Aristotle's view, representing *in outline* (my italics) a Socrates he could refer to as, indeed, 'Socrates', in contra-distinction to Soc_M, to whom he refers often as 'Plato'. But one needs to bear in mind that Aristotle's reports about Socrates offer only a few very important doctrines and salient points of method; the reports encompass only a minute number of arguments. This is compatible with Vlastos' view (1991: 50) that Plato was 'producing rather than reproducing' Socratic philosophy; and it should restrain us from commitment to the Socratic authenticity of any particular argument in Plato's early works without careful sifting of the available evidence.

Vlastos (1991: 97, n. 67), like Deman (1942: *passim*), makes an argument from the tenses used by Aristotle in his references to Socrates. Past tenses, on their view, offer an indication that the subject is the historical Socrates; present tenses suggest a literary reference. The latter one may accept; the former is more doubtful. A clear reference to the *Apology* appears in Aristotle's *Rhetoric* 1419a8–12, with Socrates the subject of two aorist tenses of verbs of speaking, and one could argue (so Zeller, *contra* Maier, both cited by Deman 1942: 63) that Aristotle believed in the essential and even detailed authenticity of the *Apology* as a report. (Vlastos, I should say, does not discuss this passage individually, relying for the *Apology*'s general authenticity mostly on the arguments of Brickhouse and Smith in their 1989: 2–10 – arguments I hope to undermine elsewhere.) But the argument is not cogent. At *Rhetoric* 1367b7–9 Aristotle used the past imperfect of a near quotation from the Socrates of Plato's *Menexenus* (235d), of which he uses the present tense when explicitly quoting the same passage later in the same treatise (1415b30–2). One wonders whether the historical Socrates should really be credited with the quoted phrase, or Aristotle with independent knowledge of its Socratic origin, or whether Aristotle has simply been careless in his use of tenses. By the so-called 'Fitzgerald's canon', the presence at 1367b of the definite article with the name 'Socrates' should indicate a reference to a literary work; but this clashes with the past tense supposed to refer to the Socrates of fact. These facts suggest an Aristotle unconcerned, over this kind of detail, whether it was or was not the Socrates of history who was talking in Plato. But in that case we should not lean heavily on the past tense at *Rhetoric* 1419a. The question whether the historical Socrates said or did not say the things Aristotle quotes from Plato (the *Apology* and elsewhere) is so utterly irrelevant to the concerns of the *Rhetoric* that it would probably be a mistake to attribute to Aristotle as he wrote it any high degree of interest in the question. (And one should beware of laying too much stress on Aristotle's use in some places of the imperfect – roughly iterative – tense and in others of the aorist – roughly factual – tense, in face of the apparent lack of any importance to the distinction in the parallel passages *Eudemian Ethics* 1230a7 and *Nicomachean Ethics* 1116b4.)

Vlastos and I differ in emphasis on the question how far to trust the early Plato as an 'account' of Socrates. Vlastos treats Plato as writing Socratic philosophy in a spirit largely faithful to the master's lines of argument; to me the dialogues read like Platonic literature, written within certain parameters of major Socratic method and doctrine but otherwise free. Whatever the reader may think on this general question, he or she cannot resolve it on the basis of Aristotle's testimony, which does not deal in the appropriate level of detail. The way lies open therefore to the arguments of the rest of this chapter. If Plato was producing rather than reproducing Socratic rhetoric in the *Apology*, as he does Socratic philosophy in the early dialogues (properly so called), then we should weigh probabilities with care before deciding to assign or not to assign this or that individual argument in the Platonic Socrates' defence to the historical Socrates.

If Aristotle's evidence is inconclusive on many points, so is the agreement with Plato's Soc$_E$ discernible from time to time in Xenophon or in Aeschines of Sphettus. Examination of individual passages would take us too far afield, but in general the dating of Xenophon's and Aeschines' works is not on a footing enabling us to dismiss the possibility that these writers plagiarised from Plato's fascinating Soc$_E$. A single example may point up this possibility: Xenophon, *Memorabilia Socratis* IV. 4. 9, the single Xenophontine passage Vlastos quotes (1991: 105) on Socrates' refusal to answer questions, happens to be about justice, also the topic in the context of Thrasymachus' very striking attack on Socrates for the same thing at Plato, *Republic* I. 337a. Here, much the most likely explanation of the facts is conscious or unconscious reminiscence by a Xenophon momentarily unheedful in literary excitement of the resultant conflict with his own general portrayal of 'Socrates' in the *Memorabilia*.

Finally (so far as concerns this already over-long note), Vlastos (97, n. 69) and others point out that Plato was not Aristotle's only source for his judgements on Socrates. I think, however, that one can derive Aristotle's testimony entirely from the combination of (a) Plato's Soc$_E$, (b) Xenophon, and perhaps others' Socratic writings, and (c) anecdotes of a common type leading up to supposed sayings of Socrates. There is little trace of any serious talk in the Academy about Socrates (and notoriously we know rather little of what did go on in Plato's Academy), except for Aristotle's apparent certainty that Soc_M represents, where he differs from or goes beyond Soc_E, Plato's own contribution; and it is not difficult to imagine Plato, on one or more *semi-public* occasions within the school, outlining the extent of his own contribution. Evidence that Plato openly, informally and conversationally discussed with Aristotle or other pupils exactly what Socrates had said is hard to find. How much importance to attach to its lack is for the reader to decide. And my readers should most certainly read also Vlastos' book.

2 Notably not only Vlastos 1991 but also Brickhouse and Smith 1989; Reeve 1989 is more cautious.

3 See, e.g., Hackforth 1933: 88–104.

4 Brickhouse and Smith 1989: 88ff.

5 Well brought out by Gladigow 1965.

6 I try to observe the distinction of Fontenrose 1978: 1 n. 1, between 'Oracle' (capitalised) for an institution such as the Delphic Oracle and 'oracle' (lower case throughout) for an oracular response.

7 E.g. Hackforth 1933: 89ff.; Brickhouse and Smith 1989: 88 (with bibliography); Reeve 1989: 25; and, emphasising what he sees as the subjective aspect of Socrates' interpretation, Vlastos 1991: 171f.

8 Wilamowitz-Moellendorff 1920: 54.

9 Gomperz 1905: 104–8; Hackforth 1933: esp. 101ff.

10 Guthrie 1969: 408.

11 1989: 91–4.

12 1989: 25.

13 1989: 26f.

14 1989: 28.

15 At *Apology* 23d Socrates says that the victims of his refutations are not angry with themselves for ignorance of which they had been unaware, but with Socrates; and that suggests no inner acceptance of his refutations.

16 Notably Coulter 1964: 303 n. 33 and (less explicitly) Meyer 1962: 72.

17 I include under the head of 'legend' the Herodotean oracle commending 'wooden walls' (ships) to the Athenians, despite Guthrie 1969: 40. See on the whole subject Fontenrose 1978 (a controversial book).

18 So in effect Hackforth 1933: 89 and others cited by Reeve 1989: 23, n. 24. Jordan (1990: 61) perhaps hedges his bets: '[Socrates] set out *as if* [my italics] to refute the oracle . . .'; but for *hos* with future participle meaning 'as if', see Euripides, *Helen* 1037.

19 See, e.g., Mikalson: 1983: 40 with nn.

20 See *Apology* 20e–21a.

21 Reeve (1989: 22) appears, without supporting argument, to accept the prospective meaning of Socrates' participle here.

22 The most plausible I have found is Herodotus I. 80.4, where, however, Godley's Loeb translation suggests he took the Greek differently. With a main verb which is not one of motion, see, e.g., Aeschylus, *Agam.*

1320, Herodotus IX. 37.2, Euripides, *Suppl.* 464, Thucydides V. 43.3. I owe these references to Stahl 1907: 722ff.

23 See *Iliad* XIV. 365, cited by Burnet 1924: 94 on 22a7.

24 See my list at Stokes 1971: 310, n. 78.

25 It is perhaps necessary to add that, though the similar passage at Xenophon, *Cynegetica* XIII. 7 has a clearly purposive import, and this chapter of the *Cynegetica* appears to borrow some ideas and even phrases from Plato's *Apology*, Xenophon need be no reliable guide to Plato's meaning.

26 Euripides, *Ion* 69–71 (with whole context) and again 1528ff. depict Apollo as himself giving out a falsehood. An Athenian audience would presumably have found this a deeply shocking depiction.

27 Notice the logical connective 'For', *gar*, at 21b5, and see Reeve 1989: 23 on the impossibility of doubt.

28 See, e.g., *Laches* 191b6–8.

29 See further below.

30 Adam 1897: 61.

31 See Sophocles, *Oed. Tyr.* 902f., Pindar, *Pythians* II. 21, and Herodotus II. 120.5; and Archilochus 122 (West), all cited by Cameron 1940: 115ff.

32 See n. 16 above.

33 Vlastos 1985: 1ff.

34 See, e.g., Reeve 1989: 36.

35 See Vlastos 1991: 82f. and n. 4.

36 On both of these see p.32ff. above and pp.60ff. below.

37 See below, pp.52–4.

38 See Guthrie cited above, p.30 and n. 10.

39 See above, n. 1 for some relevant considerations.

40 Montuori 1981b: esp. 57–146; Armleder 1966; Toole 1973–4; Fontenrose 1978: esp. 34.

41 Montuori 1981b: 87–95.

42 Reeve 1989: 21.

43 See Taylor 1917: 115, and his 1933: 74–82.

44 Reeve 1989: 14–19.

45 Taylor 1917: 111–18.

46 See Athen. *Deipnosophistae* V. 218; Plutarch, *Adv. Colotem* 1116e. Montuori accepts in his 1981b: 69 that these and other post-Classical scholarly evidence derive from Plato's and Xenophon's *Apologies*, except for the forged metrical version of the oracle.

47 Montuori 1981b: 66.

48 Von Arnim 1923: 87.

49 Isocrates in his *Antidosis* over-trumps Plato's *Apology*, as I hope to show elsewhere.

50 Amandry 1950; Parke and Wormell 1956; Fontenrose 1978.

51 Taylor 1933: 77, written before the fundamental works of scholars mentioned above.

52 See on one side Amandry 1950: 7 and Parke 1967: 85; and for doubts, Fontenrose 1978: 223 and Malkin 1987: 29ff.

53 See on one side LSJ s.v. *kleroo*; on the other, Owen 1939: 130.

54 Lobeck 1829: 814n., cited by Amandry.
55 Amandry 1950: 25f., n. 2, on Latte 1940: n. 9 and 1942: cols. 831–2.
56 1978: 219–23.
57 Herzog in Horneffer 1922: 149–70; Parke and Wormell 1956: 1, 384ff. with texts at 2, 97ff. See also Montuori 1981: 133–9.
58 Parke and Wormell 1956: 1, 385.
59 Herodotus I. 30.4.
60 So Montuori 1981b: 133–9.
61 Fontenrose 1978: 34; elsewhere Fontenrose brings the Platonic oracle as evidence in a way suggesting he views it as historical, 1978: 8.
62 I am glad to notice some points of resemblance between the explanation which follows and Vlastos 1991: 175ff., but Vlastos speaks in terms of piety rather than justice. On Socrates' ideas of justice see Vlastos 1991: 179ff.
63 See Stokes 1986: 219–26 and (much more weightily) Lloyd-Jones 1971 *passim*.
64 See, e.g., Brickhouse and Smith 1989: 137ff.; Reeve 1989: 115ff.; and Spiro Panagiotou's chapter in this volume.
65 It does not become any the less problematic for Vlastos' rendering (1991: 72) of *manteia*, 'oracles', as 'divinations'. The only divinations I know to be denoted by this word in normal Classical Greek are oracular responses.
66 From at least as early as Gomperz 1905: 107.
67 I regret that 'Socrates' Elenctic Mission' by T.C. Brickhouse and N.D. Smith, *Oxford Studies in Ancient Philosophy 9* (1991), 131–61, came into my hands too late for consideration.

2

SOCRATIC QUESTIONS

Ian Kidd

Plato is one of those rarest and most rewarding of intellectual geniuses, both a philosopher of the highest quality and also a supreme creative literary writer. But these gifts create difficulties of their own. For we are not dealing with a split personality: don in the daytime and pseudonymous writer of novels or detective stories in the evening; or yet, on a higher level, with a David Hume writing history for literary fame. The two aspects of Plato are deliberately, inextricably and organically entwined as matter and form where his philosophizing is expressed in the literary dramatic form of the Socratic dialogue. So, either to analyse the arguments and simply lay bare their relationships in logical formulation without taking account of their literary formal clothing or to read the plays without regard to their philosophical direction is of course possible and has its own rewards, but is likely to be wasteful and distorting, since one would then be dealing with one aspect out of focus, instead of with the whole. Although this is no doubt now the received view of Platonic scholarship, it cannot be said that great agreement has been reached over the operation and effect of the relationship of the two aspects, and over which is the dominant factor, for emphasis is laid now on one side, now on the other, usually objecting to over-emphasis of the opposite feature. Part of the trouble is that the Socratic dialogue illustrates a curious combination of art and science. Science aims at objectivity, and one aim of the dialogues appears to be the pursuit of objective truth and reality, as Socrates' hunt for certain infallible shared knowledge and a 'science' of morality, and as the emergence of the Theory of Forms indicate. On the other hand, an art form is especially characterised by the subjective response of the individual audience, viewer or reader. And this, in my view, was also intended by Plato; indeed, whether intended or not, that characteristic of the dialogues has certainly yielded rich fruit in their subsequent study within the history of philosophy as well as literature.

It is indeed the interpretative importance of the dramatic form that has been the subject of much recent Platonic publication, and it is a single thread arising out of this that I want to pursue. But first I should make two things clear. By 'Socrates' in this context, I mean the Platonic Socrates of the Socratic dialogues. And second, I regard the Socratic dialogues not as historical reporting or biography, nor as pure fiction or literary drama, but as philosophical faction: that is, following the definition in the *Oxford English Dictionary*, a fictional development from a base of real people, events or situations. But, and this is important, Plato wrote, created and directed the whole himself purposefully.

Now, the central dramatic feature of the Socratic dialogue is Socrates asking questions examining various contemporaries. Or so I thought until I was forced to reconsider the philosophical function of these questions by Michael Stokes' stimulating book, *Plato's Socratic Conversations*.[1] In his examination of the dramatic form, he shifts all the stress from Socrates' questions to the role of Socrates' interlocutors, which he thinks has been unduly ignored. He makes a case that it is their views which are being examined, and which are used as hypotheses for investigation, whereas Socrates himself does nothing but ask questions. So we may not look for Socrates', far less Plato's, views on philosophy in the dialogues (I would put this the other way round: not even Plato's views, far less Socrates'). In any case we must not confuse the dramatist with his characters, or the play with the author's philosophy. What is going on is an examination of currently held moral and social beliefs and standards. This point of view leads to very acute and illuminating exposition of detail, but to my surprise appeared to demote the force of Socrates' questions as being colourless or neutral. 'We can suppose', argues Stokes, 'that *all* Socrates' questions have the aim of eliciting the respondent's view, and that any other purpose is, if present at all, of secondary importance'.[2] Geared to the respondent, Socrates asks genuine alternative questions to which the respondent has the right of personal response, and is capable of saying 'yes' or 'no'. This rather qualified and predominantly dependent and negative view of the function of Socratic questions seems to me at least partly misleading, and I want to put a case for a different side of the question, for a more positive force in the directional quality of Socrates' questions. I suggest that Plato uses them to lead the movement of the argument to an end (not necessarily a conclusion) that he has in mind.

But first a brief reaction in mild protest to an overall general estimate of neutrality for Socrates' questions. In fact, the question form in whatever language is really a most complex and treacherous linguistic device. I am not persuaded that many of Socrates' questions are colourless. Even alternative questions are, and are often assumed to be, loaded. I have given up asking my wife alternative questions, because if I ask 'Are you going to Edinburgh tomorrow or on Friday?', she answers 'yes' or 'no', always to my disgust assuming that the first of the alternatives is the leading question to which you expect the answer 'yes'. But is the Socratic respondent capable of saying 'yes' or 'no'? Well, yes in theory and in implication; but Plato's characters are not live, independent, autonomous people. We must not confuse written dialogue with live television interview, as if Meno, as Plato poised his stylus to write another 'yes', caught Plato's wrist and said, 'That's enough, write down "no".' It is Plato who is writing it all, and his characters cannot in fury get up and go like John Nott in the famous Falklands War television interview, not even the aggrieved Callicles in the *Gorgias*, without *Plato's* literary permission. Otherwise we confuse faction and fact. The characters, although real people (at least the originals were real people), are Plato's own literary creations.

Nor do I believe that Socrates' questions *simply* spring from respondents' answers. When Meno defines *arete* or goodness or excellence as managing a city or a house well (*Meno* 73a6), that certainly derives consistently from the character Meno (and his mentor Gorgias). But Socrates' next question, 'Is it possible to manage a city or anything else well unless *sophronos kai dikaios* [i.e. prudently and justly]?', surely *springs from* Socrates, or rather from Plato, not from Meno. Meno may, and does, agree, because the Greek words are ambiguous, but neither the historical nor the dramatic Meno would have *originated* that point. And in that sense it is a Platonic leading question. So Socrates' questions are not always negative or responsive to his interlocutors, but can be positively directive. If the dialogues were merely dependent on respondents' views, they would be haphazard. But they are not: unlike ordinary conversations, the Socratic dialogues are organic developments. Plato himself is quite explicit about this desired ideal quality of literary work in *Phaedrus* 264c, but the description obviously applies to the early Socratic dialogues also.

But the organic control of a dialogue lies in the direction of Socrates' questions. In the famous illustration in *Meno* 82b ff. eliciting from an ignorant slave boy the answer to the problem of forming a square double in size to a given one, the boy is not instructed by Socrates, as Plato correctly insists, in the sense of being told the answer; he is questioned to develop what Plato thinks of as latent knowledge, so that he understands for himself each step as they proceed, eliminating the obviously wrong answers. This, however, cannot be done haphazardly without order or direction, as in the case of the notorious chimp who was expected on his own eventually to type Shakespeare. Socrates, or rather Plato, knows where he is going. The directive force is the questions; and this, as teachers know very well from their experience in tutorials, is a very difficult thing to achieve, and should not be attempted except by someone who knows what he or she is doing. Plato's Socrates may profess ignorance, but Plato uses him as an active and positive dialectical force, even by, or rather especially by, asking questions.

I should like to try to illustrate this, however superficially, from the *Laches*, a shortish early Socratic dialogue that is fairly clear, beautifully written, amusing and provocative. I see it less as a drama of character, where the beliefs of the generals Laches and Nicias are examined and tested (although certainly those of 'Laches' and 'Nicias' are involved), than as a dynamic dramatic philosophical dialogue orchestrated by Plato through the medium of his chief character Socrates to a problem which he feels that we (and he) should face. I am not concerned with detail (on which Stokes has often been so illuminating), but with the operational plan and structure.

The *Laches* is concerned with courage. But we only gradually come to see this through the development of the dramatic form from a particular situation. This is how faction works. Two anxious fathers, Lysimachus and Melesias, conscious of themselves having been allowed to run wild in their youth by their own famous fathers, Aristides and Thucydides, are worried about their sons' education. There is a new lecturer in town teaching weapon drill. Should they spend their drachmas on that? They sensibly consult their friends Laches and Nicias, two famous and successful generals who should know what they are talking about. Nicias, an enthusiast for the new intellectual enlightenment, is all for it. One skill will lead to another; before long the boys will find a general's baton in their chiton (181e–182d). Laches, a bluff practical soldier, is sceptical;

he has seen this Stesilaus make a bit of a fool of himself in actual battle. Anyway, mere technical skill is not enough in a tight spot (182d–184c). Impasse results. The distraught fathers turn to Socrates, who is hovering as usual, a gadfly or cleg disguised in human form. Would he like to give the casting vote? Instead, of course, Socrates starts asking questions (184d ff.). Would they actually settle this, or any other crucial issue, simply on a majority decision of Tom, Dick and Harry (in the guise of Laches, Nicias and Socrates), or rely on the advice of one expert who knows and is right? This important point comes from Plato, as is obvious from a whole series of dialogues. It is directed by Socrates' question, not from the respondents. Very well. But, asks Socrates indefatigably, do we know what we are talking about (185b)? Weapon-training, of course, say the others impatiently. But isn't that just a means to an end? If we are debating which eye lotion to apply or not, isn't it the condition of the eyes we are concerned about? What then? And here Plato hurries things on: well, are we not talking about weapon-training in relation to the end product of the youngsters' education, and isn't that the care of their minds (*therapeia tes psyches heneka*, 185d–e)? Surely that is a leading question, and from Plato through Socrates, even though it may have been prehinted; and by it the switch has been made from physical to mental or intellectual and moral education.

But isn't *arete* or moral goodness a large question, pursues Socrates. Shall we confine it to the appropriate part of *arete*, namely manliness, *andreia*, courage (190c–d)? It is Socrates who initiates that move, which turns out to be crucial. He makes no statements, but only asks questions. But these questions are vital. If the discussion is to go anywhere, it is important that the participants must agree (or disagree) each step; but clearly for the direction of the discussion, what is important is not the respondents' answers, but the kind of questions Socrates asks them, his leading questions.

Laches and Nicias, the supposed experts, agree to be questioned by Socrates on this subject, but at this point Plato permits himself a wry ironic thrust against himself. Nicias, who has some acquaintance with Socrates, ruefully remarks that he knows very well what this means (187e ff.), stringent self-examination under Socratic questioning. But benefit will result.

Laches goes in to bat first, full of confidence. Socrates asks innocently (190c): if he knows what a thing is, can he say what it is? This is a dreadful trap, but Laches agrees without hesitation.

So can he say what courage is? Laches sees no difficulty about that whatever; a man who stands fast in the ranks and fights off the enemy is brave (190e). Now in the Laches examination, while very dramatically characteristic, that is consistent, answers come from Laches, Socrates' (that is Plato's) questions make a Platonic philosophical point. In attempting to define something, Plato thinks that we can go wrong in two ways: we can set about it in the wrong way, in other words get the form of our answer wrong, and/or the content of our answer can be wrong. Laches' first answer is from Plato's point of view formally wrong, because he merely gives an example of courage, instead of defining it. We are not talking here about universals and particulars,[3] but about definition and example. Laches is saying that x is courageous, rather than courage is x. Socrates' questions quickly convince him of the inadequate narrowness of this procedure (191a ff.). He can, and does, produce contrary examples, including the Spartans courageously breaking ranks at Plataea to win the battle. Also courage has, has it not (Socrates leads with questions as usual), an extraordinarily wide field, covering, for example, illness, poverty, affairs of state, pain, fear; and courage can even be shown in the face of desires and pleasures (191d). Laches has to agree and tries again. This time he finds the right form (or at least the form that Plato is looking for): courage is *karteria tis tes psyches*, a kind of mental endurance (192b–c). But is this, that is the content, right? We know what he means by *karteria*, sticking it out, guts, bottle. But he said '*a kind of* guts'. Would he accept all guts as courage? Well, no; this time it looks too broad. Socrates prods interrogatively (192c ff.): isn't courage a fine thing (*kalon*, something we admire or value)? Intelligent (*phronimos*) endurance is a fine and good thing; but foolish endurance is surely the opposite, a hurtful and vicious thing. Therefore foolish endurance cannot be courage (that follows); therefore intelligent endurance is courage (that does not follow, but it will do as a working hypothesis). But what does that mean? Does 'intelligent' mean prudent, sensible, opposed to foolish or foolhardy? Or does it mean technically skilled as opposed to inexpert, incompetent? So Socrates (Plato) asks, intelligent in what (*he eis ti phronimos*, 192e)? He produces some examples, asking Laches whether they are examples of courage: if a City yuppie, with insider dealer knowledge, knows that by buying shares and holding out he will make money, is that courage? No. What about a doctor knowing that he will kill his patient if he gives in to his pleas for a drink, and so intelligently sticks out against it? No again. Or take Laches' own field: two armies face each other. One general knows that reinforcements are coming, that he outnumbers the enemy, that he holds the stronger position. He clearly sticks it out intelligently. But his opposite number, with the odds against him, is in a sense foolish or stupid if he sticks it out. Yet Laches thinks the latter is brave in doing so, not the former. But in that case, we now seem to be saying that the more foolish or stupid guts is courage; so intelligent guts, at least in the sense of prudence based on expert knowledge and reckoning the odds, isn't courage after all, is it?

Now, the answers given through this passage are certainly dramatically consistent with the character Laches, but it is not so much the answers that are interesting, but the questions which lead to the answers. So we notice not just Laches' dramatic discomfiture under examination of his own beliefs, but how Socrates' (Plato's) questioning is swinging attention to this peculiar and genuinely puzzling mental aspect of guts in courage. Just guts, sticking it out, is not apparently enough. But what is this key element of mind involved?

Laches retires hurt and frustrated. Socrates admonishes him; we must have the guts to continue, or Courage itself will laugh at us (194a). Nicias, the other general, whose ears have pricked up during this latter exchange, now moves in with what he thinks is a clever sure-fire winner in present company, because – and Plato makes a point of this, and it is Plato after all who is writing the whole of it: it is not a tape-recording – he suggests that the key may be a mot which he has heard Socrates himself say over and over again (194d). Ah, what is that? Well, says Nicias, you keep saying that a man is good (*agathos*) at what he is wise (*sophos*). So if the courageous man is good, he is wise; that is, courage is a kind of wisdom (*sophia*). Thus baldly and suddenly put the argument is startling, to say the least of it. For the first premise appears to mean: a man is good at what he is clever (skilled) at. But the following hypothesis seems to mean: so if the courageous man is a good man, he is an intellectually wise man. On the face of it, there is equivocation, or at least ambiguity in the use of both Greek terms, *agathos* and *sophos*. Laches at once ridicules the suggestion, not without reason. But Plato makes Socrates think it interesting and worth investigation.

Now, again what impresses here is the planned pattern of developing structure in the dialogue. The Laches episode, it is true, finishes ostensibly by showing the contradictory incoherence of Laches' views in attempting to define courage. But it does not really end in a negative blockage or *aporia* of defeat, but surely in the opening of a new question. What brought about the demolition of Laches was not the guts element, but the intellectual (*phronimos*) or mental aspect of courage; and Plato now makes the design of the dialogue concentrate on precisely that with Nicias.

So what kind of *sophia* could courage be or involve? Nicias suggests that of the terrible or fearful and encouraging (*he ton deinon kai tharraleon*, 195a). But then what is its sphere or relevance? Under questioning it appears to be a very odd one (195b ff.). It is not what is to be feared in disease, for that is the doctor's sphere; or in agriculture, for that is the province of the skill of the farmer. Why is it different? Because the doctor's skill, we are told, lies in his knowledge of illness and health, but not in whether it is *better for* a patient to live or die, which is where the fear lies. Again, the professional prophet may have the technical skill to foretell the future, but not the knowledge whether the predicted event is better or worse, and so to be feared or not, for the enquirer. So if the brave man has a *sophia*, it is a very peculiar kind of *sophia*, not a skill in a sphere, but apparently a knowledge of better and worse; that is he has a knowledge of values, or in other words he makes a value-judgement. This line of questioning is surely driving not only Nicias, but also the reader to distinguish moral 'knowledge' from knowledge as some kind of technical skill.

This intellectual link of courage with values as distinct from intellectual skill, which had been confused by both Laches and Nicias, is now strengthened in Socrates' questions by classifying courage not as being good at something or as a prudential calculating of the odds, but as being good in the sense of moral goodness, and so aligning it with the other virtues as part of 'goodness', i.e. morality (198a). Courage is still being examined as knowledge of the fearful, but Plato now makes Socrates proceed with another set of leading questions (198b ff.): fear is for the future, isn't it, because it is expectation of bad to come? So it is informed judgement of future good and bad. But Socrates suggests that knowledge of one time aspect entails knowledge of other time aspects (198d–e). If you know what *is* healthy and what *was* healthy, you will know what *will be* healthy, and vice versa. This is the whole point of science in the broadest terms. So a 'science' of morality, if there is such a thing, would be timeless. But then, *if* they are on the right track, Nicias has not, has he, defined the courageous man, but apparently the good man, although it was earlier agreed that courage was only a part of goodness. Nicias is baffled, much to Laches' joy, and here Plato stops, apparently with an *aporia*. But it is hardly negative; because what results from the impasse is not so much that they have not managed to define courage, but it would seem to follow, if their arguments in agreement so far have been correct, or at least acceptable, that before they can define courage, they would have to be able to define goodness or virtue itself, and what they mean by that.

So what are we left with? Not, I think, at the purely dramatic level, the rubble of demolition. It seems to me that greater interest from the *Laches* comes not from the exposure of the incoherence of popular current views such as Laches and Nicias held, but in the consequent problems which such *aporia* from the exposure reveals. It is the question or questions at the *end* of the *Laches* that are the important ones; and since Plato planned and wrote the whole of the *Laches*, it is to the ultimate question hanging in the air, not the answers we have had, that Plato has been leading us from the start, and so it has the final emphasis.

Are Socrates and Plato then involved? I believe so. In the first place, that the equation of value and rationality comes from the historical Socrates seems to me very arguable from the famous account from the Platonic Socrates of his intellectual development in *Phaedo* 96a ff. The much-discussed *deuteros plous*, or second voyage or tack that Plato finally embarks on in the last argument of that dialogue, surely derives from Plato himself, with its dependence on the Theory of Forms. But the abandoned *protos plous*, or first tack, which attempts to posit a straight rational *value* explanation for everything, surely then comes from the historical Socrates, or at least the picture Plato had of him. And indeed the value–rationality equation has been thought to be one of the most momentous legacies of Plato's Socrates to subsequent Greek philosophy. But in any case, in the *Laches* itself, Plato made a point of linking Nicias' starting point with Socrates, and the last section looks like an exploratory probing by Plato of a rudimentary Socratic epistemology of value. There has been much written about the Socratic dialogues exposing puzzles over the confusion between the different kinds of knowing, such as skill and expertise on the one hand and theoretical knowledge on the other. No doubt this is involved, but I would rather suggest that the basic problem confronting Plato was the identification of the very peculiar and puzzling characteristics of moral knowledge and value-judgements and standards. And so the questioning *aporia* at the end of the *Laches* exposes some of the puzzles and inadequacies of what he took to be Socrates' approach. But the questions he left us with, and they were real questions, were also there for himself, and although the dialectic unpeels some of the difficulties, and may even point to future ways of tackling these, as Plato himself did later, in the *Republic* for example, I doubt whether Plato at this point had an answer for himself, although he was facing himself as well as his characters with the question.

Finally, let me return to my starting point, and to some aspects of the dramatic form which Michael Stokes amongst others has made us face. It does not seem to me generally that 'Plato, like other writers of drama, keeps aloof from his readers.'[4] The dramatic form by itself does not exclude him. Plato is surely a philosopher using dramatic form rather than a dramatist using a philosophical theme. In any case, in the middle and late dialogues the personal significance of interlocutors can fade. It does not greatly matter in the *Symposium* who Diotima is; while 'Theaetetus' in the dialogue named after him is simply an intelligent young man, and Plato seems to be arguing mainly with himself. But the dialogue form is retained, and must then be for a dialectical rather than for a purely dramatic purpose.

So the dramatic form is exemplary Platonic philosophizing, neither historical record nor theatrical play, and cannot have been there for show, fashion, entertainment or fun, but was created because it was actually necessary for Plato, when writing, to philosophize thus. The actors in his dramas represent real people, partly at least because Plato was a humanist, and believed that the questions of philosophy, as he understood philosophy, were not esoteric games, but crucial for all of us and the way we live; and indeed that attitude he took from Socrates. But Laches, Nicias and the rest were of course dead by the time he wrote the dialogue. Laches died in battle before Plato was ten, most likely. They and their answers are no more than the matter or *hyle* on which he imposed the form of Socratic questioning, by which he involves us, his readers and himself. For since philosophy for Plato is maieutic or zetetic (as Diogenes Laertius (III. 49) put it), not dogmatic like sophistic instruction, but a questing self-examination, and so self-discovery, for *latent* knowledge and truth, a natural model is the dramatic form of the progressive Socratic conversation or dialectic as the dynamic operational mode. The dialogue form illustrates the importance of three things: (1) the elicitation of latent knowledge, which requires prodding; (2) the testing in agreement of each step in the process of the developing argument as it occurs; (3) the direction of the argument. For the movement and development is not haphazard, but purposefully led. And what I have been suggesting is that the directive spring or *arche* of this material is Socrates' questions: that is *Plato's* questions. If they had been primarily directed to that fascinating but dead fifth-century society of Socrates, they would be barren. They are directed partly to himself, because apart from a rather more dogmatic phase in the middle period of his writing, which the splendour of a work like the *Republic* puts in false perspective for us, Plato remained zetetic, self-critical and exploratory to the end. But presumably the published exoteric Socratic dialogues are mainly directed to the reader, to stimulate us to examine the flow of the argument, and face those ultimate questions to which we are led, for ourselves.

NOTES

1 Stokes 1986.
2 Stokes 1986: 30.
3 As has been suggested by Nehamas 1975–6.
4 Stokes 1986: 29.

3

SOCRATES AND CIVIL
DISOBEDIENCE

Spiro Panagiotou

I

In this chapter I am concerned with the interpretation of Plato's
Crito. My principal thesis is two-fold. I shall argue, first, that in
the speech he is made to rehearse on behalf of the Personified
Laws of Athens (henceforth, PLA), Socrates contends that on all
occasions the good citizen must ultimately obey the state. I shall
then suggest that this view on the good citizen's obligation to the
state cannot and must not be attributed also to Socrates himself,
by showing that the views he expresses in his own person differ
fundamentally from the views he expresses on behalf of the PLA.
The principal thesis of this chapter forms part of a much larger
thesis, concerning the interpretation of Plato's *Apology* and *Crito*,
which has intermittently engaged my attention over the past few
years. I think that I ought to sketch out this larger thesis in the
hope that the reader may appreciate the connection between the
concerns of this chapter and the larger issue of Socrates' position
on 'civil disobedience'.

The larger thesis goes along the following lines. In the *Crito*,
Plato canvasses three distinct positions as to the obligation, on
the part of a *virtuous* citizen, to obey the laws or orders of
his state. Crito's own speech (44b5–46a4) represents the position
that, when confronted with a law or order he considers unjust,
the virtuous citizen must disobey it. Indeed, Crito proclaims that
in such circumstances the virtuous citizen must disobey in the
name of virtue (45d–e). When talking in his own person, Socrates
represents the position that, when confronted with a law or order

he considers unjust, the virtuous citizen must disobey it, *provided* that his so doing treats the state neither 'unjustly' nor 'badly'. The difference between Crito and Socrates is over what they mean by a 'virtuous' citizen. Socrates' virtuous citizen adheres strictly to the two principles enunciated at 49a–e: (1) one must never treat anyone (a) 'unjustly' or (b) 'badly',[1] even in retaliation,[2] and (2) one must abide by one's just agreements.[3] Crito's virtuous citizen also would certainly embrace (2) and (1a), but I very much doubt that he would embrace also (1b) or the qualification 'not even in retaliation'.[4]

Finally the position of the PLA is that the virtuous citizen, as understood by Socrates, is obliged to obey any and all laws or orders of the state. That is, the PLA contend that notwithstanding his sincere belief that what he is being required to obey is unjust, the virtuous citizen must obey, unless he manages in fact to convince the state that his perception of the issue is correct or the state's own perception wrong. The position of the PLA amounts to what we may call the blind-obedience-to-the-state position.[5] The fundamental difference between the Socratic position and that of the PLA is that whereas Socrates thinks that a virtuous citizen may disobey in consistency with the two principles of 49a–e, the PLA think that he cannot. As far as they are concerned, disobedience to the state cannot fail to treat the state either 'unjustly' or 'badly' (indeed both), and, hence, the virtuous citizen cannot disobey without violating one or the other of the moral principles which supposedly circumscribe his life of virtue.

In canvassing the three positions outlined above, Plato intends to offer the Socratic position as the compromise between the Individualist (in some sense) position of Crito and the Collectivist position of the PLA. Underneath the tension between these two positions, there lies for Plato the conflict between morality and law, as well as the matter of their possible reconciliation. Crito believes, obviously, that there may well be conflicts between morality and the law and that in such cases morality is paramount. The PLA, on the other hand, believe that there is, and can be, no such conflict, since the pronouncements of the state (i.e. laws, judgements, orders) are *prima facie* just (i.e. in accordance with morality) or, after successfully meeting challenges by citizens or going unchallenged, *in fact* just. Hence, on their view, the virtuous citizen never has any principled reason for disobeying, since the state never requires its citizens to do anything unjust.[6] The good (obedient) citizen is also a good (virtuous) person.

Socrates himself believes, with Crito, that there may well be conflicts between morality and law and that in such cases morality is paramount. However, unlike Crito, Socrates would also insist that the highest moral life should embrace the two principles of 49a–e. Though embraced on the ground that any act of 'injustice' or 'bad treatment' of others redounds on the agent (49b4–6), the two principles commit their holder to the position that the good person, contrary to what Crito suggests, cannot throw to the wind the claims others have not to be treated 'unjustly' or 'badly' (the 'others' include also those one may regard as one's enemies). Accordingly, if he is to disobey, the good person must do so in a way which treats the state neither 'unjustly' nor 'badly'.

That it is possible, according to Socrates, to disobey the state without treating it in either way is evident, on certain assumptions, from Socrates' own defiant stand against the hypothetical proposal of the court at *Apology* 29c ff. Assuming that the defiant Socrates of the *Apology* operates under the two principles of the virtuous person in the *Crito*,[7] then obviously he thinks that his would-be non-compliance treats the state neither 'unjustly' nor 'badly'. However, how exactly, on his view, virtuous disobedience accomplishes such a thing is a much more complex and contentious issue. For neither the text of the *Crito* nor that of the *Apology* tells us anything directly on the issue. For this we must rely on scholarly ingenuity and the hints of the text.

There are hints in both dialogues which together point to the interpretative position that Socrates believes that the disobedient citizen treats the state neither 'unjustly' nor 'badly' as long as: (i) he disobeys only what he considers to be unjust laws, orders or judgements,[8] but (ii) he abides ultimately by the penalties or sanctions imposed for non-compliance.[9] In explaining the above conditions, suffice it to say the following. (i) In disobeying an unjust law (order, judgement), the citizen is not himself doing anything unjust to the state. He is refraining from injustice and may well be doing something just.[10] (ii) Still, this does not mean that the disobedient citizen may not be treating the state 'badly'.[11] There is a sense in which disobeying the pronouncements of the state is, or becomes, destructive of its authority. Since he holds the absolute principle that one must never treat anyone badly, the virtuous disobedient person must obey (accept, abide by, acquiesce in) the state's pronouncements at the level at which their violation becomes destructive of it. This is reached at the level of the penalties or sanctions the state may impose for non-compliance with its pronouncements. However, an important qualification must be understood here. The virtuous disobedient citizen cannot obey (accept, abide by, acquiesce in) any and all sanctions the state may see fit to impose. He cannot and must not accept sanctions which require him to violate the moral principles for the sake of which he is disobeying in the first instance.[12]

The position on 'civil disobedience' I ascribed to Socrates in the previous paragraph will not be found directly in the text of the *Apology* or of the *Crito*. I believe that the various component elements of this position are indeed present therein, but they are not put together by Socrates himself as I have suggested here. Nevertheless, it is a position which students of Socrates' thought, particularly as portrayed in the *Apology* and the *Crito*, should find plausible and in some sense natural, were it not for the speech of the PLA in the *Crito*. For in it they argue for blind obedience to the state and thereby contradict the defiant stand of Socrates in the *Apology* and the stand of anyone who adheres strictly to the principles of *Crito* 49a–e. Whereas he feels the need for principled disobedience, the PLA absolutely do not.

Evidently my larger thesis regarding the interpretation of the *Apology* and the *Crito* depends for its very plausibility on drawing, in the first place, a very sharp line in the *Crito* between the views of Socrates, when he speaks in his own person, and the views of Socrates when he speaks on behalf of the PLA. Accordingly, drawing and defending such a line is the main task I have set for myself in this chapter. This is of course easier said than done, especially since some serious objections may be and have been raised against such a project.

First, the motive for drawing such a line, namely the alleged contradiction between the views of Socrates and the views of the PLA on obedience to the state, may seem otiose. The alleged contradiction turns also on attributing to the PLA the blind-obedience view, and such attribution is, it may be felt, far from being textually warranted. Second, such a sharp line seems to fly directly in the face of the text. The Socrates who talks throughout the *Crito* in his own person seems to agree with the Socrates who, subsequent to 49e, talks also on behalf of the PLA. Indeed, in explaining at the end of the dialogue his decision to heed the PLA's exhortations (54d2 ff.), Socrates (in his own person) says that the 'sound of their words' drowns all other considerations out of his mind (54d4–5). Accordingly, the objection may continue, unless some argument is offered to show that Socrates, despite appearances, does not see eye to eye with the PLA, any contradictions or conflicts one is bent on descrying between his and the PLA's position would have to be regarded as arising within the Socratic position itself. Furthermore, the kind of arguments one might offer must be independent of the argument that Socrates and the PLA hold opposing views regarding obedience to the state. For, showing that the PLA argue for blind obedience does not also show necessarily that Socrates would not or does not agree with it. The blind-obedience view need not on its own be inconsistent with the Socratic principles of *Crito* 49a–e. Whether or not it is inconsistent depends also on the sorts of considerations and arguments the PLA adduce for it.

Obviously, I need to address the cluster of concerns and objections raised above. I shall try to do so in the following sections of the chapter. In section II, I shall take up the issue of the textual warrant for attributing the blind-obedience view to the PLA. In section III, I shall try to show some aspects of the fundamental way in which Socrates' views differ from those of the PLA.

II

In his valuable study on Socrates, Richard Kraut[13] argues against understanding the speech of the PLA as enjoining blind obedience to the state. He contends that the speech may be interpreted as allowing room for justified disobedience under certain circumstances. Kraut is led to this view by his desire to remove at once two inconsistencies which, in his opinion, confront any reader of the dialogue who is bent on descrying the blind-obedience view in it. The first inconsistency is between the *Apology* and the *Crito*. The Socrates of the *Crito* who, on the blind-obedience reading, urges that a citizen must obey all the laws or orders of the state, comes into conflict with the Socrates of the *Apology* who declares that he would defy an order of the court prohibiting him from practising philosophy (*Apology* 29c–d). The second inconsistency is internal to the *Crito*. At 49a–c Socrates embraces the absolute principle that one must never do anything unjust. Now, if he is committed, along with the PLA, to the view that a citizen must comply with any and all laws or orders of the state, Socrates finds himself in the uncomfortable position of being unable to live up to both commitments on those occasions on which he sincerely believes that what the state orders him to do is unjust. Either, consistently with his commitment to blind obedience, he must always obey the state in (occasional) contradiction to his principle of never doing anything unjust, or else, consistently with the latter principle, he must (occasionally) do something unjust in contradiction to his commitment to blind obedience.

On Kraut's view, the source of both inconsistencies is the scholarly insistence on interpreting the speech of the PLA as advancing the blind-obedience view. Hence, he believes, if we abandon this interpretation in favour of his own, we eliminate both inconsistencies at once. Kraut offers both logical and textual grounds for rejecting the blind-obedience interpretation. His logical grounds have to do with his thinking that the blind-obedience reading of the *Crito* is inconsistent with Socrates' commitment in the same dialogue to the principle of never doing anything unjust, and with Socrates' determination in the *Apology* to defy an unjust order of the court. Or, as Kraut might put it more generally, the blind-obedience interpretation is inconsistent with the Socratic recognition of the need for disobedience.[14] When it comes to textual evidence, Kraut does what is, I suppose, the only thing one could do under the circumstances: he constructs a negative case against the main prop in the blind-obedience interpretation, namely understanding the verb 'to persuade' in the PLA's formula 'persuade or obey' (*peithein e poiein*) to mean 'to persuade successfully'. On this understanding of the formula, the PLA mean to assert that, when confronted with a law or order he considers unjust, the citizen either must convince the state that his view is right or else, if he fails to convince, he must obey.[15] According to Kraut, we are not warranted in taking *peithein* to mean 'persuade' as opposed to 'try to persuade' and, in any case, even the sense of 'persuade' does not necessarily lead us to the blind-obedience interpretation. How so?

In his opinion, one's understanding of *peithein* as 'persuade successfully' proceeds on two 'mistakes':

First, it is simply not true that whoever says 'persuade so-and-so' will tolerate no failure. Imagine a government official telling his subordinate, 'You must persuade Mr Jones to vote for our bill.' Nothing in this command suggests that the subordinate will be blamed for anything less than success. There is only the smallest of differences between 'you must persuade' and 'you must try to persuade'. The latter expresses the speaker's awareness that persuasion is not entirely in the hearer's power, and it signals a willingness to tolerate honest failure. But someone who says 'you must persuade' may be equally tolerant. We do not have to say 'try to do X' every time we realize that the hearer may not be able to do X through no fault of his own. Therefore, even if the Laws [i.e. the PLA] say 'persuade or obey' rather than 'try to persuade or obey', that fact does no damage to my interpretation. They are not thereby making successful persuasion a necessary condition of justified disobedience.[16]

And second:

In the present and imperfect tenses, Greek verbs can have . . . a 'conative' force; that is, a word that means 'to do X' can in the right context mean 'to try to do X' . . . Wherever the Laws tell the citizen that he must persuade or obey, the tense of *peithein* (persuade) is present, and so the Greek is more ambiguous than we may have realized. That is where the second mistake occurs: the Laws do not necessarily mean 'persuade or obey' rather than 'try to persuade or obey' . . . For reasons I have just given [i.e. in the first passage above], even if the Laws mean 'persuade or obey' rather than 'try to persuade or obey', their doctrine makes room for disobedience. So I think it is an arbitrary matter whether we translate *peithein* by 'persuade' or by 'try to persuade'.[17]

Let us examine how Kraut shows that *peithein* in the formula is linguistically ambiguous. His argument in the first passage above is, I suppose, this: since in the present tense Greek verbs can have a conative force, and since wherever the PLA use the formula, the tense of *peithein* is present, *peithein* in the formula *may* have a conative force. Hence, 'the Greek is more ambiguous'. Formally this is a valid argument. But what exactly does it show? That the Greek is ambiguous? Well, 'is ambiguous' is here being used ambiguously. Does Kraut mean that the Greek is *potentially* or *in fact* ambiguous? If the first, he is surely right. His argument does show that the word is ambiguous and, hence, that any linguistic context containing it *may* be ambiguous. But this argument does not show what Kraut requires for his interpretation, namely that each and every one of the three particular contexts in which *peithein* in the formula occurs is *in fact* ambiguous or, what comes to the same thing, that none of the three contexts can help us to resolve the ambiguity and determine the sense of *peithein*.

I am prepared to admit that the last of the three occurrences of the formula, the one at 52a2–3, is indeed irremediably ambiguous in the sense that there are, as far as I can see, no specific indications in the immediate textual context to help us decide on the sense of *peithein* therein. There is, however, a fairly broad textual indication which should incline us to think that here too *peithein* means 'to persuade'. In any case, there are specific indications in the text which are decisively in favour of 'persuade successfully' in the first two occurrences of the formula, at 51b3–4 and 51b9–c1.

We ought to bear in mind that the speech of the PLA is solicited as a response to a question raised by Socrates at 49e9–50a3. The question is whether a citizen does or does not violate the principles enunciated at 49a–e whenever he escapes from prison 'without having convinced the city' (*me peisantes ten polin*, 49e9–50a1).[18] That is, the problem is posed by or for someone who has already tried but failed to persuade the state of his innocence. This circumstance informs the response of the PLA throughout their speech. They develop their own position in response to, and in the light of, Socrates' own particular situation. Accordingly, any plausible interpretation of their speech must start with and account for the fact that they in effect tell Socrates in particular (as opposed to any would-be disobedient in general), 'You must obey because, among other things, you have failed to persuade the state of your innocence.' This, admittedly broad, textual feature should be sufficient warrant for thinking that even the *peithein* at 52a2–3 is meant as 'persuade'.

Turning now to the specific textual indications, consider the first occurrence of the formula, at 51b3–4, which reads as 'either persuade the state or do what it orders you'. The formula is offered here as part of a long list of propositions which, according to the PLA, the virtuous would-be disobedient citizen has forgotten in his 'wisdom' (51a6 ff.). In other words, the PLA are saying to the disobedient citizen, 'You have forgotten, among other things, that you must persuade or do.' Now, surely, one thing the PLA cannot accuse Socrates of (or the citizens on whose behalf Socrates poses the question of 49e9–50a) is that he has forgotten *to try to persuade*, since he did try to persuade at his trial, albeit unsuccessfully. Accordingly, at this juncture the PLA must be reminding the would-be delinquent citizen not that he must try to persuade or do but rather that he must succeed at persuading or else do.[19] There is a yet more telling piece of evidence for this.

It is obvious that the PLA address their remarks specifically to those citizens who entertain the possibility of disobeying on moral principle, i.e. to those who claim to have moral objections to what the state requires them to do. Now, depending on which understanding of *peithein* we attribute to them, the PLA would be addressing their remarks to two *different* sub-groups of would-be conscientious disobedient people. If they were informed merely by the necessity of the citizen's *trying to persuade* the state, the PLA's remarks would be properly addressed to those who have objections but who do not voice them. In contrast, if they were informed by the necessity of *successfully persuading* the state, the PLA's remarks would be addressed to those who not only have objections but also voice them, i.e. to those who engage in the process of persuasion. In the case in hand, the PLA clearly address their remarks to the would-be vocal disobedient people. If this were not so, it would be pointless for the PLA to remind the citizen, as they do immediately after they list the formula 'persuade or obey', that he must suffer whatever the state commands 'holding his peace' (*hesuchian agonta*, 51b4–5). Those who do not voice their objections cannot be urged to obey *without demur*. It will not do to suggest that the PLA's present reminder is of a more general nature in that it is addressed to *all* citizens, informing them that they are to obey quietly, in the first instance, whatever the state commands. Given their invitation to the citizens to challenge whatever law or order they consider unjust, the PLA cannot be understood to be saying also that citizens are, in the first instance, to obey quietly. Allowing challenge and requiring acquiescence in the first instance cannot go hand in hand. The reminder 'holding your peace' must therefore be directed to those citizens who have already voiced their objections but who have failed to move the state. It is these citizens who must now obey without demur; who must obey despite their objections.

The second occurrence of the formula comes at the end of the list of the supposedly forgotten propositions. The citizen is now to 'do everywhere what the city and the fatherland command or persuade (*peithein*) it where justice lies' (51b9–c1). The point that persuasion is about 'where justice lies' is necessitated by, and looks back to, another item in the list of 'forgotten' propositions. Having told the citizen that he must quietly do or suffer what the state commands (51b4–6), the PLA go on to claim, and add as yet another proposition that the disobedient citizen should do well to remember, that 'that's how justice is' (51b7).[20] Given this claim by the PLA, it would be extremely odd for them to invite the citizen, barely two lines later, 'to do what the state commands or *to try* to persuade it where justice lies'. Unless they lost their nerve in the intervening lines, the PLA are now telling the citizen that he must either do what the state commands or else convince it *in fact* that it is wrong in thinking that justice lies with what it is requiring him to do.

The textual considerations adduced above are sufficient to show that *peithein* in the first two occurrences of the formula has the 'achievement', not the conative, sense. Given the fact that nothing changes in the PLA's sentiments between the first two and the third occurrence of the formula, I should think that we must understand *peithein* at 52a2–3 also to have the 'achievement' sense. Let us now turn to Kraut's claim that even this sense does not necessarily lead to the blind-obedience interpretation of the PLA's position. He argues to this effect by considering a number of examples which, I suppose, he thinks are analogous to the *Crito* formula, 'persuade or obey'.

The example in the first of the two passages quoted earlier, 'You must persuade Mr Jones to vote for our bill', is irrelevant, since it is not analogous to the *Crito* formula. What would be analogous is, I suggest, the following variant of his example: 'You must persuade Mr Jones to vote for our bill or tender your resignation.' The natural interpretation of this and of the *Crito* formula is that the speakers are after success, that they will tolerate no failure on the part of the addressee. It is, in part, a sign of their intolerance of failure that they stipulate an alternative as a kind of penalty or price to be paid for failure at the first task. Furthermore, their intolerance of failure is reflected in the fact that the alternative they stipulate is indeed something the addressee can successfully do, because it is something completely within his power to do, i.e. to tender his resignation or to obey, however much he may dislike it or think it unfair or unreasonable. The failure the PLA are intolerant of is failure at both persuasion and obedience (see 51e7; 52a2–3). On their view, the citizen must do one or the other, and he is certainly able to do one of them.

Kraut will no doubt point out that my reading of the formula and my objections to his position proceed on the assumption that the command *peithein e poiein* is of the type: 'either do A or else, if you fail, do B'. But, he will continue, the *Crito* command is of the 'far more indefinite type', namely 'do A or B', and such commands may be ambiguous in the sense that 'someone who is told to do A or B does not necessarily have to do B if he fails at A'. He may ask us to consider his example of the father who tells his son to 'clean either the kitchen or the dining room floor'. Supposing that he chooses the first task and that, after much effort, he fails to remove the dirt spots, the boy, according to Kraut, is not required now to clean the other floor. For, 'the father . . . has simply failed to say what is expected of his son should the floor prove uncleanable; and similarly, we have to admit that the Laws do not tell the citizen what to do if he tries to persuade but the jury proves unpersuadable.'[21]

Leaving aside for the moment the fact that the father's command is not quite analogous to 'persuade or obey', the following may be said. The plausibility of the claim that 'the father has not stipulated what is expected of the boy should the floor prove uncleanable' depends on what 'floor' refers to. If it refers to both the kitchen floor and the dining room floor, then Kraut is right. But, I should think, the father's command does stipulate what is expected of the boy in the event where *whichever* of the two floors he tries first proves uncleanable. If, say, he tries the kitchen floor first and it proves uncleanable, then he is certainly expected at least *to try* to clean the dining room floor. Think of the analogous example where X says to Y: 'Close the door or the window.' Suppose that the door is hopelessly stuck. Would we normally think that Y has complied with the request if, after trying unsuccessfully for some time to close the door, he walks away without doing anything at all about closing the window? It is true that in extreme cases, where the addressee may spend inordinate time or effort at the first task without accomplishing anything, we may excuse him from trying to deal with the second task, though our motive for so doing would typically be pity or frustration or irritation. In general, however, Kraut's point that the father has not stipulated what is expected of the boy applies only to the eventuality of both floors proving uncleanable, but not also, as Kraut thinks, when one or the other proves so.

If we follow my analysis of Kraut's example, we must say analogously that if the state proves 'unpersuadable', then the citizen is required at least *to try to obey*. Furthermore, and here the two cases are not analogous, the command in the *Crito* does not envisage any such eventuality where both tasks prove 'undoable'. It would be a complete misunderstanding of the PLA's speech to raise the question, 'What happens if both the state proves unpersuadable and the law, or order, in dispute is unobeyable?' and to answer it by saying, 'Well, the PLA do not stipulate what is expected of the citizen in that event.' The PLA do not entertain such an eventuality because for them the task, as it were, of obedience is within the power of the citizen to carry out, regardless of any moral impediments he may feel to be in the way of doing the particular thing commanded (see 51b–c).

We must keep apart two very different things: the particular task the citizen is commanded to do and the citizen's obedience to the command. Particular tasks commanded, for example 'take the hill', may not be entirely within the citizen's own power to accomplish. All he can do is to try to accomplish them, and the PLA themselves would expect no more. However, obeying or complying with the command issued is itself entirely within the citizen's own power. The citizen does *obey or comply with* the command whenever he *tries to carry out* the task commanded. It is crucial to realise that the PLA believe that there are no occasions on which a citizen finds it impossible to obey. They are not interested in the mental state, intentions, feelings, attitudes and so on of the citizen vis-à-vis the task commanded. The PLA are concerned with the citizen's *actions*. Indeed, they define the citizen ultimately by his actions (see 51c6–53a7, and especially 51e3 and 52d5). In so doing, they proceed on the Hobbesian notion of freedom of action as the 'absence of external impediments to motion'. In the case of the task of obeying a given command, as opposed to the task of carrying out the activities commanded, there are, according to the PLA, no such external impediments and hence no impediments at all. In a sense, then, the act of obeying, for the PLA, is not a *task* at all, and certainly not a task at which the citizen may fail through no fault of his own. In their view, whoever disobeys does so not because he cannot but because he does *not wish* to obey. The PLA's formula 'persuade or obey' requires of the citizen that he produces by his actions one or the other of two states of affairs: either obedience or persuasion. The good citizen is one who does produce one or the other, while the delinquent citizen is the one who produces neither. And he is so delinquent because one of the alternatives – obedience – is certainly always within his own power to produce.

III

No doubt there are some views Socrates shares with the PLA. But I deny that they see eye to eye on everything, or that they share the same moral outlook and hence that they are to be identified. The speech of the PLA could not and would not have been delivered unaltered by Socrates. His intimating that the words of the PLA drown everything else from his mind and his eventually heeding their exhortation to stay need mean no more than that he agrees with their advice to stay and die, but not also that he agrees with all the reasons they offer.[22] There is a dramatic feature of the text in the last third of the dialogue which, though admittedly puzzling, does seem to militate against identifying Socrates with the PLA in any case. The PLA consistently direct their remarks to Socrates (by using the second person singular), and this in spite of the fact that Socrates has already set up the hypothetical escape as a *joint project* between himself and Crito. Not only that, but whenever he is about to respond in his own person to the PLA's remarks, Socrates makes a point of asking Crito how 'they' are to reply. There is only one exception to this practice, but it is the sort which proves the rule. For it concerns something unique to Socrates, his not going away from Athens (see 52a5). Dramatically, Socrates, as the mouthpiece of the PLA, does not seem to know what Socrates says in his own person.

It is part of Kraut's view that the PLA are not to be identified with the sum total of the ordinary, specific laws of a state or with the state itself.[23] In his opinion, they operate at the higher level of jurisprudential thinking. They articulate the legal philosophy of Plato's *Crito*. Kraut also thinks that the PLA carry out their jurisprudential function in an ideal context. And it is in this lofty capacity, as ideal legal philosophers, that they are to be identified with Socrates. For they, just like Socrates, recognise that there is a fundamental distinction between virtue and law, that law and virtue may come into conflict and, finally, that one may disobey the law in the name of virtue.[24]

I myself do not think that the PLA operate, or are meant to operate, at an ideal level. They are doing legal philosophy, all right. But the principles and views they expound are meant to explain and justify the position that the state of Athens of Socrates' time (or of any state of the same type) would take against any disobedient citizen. In any case, the proof of the pudding is in the eating. Does their speech reveal that they share Socrates' recognition of the fact that virtue and law may come into conflict, or do they accept in the same spirit the principles by appeal to which Socrates himself thinks that the conflict ought to be resolved?

The possibility of conflict, and hence the fundamental distinction, between law and virtue is raised explicitly by Socrates and Crito in their rejoinder to the PLA's first argument (50a8–b5). Their rejoinder is that the state has wronged them (*edikei hemas he polis*) in not judging their case correctly (50c1–2). Socrates and Crito draw attention to the fact that the pronouncements of the state, represented here by the court, may not, and in Socrates' own case do not, coincide with what they themselves at any rate believe to be just. How do the PLA respond to this charge?

They do not, initially at all events, deny it. Indeed, the way they respond immediately, at 50c4–6, gives the impression that they accept the charge and that they will in the sequel go on to try to defuse it by appealing to the Citizenship Agreement Argument. I take it that in supposedly accepting the charge at this juncture, the PLA would also evince their own recognition of the possible conflict and, hence, distinction between law and virtue. They continue to give this impression throughout their speech. At 51e7 they appear to concede that the state (or its laws) may do some things 'not well'. At 52e4–5 they again appear to concede that the 'agreements', or the things which the citizen has agreed to perform, may not be just. Finally, in their summation of their speech (54b2–d1), the PLA claim that in escaping, Socrates would be 'returning injustice with injustice and bad treatment with bad treatment' (54c2–3), and this clearly suggests that they themselves think that Socrates has suffered an injustice. Given all this, one may be inclined to find the same sentiment expressed in the PLA's second argument (50d1–51c4). That is to say, one may be inclined to think that the PLA's intention here is to allow, on the one hand, that the state may sometimes treat citizens unjustly but to insist, on the other hand, that the aggrieved citizen must nevertheless not retaliate in kind. All indications so far cited give the reader the impression that the PLA recognise and accept the distinction between law and virtue, that they concede the possibility of conflict between the two, and that they accept that in Socrates' own case they have in fact come into conflict.[25]

In one respect and after a certain fashion, this impression is correct; otherwise, quite erroneous. The PLA recognise and accept the distinction between law and virtue. They do not, however, concede the possibility of conflict between them, nor, of course, do they accept that there is such a conflict in Socrates' own situation. It is an absolutely crucial item in the text of the *Crito*, and one which any plausible interpretation of the text must take into account, that between the time they supposedly accept the charge of state wrongdoing (i.e. 50c4–6) and the time they sum up their speech, the PLA certainly appear to shift their ground. For they claim in their summation that Socrates has been wronged *not by the laws or the state*,[26] but by particular men. It is not necessary to assume that the reference here is to the jury sitting on Socrates' own case. Almost certainly, the PLA are thinking of Socrates' prosecutors.[27] In any case, it should strike us as odd that the PLA begin by accepting, albeit by implication, the charge of state wrongdoing and conclude by denying it. Have they changed their tune, or do they hold inconsistent views on this score? Neither.

The problem is our inclination, understandable under the circumstances, to think that the opening lines of the PLA's response to the charge concede the facts contained therein, when in truth they seek to deny them by suggesting that the bringing of the charge does not ultimately square with their understanding of the Citizenship Agreement. The dialectical move used is the one where you counter your opponent's claim by suggesting that it contradicts a point yet to be made or a conclusion yet to be reached. If your opponent is unable to appreciate the move, you then go on to spell it out for him. Socrates is lost, hypothetically, for words (50c6–7), and the PLA embark now (50d) on the long series of considerations which will culminate in the Citizenship Agreement Argument. The PLA entertain the charge of state wrongdoing not in order to go around it but in order eventually to deny it.

The PLA's considerations against retaliation vis-à-vis the state, which are developed in terms of the analogy of retaliating against one's father or master, are interesting, especially for what they neglect to mention. Contrary to what one might expect in an argument supposedly on the evils of retaliating *in kind* (for example against injustice), the PLA do not mention, let alone concede, even indirectly, the fact that the state may and sometimes does treat citizens unjustly. When they refer specifically to Socrates' own case, they phrase their question (51a2–7) with, 'if we try to kill you, thinking it to be just' (51a3–4). It does not occur to them to phrase their question along some such lines as: 'if we try unjustly to kill you', or 'if we try to kill you, even unjustly', or 'if we try to kill you, thinking it, incorrectly, to be just' and so on. It does not occur to them because they are already on the way to arguing that the pronouncements of the state are, in the first instance, *prima facie* just and ultimately just *in fact*. This is exactly what they argue in the sequel (51a7 ff.), when they claim not only that a citizen must do and suffer whatever the state commands (51b3–c1) but also that 'this is how justice is' (51b7). The latter point amounts to the claim that whatever the state commands is just. This, as we saw earlier, is made abundantly clear by the PLA's qualification that the citizen must do what the state commands, or else persuade it 'where justice lies' (51c1).[28]

This way of putting the matter may seem unfair. For the PLA concede that a citizen may disagree that a particular command of the state is just and, more importantly, they seem to recognise that the citizen may well be right in so thinking. True enough. However, they also contend that in such cases of disagreement the onus of proof is on the citizen, while the success of the proof lies entirely in the judgement and discretion of the state. This suggests the following interpretation of the PLA's position. There is just the *theoretical* possibility of conflict between the demands of the state and those of justice and morality. However, in a state in which laws are generally framed well, or for the benefit of all citizens (see 50d1–e2; 51c9–d1), there is a natural presumption that any particular law or order of the state will be in accordance with justice. In the event that a citizen thinks otherwise, we do not immediately have a conflict between law and morality but, rather, given the fundamental citizenship facts presented in the Citizenship Agreement Argument, a dispute between two different perceptions as to where virtue lies: the citizen's and the state's. The Citizenship Agreement, furthermore, specifies how such disputes are justly resolved.

One cannot over-emphasise the importance of the fact that the PLA pit only what the citizen *thinks* or *claims* is just against what the state thinks on the matter. In the instances I cited earlier, in support of the view that the PLA allow the possibility of state wrongdoing, they allow it only in so far as it is something the citizen may think or claim. The point is patently obvious at 52e4–5. The 'agreements' may *appear* to be unjust to the citizen (*ephainonto soi*). At 51e7, where they appear to concede that the state may do some things 'not well', they simply state that the disobedient citizen 'neither obeys nor convinces us *that*[29] we are doing some things not well'. At 51a6 the disobedient citizen, regarded as retaliating against the state, is said to be trying to kill the state and *claiming* that in so doing he does right. The citizen's behaviour is contrasted with the state's treatment of the citizen and his claim to its claim that its treatment of him is just (51a3–5). The PLA concede not that the state may do, or ever does, wrong but rather that the citizen may think that it does.

At the same time, the PLA contend that the burden of proof is upon the citizen and that he may be said to succeed only if he brings the state, by means of arguments, around to his way of thinking. Whatever happens, the state will act justly or rightly. If, on the one hand, the citizen convinces it, it will presumably act in accordance with his view.[30] If, on the other hand, the citizen fails and the state remains unconvinced, the original law or order stands,[31] because it is now in fact just. This doctrine finds its ultimate and natural conclusion in the claim, made indirectly in the summation of the PLA's speech, that the state is blameless.

The PLA also contend that a disobedient Socrates would violate his principle (2), that 'one must abide by those things one has agreed to, provided they are just'. I believe that the PLA can plausibly so contend only by proposing a, or interpreting the, Citizenship Agreement in such a way as to make it inevitable and necessary that *any and all* acts of disobedience are inconsistent with this principle.

In the Citizenship Agreement Argument (51c6 ff.), the PLA argue that the citizen agrees, implicitly, to obey all laws and commands of the state (51e3–4) or, generally, to conduct his civil life (*politeuesthai*) in accordance with the standing laws and practices of the state (52d3–5). This contention is not sufficient in itself for justifying the claim that in disobeying the sentence of the court Socrates would be acting in violation of his principle (2). For the principle refers to the 'justice' of what the citizen has agreed to and, hence, certainly at least to the citizen's own perception of the justice of the things he has agreed to.[32] For this reason, the PLA contend also that in agreeing to abide by the laws and practices of the state, the citizen agrees that such laws and practices are just.

They argue that a citizen's acts of omission (his continued residence in the state, 51e1) or commission (his begetting future citizens, 52c3) are signs not merely of his agreement to abide by the standing laws and practices but also, and in the first instance, of *his own approval* of such laws and practices. For his acts of omission or commission arise out of his own *liking* of such laws and practices (51d4; 52b1–c3) and out of his thinking that the things he has implicitly agreed to are just (52e3–5).[33]

However, even when armed with this contention, the PLA still cannot argue that Socrates is contradicting his own principle. In order to establish that conclusion, the PLA must show that Socrates has himself agreed that the judgement of the court is just. How, then, can the PLA possibly argue that a disobedient Socrates would be contradicting his own principle, when Socrates himself thinks that the judgement of the court is unjust?[34] They might contend that Socrates has implicitly agreed that any and all judgements of a court are just and, hence, that the judgement or sentence in his own case is just. Accordingly, their point might be that Socrates' express charge that the state treated him unjustly (in not judging his case correctly) contradicts his standing, though implicit, admission in the Citizenship Agreement that all court decisions are just. This is, I think, exactly what they wish to argue, and it fits in with the opening lines of their response at 50c4–6. However, how exactly they argue to it I am not certain, though I believe that they proceed along the following lines.

They do not argue simply that a citizen enters into an agreement, which he himself considers just, to do *anything* the state commands him to do, even things he might consider to be unjust. Their argument is much more subtle and devious. The citizen enters the agreement recognising and admitting that whichever particular thing the state commands is itself *prima facie* just. In the PLA's view, the Citizenship Agreement is to the effect not merely that a citizen must do what the state commands but also that in case of dispute the citizen must either persuade or obey. The 'persuade or obey' formula is part and parcel of the Citizenship Agreement. This is most clearly brought out where the PLA point out the three ways in which the would-be disobedient citizen offends the state (51e5). The third way is, as they put it, 'that though he has agreed to obey us, he neither obeys nor persuades us *that*[35] we are doing something not well' (51e6–7).[36] On the PLA's view, in entering into the Agreement the citizen realises and accepts that what the state commands is presumed to be just, that in case of dispute he carries the burden of proof, and that his proof is successful only if he manages to persuade the state. Accordingly, whenever there is a dispute as to the justice of a particular command, then the issue, as determined by the terms of the Citizenship Agreement, is simply whether the citizen can persuade the state that its command is not just. Unless he convinces the state to this effect, the citizen is bound, in virtue of the Agreement, to do what the state commands, because the thing commanded is now in fact just, notwithstanding his continuing perception that it is not.

Would Socrates or the good man agree with this position? The question does not admit of a simple 'yes' or 'no' answer. Socrates or the good man might agree that the citizen does indeed enter into the Agreement admitting that whatever the state does or will command is – or may be – generally presumed to be just. He would accept this presumption in view of his knowledge, as a mature person, of the current and past performance of the state and of his implicit recognition of this record as being up to now generally good (see 51d3–e3). However, on the evidence of problematic instances in the state's record and out of his own awareness that no state is morally perfect or infallible, the good and sensible person would insist that this general presumption holds only for as long as no citizen objects, in point of moral principle, to a particular edict of the state. When a citizen so objects, we then have a dispute with no presumption in favour of either party.[37] What does or does not follow from here on depends on the method used for resolving disputes between state and citizen. Though they proclaim that theirs is the method of persuasion and not force, the PLA have, as I shall try to show presently, a rather un-Socratic conception of what is involved in the dialectico-persuasive enterprise.

Socrates refers to the escape from prison in a number of ways: 'to go out of here without the permission of the Athenians' (48b12–c1); 'to go out of here while the Athenians are unwilling' (48e3); 'to go out of here without convincing the Athenians' (49e9–50a1). He recognises that these locutions mean no more than 'break out of prison', since he refers to the escape also as *apodidraskein*, though he does also suggest that it does not matter what one calls it (50a6–7). However, the very terms he uses are important because they allude to his views regarding the place of persuasion in one's relations with the state. Obviously, he regards as an indispensable element in his decision his considering whether or not the Athenians are 'willing' or 'convinced'. But how much weight does he allow to such considerations? We have some evidence to help us with this question, though it is concerned with the place of persuasion in one's private associations.

Looking back to their previous discussion, Socrates invites Crito at 48d8 ff. to argue, if he has any arguments, against what he – Socrates – will be saying presently on the crucial issue before them: 'is escaping right or wrong?' (see 48c–d). Indeed, Socrates promises, 'you argue successfully against it and I will be convinced' (48e1). However, if Crito has no such arguments, he must really stop telling Socrates the same old thing, that he should get out of prison 'against the will of the Athenians' (48e3), because, as Socrates puts it, 'I myself place a lot of weight on our doing these things after persuading you and not against your will' (48e3–5). A number of things should be noted here. Socrates' promise that he will be persuaded by a successful opposition is really an avowal of his openness to reason and argument, provided that the arguments are on what he considers crucial to the issue at hand. It is no more than a reiteration of the principle, with which he introduces his response to Crito's speech, that he will be convinced by nothing except the reason or argument that appears best to his own way of thinking (46b4–6). At the same time, however, he places a great deal of importance on persuading his dialectical opponent. Indeed, he believes that this concern should be reciprocated, and implicitly accuses Crito of not doing so, in so far or as long as he fails to present arguments on *what is crucial* to the issue before them. The reason why we should place weight on persuading our dialectical partners has to do, apparently, with the fact that 'acting without being persuaded' is tantamount to 'acting against one's will'. This is, I take it, the force of the contrast between *peisas se* and *alla me akontos* at 48e4–5. I shall elaborate on this reason below.

Having done all this, Socrates next invites Crito to consider the 'starting point' of their enquiry, which of course will turn out to be the two principles of 49a–e, in order to see whether 'it is to his satisfaction' (48e5–49a1). That Crito should himself find the starting point to his satisfaction is related to the requirement, brought out by Socrates a bit later, that Crito should agree to the Socratic principles out of his own heart-felt conviction. Or, as Socrates tells him, 'make sure that in agreeing to these you do not agree against your own opinions' (49d1). When generalised with respect to the dialectical participants, this requirement is to the effect that *all* participants must be *personally convinced* of whatever propositions they are agreeing to.

It may be felt that I have also generalised with respect to the propositions involved, and illegitimately so, since the text is concerned only with 'first principles'. Though admittedly the concern is specifically with first principles, the requirement is surely meant to apply also to any and all the steps in the dialectico-persuasive process. When he invites Crito at 49a1–2 to respond to what is being asked in the way he thinks best, Socrates surely has in mind the following two things. First, what Crito thinks best is what Crito is personally convinced of. Second, the invitation is not confined to the enquiry into first principles but is extended to the enquiry subsequent to their enunciation. This does not mean that the participants hold their heart-felt principles tentatively but rather that, even after they embrace the same principles, there may well be items with respect to which any one of them may raise the question, 'Am I personally convinced of this?' This is *one* reason why throughout the PLA's speech Socrates asks for Crito's own responses. Agreeing to first principles is merely a *necessary* condition for any subsequent 'common deliberation' (see 49d2–4).

The requirement that *each* participant be personally convinced of what he is agreeing to is necessitated by the fact that the aim of the dialectical exercise is *action*. To act on opinions one does not really hold, or which are contrary to one's own opinions, is to act against one's own will or, at the very least, against one's best judgement. The requirement that *all* participants must be so convinced is necessitated by the fact that the action is supposed to be *common* or *joint* (see 48d6–8). Accordingly, participants must all agree not only about first principles but also to every step in the process, since the action undertaken, the very last step in the process, must be one they could *all* live with. It is important to note that Socrates treats the dialectical exercise as a joint deliberative process which ensues in 'common directives for action' (see 49d3).[38]

But even in this special context, in which the dialectical exercise aims at a common project,[39] Socrates says merely that he places considerable, not absolute, weight on persuading his dialectical partner on the course of action to be chosen. What he places absolute value on, in so far as he regards it as an indispensable element in the exercise, is one's *trying* to persuade one's partner.

Even if he should fail to persuade Crito, Socrates may still go on to do what he considers best. Now, is the Socratic requirement of merely *trying* to persuade applicable also when one's dialectical partner is the state? I cannot see any reason why it could not be, apart from the fact that in their own speech the PLA insist that the citizen must *succeed* at persuading the state.[40] The fundamental context in which one tries to persuade the state is certainly the same as when one tries to persuade one's private partner. When the state requires a citizen to do some thing or other, the citizen does indeed become involved in a *joint* or *common* project with it, unless of course one thinks of the citizen, along with the PLA, as being merely an instrument of the state. I should think that, as far as Socrates is concerned, just as he and Crito are conspirators in the escape, the citizen and the state are prospective 'co-doers' of the action the citizen is at any time required to perform. Given that the citizen is invited to participate in a dialectico-persuasive process and that he is not a mere instrument of the state, Socrates would apply the same requirements to public as he does to private dialectic.[41]

It may be felt that in the very passage where he juxtaposes, in order to contrast, 'persuading someone' and 'acting against someone's will', Socrates accuses Crito not only of not trying to persuade him – on account of his using irrelevant arguments – but also of pressing him to act against the will of the Athenians (48e). Given the latter complaint and Socrates' own situation, i.e. his having tried unsuccessfully to persuade, one may be tempted to claim that Socrates is here telling Crito to stop urging him to escape against the will of the Athenians precisely because he – Socrates – has failed to persuade them. This understanding of the text implies either that Socrates places absolute value on persuading one's dialectical partner or that he places relative value on 'private' but absolute value on 'public' persuasion. The first alternative is clearly at odds with the text. The second alternative proceeds from misunderstanding both the tenor and structure of Socrates' remarks to Crito. His complaint is that Crito's reasons for escaping are misdirected. It is in the light only of this miscarriage of Crito's project that Socrates asks him to refrain from pressing him to act against the will of the Athenians, and not because, supposedly, Socrates has already failed to persuade them.[42]

It is interesting to see what the PLA contrast 'persuade' with. It may be recalled that they remind the citizen that he must obey the state or else 'persuade it where justice lies' (51c1). Immediately after, they continue, 'Forcing (*biazesthai*) your mother or father is impious; forcing the fatherland is much worse than forcing them' (51c2–3). There is no doubt that 'forcing' is contrasted to 'persuade' in the previous line. The PLA are of the view that when X acts without convincing Y, X does violence to Y when, at any rate, Y happens to be the state.[43] This view is often used in a democracy to bamboozle dissidents into submission. The political philosopher Plato sees the same contrast between persuasion and force, but then he thinks that force is all right provided that it aims at and produces benefit. Socrates, on the other hand, seeks to persuade and wishes, in return, to be persuaded.[44] If the persuasive enterprise fails, then one must act as one sees fit, provided one treats others neither unjustly nor badly. To act without convincing others is not to force them but to act as they would not. This means simply that they and you no longer have a common project.[45] Socrates would not deny the state's claim to obedience from the unpersuaded citizen, but he would also grant the citizen the right to refuse it. I very much doubt that he would accept the PLA's understanding of the dialectical exercise, for, according to it, he would be breaking one of his cardinal rules every time he acted contrary to the views of his dialectical partners. His speech on the counter-penalty in the *Apology*, especially his first and outrageous proposal (36d), is informed by his sense of the enormous incongruity involved in acting against his own convictions (37b2–5), despite what the court thinks or is convinced of (37a5–6). Similarly, I very much doubt that he would accept the PLA's conception of the Citizenship Agreement, for according to it he would be breaking both of his principles every time he acted on moral principle contrary to what the state required him to do.

It may be thought that we should understand the PLA's comments about the citizen forcing the state in the light of their already expressed belief (50a8 ff.; 51a5) that the disobedient citizen destroys or harms the state. However that may be, the reason for appraising the dissident's action as violent is not, and cannot be, the fact that he is acting without convincing the state but, rather, the fact that his action turns the state upside-down and in some sense destroys it. The PLA suggest that apart from its harmful consequences, the dissident's action is also violent on account of its being undertaken despite his failing to convince the state. Socrates may well agree that disobedience is at some level violent or harmful to the state in so far as it upsets it. But he cannot agree that disobedience is violent or harmful on account of its being supposedly action undertaken without first convincing the state.[46]

NOTES

1 The terms *kakos poiein* and *kakourgein*, which I translate as 'to treat badly', mean in the present context 'to injure', 'to do harm' or 'to damage' as opposed to benefiting someone in a palpable way. Some commentators think that the terms mean, much like *adikein*, 'to wrong' someone in a fairly broad sense. See, e.g., Kraut 1984: 25 n. 1; 26 nn. 2, 3; 27–8; Bostock 1990: 2. Socrates' statement at 49c7–8 that '*kakos poiein* does not differ at all from *adikein*' need not imply the semantic identity of the terms or, surely, the identity of the formal criteria for assessing bits of behaviour as examples of either 'unjust' or 'bad' treatment of others. It may amount simply to the claim that 'unjust' and 'bad' actions are indistinguishable from the point of view of moral evaluation: e.g. that 'bad' actions are, like 'unjust' actions, evil and shameful to the agent (see 49b4–5). This reading of 49c7–8 fits in with the sense of the immediately preceding question, at 49c4–5, 'is *antikakourgein dikaion* or not *dikaion*?', if we take, as we may, its sense to be 'is *antikakourgein* [or *kakourgein*] a kind of just or unjust action?'. In general, the tenor of the entire passage (49a–e), especially the language used regarding retaliation, with its liberal use of the *oute . . . oute* construction, makes it reasonably certain that *adikein* and *kakos poiein* are used to designate different notions. Without such difference the PLA's argument later on, at 50e5–51a7, would be nonsensical. In assuming this difference the PLA follow earlier Socratic usage. They do differ from Socrates on this issue in thinking that the two notions are indeed morally distinguishable. For example, they seem to think that one (or, at any rate, the state) may treat another 'badly' provided that one does so 'justly'.

2 Socrates qualifies (1a), but not explicitly (1b), with 'intentionally' (*hekontas*, 49a4). Given the notion involved in (1a), I should think that *hekontas* here means 'wittingly'. I suppose that (1b) is to be similarly qualified.

3 'One must do the things he has agreed to, provided that they are just' (49e6–8; 50a1–2). I should think that this is a special case of (1a) above. One way in which you may treat another 'unjustly' is by violating a *substantially* and *procedurally* just agreement with him. As stated here, the principle distinguishes between *the agreement* to do *x* and the *moral quality* of *x*. As far as the Citizenship Agreement itself is concerned, the PLA seem to preserve this distinction. For they eventually adopt (implicitly) the position that the Agreement itself is procedurally just, because effected in the absence of the 'duress' conditions outlined at 52e1–3, and substantively just, because the things the citizen (implicitly) agrees to are things he is presumed to *like* (or, at least, find bearable).

4 Crito would not and does not consider the escape unjust. Only in that

case would he regard it as a retaliatory action, i.e. as returning injustice with injustice. See 45c5–d8. There is an ambiguity in Socrates' terminology about retaliation. He uses only the formulae 'returning injustice with injustice' and 'returning bad treatment with bad treatment'. Surely he is, and must be, also against 'returning injustice with bad treatment' and 'returning bad treatment with injustice'. I am not sure that Crito would think it wrong to return injustice with bad treatment.

5 For what I mean in ascribing this position to the PLA, see p.98 and n. 15 below.

6 See n. 28 below.

7 This assumption would be readily granted in connection with the principle of not treating others unjustly. See n. 10 below. It should also be granted in connection with the principle of not treating others badly. It is true that Socrates is not made to say anything in the *Apology* about treating others badly (harming) or about retaliation. I should think this is natural under the circumstances. The *Apology* is especially concerned about justice because the indictment against Socrates was about his 'injustice' to the city. Quite properly, Plato is not concerned in the *Apology*, as he is in the *Crito*, to outline the virtuous person's reasons for acquiescing in an unjust sentence, which would occasion the introduction of the principles about not harming and about retaliation. But we are bound to assume that the Socrates of the *Apology* holds these two principles, if only because he is made to hint in the *Crito* that (1a) and (1b) are principles he has held for some time now (see 49a6–8 and 49d–e).

8 This condition stipulates that the disobedience is principled; that it proceeds from the citizen's sincere wish to act so as to avoid violating any one of the principles of *Crito* 49a–e. When the disobedience is to a court judgement, appropriate qualifications are to be understood, depending on whether the judgement requires the citizen to act in a certain way or imposes certain sanctions on him.

9 In the *Apology* Socrates declares his willingness to accept both the penalty of death already imposed by the court (39b4–6) and the penalty of death attached to non-compliance (30c1) with the hypothetical condition that he refrain from philosophizing (29c6–d1). He offers no reason here for accepting or acquiescing in such penalties apart from the cryptic 'perhaps it was meant to be so and I think it fair' (39b7–8). But we do have some clues as to his reasons in the *Crito*. See n. 11 below.

10 In the *Apology* Socrates defends all the instances of his non-compliance with the authorities on the general grounds that he is 'fighting for the just' (32a1), or 'siding with law and justice' (32b8–c1), or that his ultimate concern is 'to refrain from doing anything unjust or impious' (32d2–3). At 35c7–d1 he asks the jurors not to require of him to engage in practices which he himself considers to be 'neither good nor just nor pious'.

11 I take it that the PLA's first argument (50a8–b5) impresses Socrates at some level. The argument is directed at all acts of disobedience, principled and unprincipled. It suggests that ignoring, for whatever

117

reason, the authority and finality of a court's disposition of a case leads to lawlessness and, hence, to the destruction of the state. See Panagiotou 1987a: 38–44. *Tas dikas tas dikastheisas* in 50b8 is ambiguous in that it refers to a 'disposition' which may involve (at least) the constitutionality or legality of a specific law, or the application of specific laws to particular instances, or the verdict of guilt or innocence, or the penalties or sanctions to be imposed. In addressing Socrates' own case, the PLA may be thinking specifically of the last alternative. In any case, I think that Socrates would find it persuasive only in so far as it concerns the violation of court decisions regarding sanctions. This is, in my opinion, the reason why he does not escape: that is, so that he does not violate principle (1b).

12 See Panagiotou 1987b: 58–60.

13 Kraut 1984.

14 This recognition is explicit in the *Apology* but implicit in the *Crito* (in the espousal of the principles of 49a–e).

15 See Allen 1980: 104; Grote 1865: 300; Guthrie 1969: 146, 412–13; Santas 1979: 25; Taylor 1937: 168; Woozley 1979: 71. This is how I understand the blind-obedience view.

16 Kraut 1984: 71–2.

17 Ibid., 72–3.

18 Socrates is not necessarily talking literally about a possible attempt to persuade the state *to let him now out of prison*. The reference to *peisantes* may be to the original trial, and not to any possible current attempts to convince the state to release him. The sense of this part of his question would then be: 'If we get out of here, after failing to convince the court of my innocence. . . .' The use of the aorist participle probably supports this reading.

19 Unless, of course, one thinks that the PLA are referring not to the attempt at persuasion at the trial but to an attempt now to secure his release from prison. See n. 18 above.

20 My understanding of *kai to dikaion houtos echein* (51b7) may strike some as dubious. It may be thought that the Greek sentence may mean simply that it is just for the state to command the sorts of things mentioned in the text. That is, the state does justly command citizens to fight and die for it, etc.; and the state commands justly that sentences be deemed valid and carried out ('justly' in the sense that it is just for the state to command it, not that it is just for this or that particular sentence to be carried out). This understanding of the sentence is, to my mind, most unnatural in the context of 51b–c. It makes the PLA unconcerned about the justification of the things the state asks its citizens to do; they are rather concerned about the 'propriety' of the state's having certain powers. That may well be true. But it is not and cannot be their only concern. The charge at 50c1–2 raises the issue of justification, and the above understanding of 51b7 would make the PLA's response irrelevant. But the PLA themselves show their concern for justification when they disclose their belief that the sentence of death is just. So, they are concerned not merely (if at all) about the propriety of the state's having certain powers (a fact which

118

neither Socrates nor Crito seem interested in disputing) but also, if not exclusively, about the justification of particular edicts or actions of the state. Otherwise, their talk about 'persuading the state where justice lies' would make no sense.

21 Kraut 1984: 74.

22 See Calvert 1987: 21–2. The view, held by Grote (1865: 302) and Kraut (1984: 57–8, 79), that Socrates 'applauds' or 'endorses' the PLA's position is an exaggeration.

23 My current concern is independent of this issue, since my point is that the PLA, whatever their precise function, do not agree that Socrates has been treated unjustly by the state (court).

24 Kraut 1984: 66–9, 81–2.

25 They certainly give this impression to Kraut (1984: 66). Reeve also (1989: 119–20) takes 50c1–6 to indicate the PLA's agreement that the court was wrong to find Socrates guilty.

26 Throughout their speech, the PLA, which I regard as representing the totality of Athenian laws and public practices, do not distinguish between themselves and the state, or between themselves and the judicial system. At 51a2–7 they treat Socrates' condemnation to death *by the court* as something which *they themselves* are doing to him. The context makes it absolutely clear that they have Socrates and his own case in mind (see 51a6–7). In their references to the *polis* or the *nomoi*, the PLA, I reckon, lump together every aspect of what we may call the Public Domain (*to demosion* or *to koinon* – see 50a8) and pit it against the Private (*to idion*). By the by, the disclosure at 51a3–4 of their belief that the sentence of death is *dikaion* is proof positive that the PLA do not agree with Socrates on this issue.

27 See Taylor 1933: 121, and Taylor 1937: 173. The Athenians viewed the state, represented by the courts, as being above the disputes going on in the courtrooms. Even in public cases, i.e. where the public interest was involved, the dispute is seen as being between private litigants. There were no 'crown attorneys' or 'public prosecutors' as such. In this sort of ideological climate, it would be natural to regard the state as blameless.

28 I think that the PLA also see the state as morally continent: that is, it would never do, or require citizens to do, what it believed were unjust things. If a citizen succeeded in persuading the state that what he was being required to do was unjust, it would no longer require him to do it.

29 So Fowler in the Loeb edition and Allen 1980: 125. This reading of the line is the only one that makes sense, if *peithein* here does mean, as I think it does, 'persuade' and not 'try to persuade'.

30 In other words, the state is assumed to be 'continent'. See n. 28 above.

31 In the case of court judgements, it is understood in advance that the outcome of the persuasive exercise is or will be just, unless the litigant challenges the court's decision. According to actual Attic legal practice, such a challenge must be issued during the trial and before the verdict is known. See Harrison 1968–71: 192–3.

32 The 'justice' of what the citizen has agreed to refers to the justice as it is perceived jointly by all the parties to the agreement (i.e. the state and the citizen).

33 I am not sure what the PLA refer to by their frequent use of the terms *homologias* and *sunthekas*: 'things agreed to' or 'the agreement itself'? It appears that, on their view, *liking x* is tantamount to believing that *x* is *substantively* just, while the absence of the 'duress' elements outlined at 52e1–2 accounts for the *procedural* justice of the agreement to do *x*.

34 At 50c1–2 Socrates and Crito suggest that the city treated them unjustly. The Socrates of the *Gorgias* reveals, by one of his examples at 480b8, that he himself thinks the state capable of 'injustice'. In the same sentence he mentions also that one's parents may be unjust!

35 For reading *that* here, see n. 29 above.

36 The sense is: 'though he has agreed to obey or persuade us, he does neither'. Their referring to only one alternative – obey – may be explained by the fact that they look back to 51e1 ('. . . but whoever stays here . . .'), which outlines the condition which signals one's implicit agreement to obey what the state commands. The PLA are now sketching another of the many ways in which, or principles by which, the city conducts its affairs and which the mature citizen is presumed to know and to agree to: the principle of 'persuade or obey'. See n. 40 below.

37 The PLA derive the presumption in favour of the justice of the state's edicts from two very different sources. In the second argument (50d1–51c4) they apparently derive it from the state's natural and inherent superiority over the citizen. In the third argument (51c6 ff.) they apparently derive it from the state's record of performance and the citizen's own appreciation of its record. The latter source of course opens a 'can of worms', which the PLA promptly seek to seal by incorporating the formula 'persuade or obey' into the Citizenship Agreement. This allows them to claim that though it may be questioned by the citizen, the state's record does ultimately contain only *just* items!

38 In view of *ta bouleumata* in 49d5 I doubt very much that *koine boule* means, as it is sometimes translated, 'common ground'.

39 Come to think of it, the present context is not that special for Socrates. All dialectical endeavour aims at common action, the discovery and pursuit by all participants of the Good Life.

40 In Demosthenes 24 (Against Timocrates). 76, it is said that democracy, contrasted to oligarchy and identified with the rule of law, enacts laws which 'speak to the conduct of future affairs [but] . . . *meta tou peisai tithentes*'. In the *Statesman* Plato refers to the doctrine, held by *hoi polloi*, that 'if anyone knows of any better laws than the old [standing] ones, he must legislate having first persuaded his own city, but not otherwise' (296a4–9). In insisting on successful persuasion of the public, the PLA simply follow a general democratic principle.

41 This may sound far-fetched to some modern ears. But we should bear in mind that Socrates is thinking of a fairly narrow field over which the citizen may legitimately claim absolute autonomy: the Good Life. His

Good Life has nothing to do with life, physical liberty, or property, claims of absolute autonomy over which would render the position I am imputing to him quite eccentric.

42 The explanatory clause *hos ego peisas se . . . all me akontos* at 48e4 looks back not to the preceding clause *hos chre . . . apeinai*, but to the clause at 48e1, *. . . antilege kai se peisomai*.

43 Though they do not explicitly say so, the PLA believe, I suppose, that the state's acting without convincing the citizen does not count as 'violence'. If the unpersuaded citizen refuses to obey and the state intervenes to punish him, then, given their conception of the Citizenship Agreement, the punishment is not 'forcing' him, because 'just', but merely treating him 'badly'. 'Violence', on their view, is unjust bad treatment or harm.

44 See *didaskein kai peithein* (*Apology* 35c2); *lege kai didaske* (*Crito* 49e2); *antilege kai se peisomai* (48e1). See also the connection made in the *Gorgias* between *episteme/didaskein* and *peithein*.

45 This might explain at a deeper level Socrates' hesitation to take part in conventional political life. His sentiments and views are rather suited to the life of a society of friends who at the end of the day may agree to disagree and go their own ways. Given this fact, the only concrete political project he might congenially undertake for the benefit of his fellow citizens would be precisely the sort of social mission he did in fact and so religiously pursue: approaching people individually or in small groups and trying to persuade them what is best for them as human beings.

46 I am grateful to Brian Calvert and, especially, Michael Stokes for their numerous and frank comments on earlier versions of this chapter. I am sure they are still not convinced. I made the final revisions during one term I spent as Research Fellow at St John's College, University of Durham. My thanks to the University, to the Principal, Dr Anthony Thiselton, and to Dr Peter Forster.

4

SOCRATES VERSUS
PROTAGORAS

Malcolm Schofield

INTRODUCTION

What is the *Protagoras* about? An obvious and correct answer is: virtue. But it is an answer derived from consideration solely of the content of the arguments of the dialogue. Does reflection on its form yield another answer?

In the bad old days questions about the literary properties of the Platonic dialogue were not much canvassed by philosophical readers – unless they happened to be Straussians or (in even older days) Neo-Platonists. The flavour of the 1980s was rather different: the relation of form to content has become a prime subject of philosophical interest, sometimes handled gushingly or flat-footedly, but at best with tact and sophistication, as in the books of C. Griswold and G. R. F. Ferrari on the *Phaedrus*.[1] Therefore no apology is needed either for posing the question about form with regard to the *Protagoras* or for expecting it to yield dividends, especially given universal agreement on the exceptional literary brilliance of the dialogue.

THE FRAME

Some dialogues are written as dramas, with parts assigned to a cast of characters: for example *Laches, Gorgias, Meno*. Others are narrations by Socrates of conversations to which he had been party: for example *Charmides, Republic*. These give Plato the opportunity for elaborate scene-setting, sometimes rich in philosophical significance, and for lavish authorial irony and other forms of charm.

The *Protagoras* resembles the *Symposium* in beginning with a short dramatic encounter between two characters (*Protagoras*: Socrates and an unnamed companion; *Symposium*: Apollodorus and a similarly unnamed companion) framing the main dialogue, which is reported by one of them – although in the *Symposium* this is a report by Apollodorus of a report by Aristodemus (anticipating the Chinese box effect of the *Parmenides*). These degrees of complexity in presentation are presumably designed for more layers of textual self-reference and self-interpretation than is possible in the straightforward narrative form.

In the *Protagoras* the frame conversation (309a–310a) has a clear and simple point: to initiate the warnings about the reality of Protagoras' alleged wisdom and about its attractiveness which continue through the conversation with Hippocrates that follows.

But the frame frames the whole of the rest of the dialogue, not just this first stretch. A hypothesis suggests itself. The *Protagoras* will explore the difference between the true Socratic wisdom and the mere reputation for wisdom which Protagoras has acquired and in his final words in the dialogue (361e) predicts Socrates will acquire. True Socratic wisdom is what is illustrated in the discussion with Hippocrates, and particularly by the demonstration of the Socratic method of argument it embodies. The parade of the shadow of wisdom is introduced by the echoes of the Homeric Hades and its shades which punctuate the description of Protagoras' promenade in the house of Callias (314e–316a), and is epitomised by the agonistic conception of argument that is illustrated throughout the discussion with the sophists and thematised in the interlude on procedure set at the dead centre of the dialogue (334–8: the *Protagoras* is 309–62 in the Stephanus edition).

THE CONVERSATION WITH HIPPOCRATES

The beginning of the encounter with Hippocrates is one of the most hilarious in a highly entertaining piece of writing (310a–311a): I commend the sparkling English version of B. A. F. Hubbard and E. S. Karnofsky.[2]

> Early this morning, when it was still pitch dark, Hippocrates, Apollodorus' boy, the brother of Phason, started hammering at my door with his staff; and when someone opened up, he came rushing straight in and said at the top of his voice:

123

'Socrates, are you awake or asleep?' And recognising his voice I said: 'Oh, it's Hippocrates. Nothing up, is there?'

'Nothing but good', he said.

'That', I said, 'really would be good news. But what is it, and why have you come round at this hour?'

'Protagoras has come', he said, standing beside me.

'Yes', I said, 'the day before yesterday. Have you only just found that out?'

'Of course', he said; 'well, yesterday evening, that is.' And groping for my camp bed, he sat down by my feet and said: 'Yes, in the evening, rather late actually, after I got back from Oenoe. Satyrus, my slave, was on the run, you see, and I was going to tell you that I was after him, when something came up and put it out of my head. And after dinner, when we were off to bed, my brother tells me Protagoras has come. And even then I set out to tell you straight away, but then it occurred to me that it was too late. But as soon as I had slept off my fatigue, I got straight up and was on my way here, as you see.' Knowing how bold and volatile he is, I remarked: 'But what has this got to do with you? You don't have some charge to bring against Protagoras, do you?'

'Indeed I do, Socrates', he laughed: 'that he alone is wise (*sophos*), but is not making me wise.'

'Oh yes he will, by Zeus', I said; 'if you give him money and persuade him, he will make you wise too.'

'Oh by Zeus and all the gods, if it were just a question of money', he said, 'I should spare none of my own or my friends' possessions. But that is just what I came to see you about – to get you to talk to him for me. I am rather young, and I have never seen Protagoras before, or ever heard anything he has said. I was still a child when he was last in town. But after all, Socrates, everyone is praising him and saying that he is very clever (*sophotatos*) at speaking. But why don't we go there so that we can catch him in? He is staying with Callias, the son of Hipponicus, so I've heard. Come on.'

And I said: 'Let's not go there yet, my dear fellow; it's still early. Let's get up instead and go out into the courtyard where we can take a few turns until it gets light. Then we can go. After all, Protagoras spends much of his time indoors; so you needn't worry; we shall probably catch him in.'

Notice the studied informality of the scene. Notice the irony of making the naive teenager go to Socrates not as *sophos* but as friend and father confessor. Notice the illusion of his thought that Protagoras, of whom he knows nothing, is the only true *sophos*. Notice the Socratic jibe at Protagoras' mercenary motives. Plato has quickly constructed an opposition between Socrates' lack of pretension and a grandee whose credentials are already under suspicion.

Now follows a paradigmatic Socratic conversation, sadly neglected by scholarship.[3] That is, what Socrates goes on to say to Hippocrates is not only precisely the sort of thing we expect of the Platonic Socrates, but a sequence of conversations designed specifically to *demonstrate* the true nature of philosophical discourse as it should be practised: in a cooperative spirit of enquiry into the truth. The paradigm consists of three elements. It is unemphatically presented, and indeed understated, with the lightness and gentleness of touch appropriate to the ingenuousness of the interlocutor. But it is a paradigm for all that.

First comes a cross-examination by Socrates of his young companion in familiar style (311a–312e). It is in fact a classical example of the Socratic elenchus: not in extracting from an interlocutor a series of admissions which turn out to conflict with a thesis sincerely advanced by him, but in proving to Hippocrates that something he thinks he knows is actually something he really has no idea about. The key passage is 312b–e:

> 'Well, do you know what you are about to do, or don't you realise?' I said.
> 'How do you mean?'
> 'That you are about to place your own soul (*psuche*) in the care of a man who is, as you say, a sophist; although I should be amazed if you knew just what a sophist might be. And yet if you don't know that, you don't know whether the thing to which you have entrusted your soul is good or bad.'
> 'I think I know', he said.
> 'All right, tell me: what do you consider a sophist to be?'
> 'So far as I am concerned', he said, 'he is what the word implies: someone who has knowledge of wise things (*sopha*).'

Wise at what? He knows how to make people clever at speaking, says Hippocrates. About what?

'What is this subject about which, being knowledgeable himself, the sophist makes his student knowledgeable as well?'
'Oh dear', he said, 'now I have nothing left to say.'

In a recent article Hugh Benson rightly argues that the immediate
aim of the Socratic elenchus is the testing of the interlocutor's
knowledge, and in practice the elimination of the false conceit of
knowledge. He goes on to suggest that, with two possible exceptions, the short elenctic dialogues give no evidence for Socrates'
method once false conceit has been purged.[4] The *Protagoras* supplies
the deficiency: the next stage is exhortation or protreptic (313a–
314c), which must accordingly not be reckoned proprietary to the
Euthydemus and dialogues later than the *Euthydemus*. Having got
Hippocrates into a chastened and receptive frame of mind, Socrates
warns him in a sustained and eloquent passage of the danger he is
in, proposing as he does to entrust his soul to someone of doubtful
credentials. The sophist is like a retailer who has no notion whether
his wares are really good for the consumer. But you cannot examine
the sophist's wares prior to consumption as you can with food and
drink. They have already entered the soul and had their effect before
scrutiny is possible. A later section of the chapter will comment
further on the dangers of exposure to sophists. For the present
we may note Socrates' concern for the soul of his interlocutor,
familiar to us from, for instance, the *Apology* and the *Charmides*,
and reflect on the moral he draws, which is unhelpfully unspecific
and ironically self-deprecating (314b):

'Let us consider all this, then, and with those older than us. For
we are still rather too young to sort out so great a matter.'

There is still a final stage of the conversation. On their way to
Callias' house Socrates and Hippocrates engage in philosophical
discussion, not further described, which they do not interrupt
but pursue in the porch of the house until they reach agreement
(314c; compare the famous case of Socratic concentration during the
Potidaean campaign retailed by Alcibiades in the *Symposium*, 220a–
d).[5] Plato here gives us the merest hint of what might lie beyond loss
of false conceit and response to protreptic: a cooperative exercise,
resulting in agreement between the parties concerned, and pursued
to completion. We are surely to contrast the end of the conversation
with Protagoras, who bids Socrates finish the argument on his own
(360d), accuses him of a competitive motivation which is elsewhere

in the dialogue portrayed as the hallmark of the sophist (360e), and has better things to do (361e) than try to get to the bottom of questions Socrates takes to be fundamental to the Good Life (361c–d).

It is of course something of a paradox that after insisting so on the dangers of sophists Socrates still allows Hippocrates to meet and listen to Protagoras. But after initial introductions (316b–c, 317e–318e), Plato forgets Hippocrates. The young man has served his turn, which was to be the partner in a proper Socratic conversation.[6]

THE DOOR

Entry to the house of Callias is prefaced by a scene of low comedy (314c–e) in which Socrates argues with the doorman, and obtains admission only at the second attempt, having had the door slammed in his face and then locked first time round. This is not the only significant passage through a door in Greek philosophy. Parmenides had left the realm of mortal opinion for that of divine *logos* through the gates of the paths of day and night, which Justice had to be persuaded to open.[7] In its humble way the episode in the *Protagoras* likewise emphasises the huge difference between the Socratic discourse we have just heard and the sophistic debate we are about to witness.

Hippocrates has been given to understand that consorting with Protagoras may threaten his soul with danger. Is Socrates too in danger? Plainly he is too adroit and wary a dialectician to imbibe Protagoreanism uncritically. A subtler problem confronts him.

The conversation with Hippocrates has taken place on Socrates' ground: literally, since it begins in his house and continues in the public space where Socratic dialogue is habitually conducted; metaphorically, for it is a private talk between friends, undertaken for the moral and intellectual benefit of the interlocutor. The conversation with Protagoras, by contrast, is conducted on alien territory in someone else's private house, indoors – that is no accident, but Protagoras' frequent custom (311a). And although Socratic elenchus eventually dominates the occasion, it begins not exactly on Protagoras' terms, but certainly in the style of a public debate between intellectuals competing for the attention of an audience.

Private faces in public places
Are wiser and nicer
Than public faces in private places.

There is much in Socrates' performance that is just that – a performance, by a Socrates who is not altogether himself, if we judge by the standard of the shorter elenctic dialogues (and the *Apology*) which the conversation with Hippocrates has called to mind.

Consider briefly three of the contributions he makes to the discussion in the house of Callias. After some prodding Protagoras defines his prospectus. He promises to teach a pupil 'good judgement (*euboulia*) both about his own affairs, to the end that he might best manage his personal estate, and about the city's, to the end that he might be in the strongest position to conduct, in speech and action, the common business of the city' (318e–319a). How does Socrates challenge this? Not as a Socratic Socrates would, with an elenchus. He develops on his own account two counter-arguments for the proposition that virtue cannot be taught (319a–320c). It seems unlikely that the case he puts is original. The teachability of virtue was a well-known topic of sophistic debate;[8] and at any rate the second of the two arguments is found in the sophistic compendium *Dissoi logoi* (Diels-Kranz 90.6).[9] No less un-Socratic is Socrates' conduct in the interlude on procedure (334c–338e), which I shall discuss shortly: gamesmanship is the only word for it. Finally, in the episode devoted to criticism of Simonides' poem (338e–347b) Socrates first adopts blatant delaying tactics (339e ff.) until he has thought out a line of defence, and then launches at Protagorean length into an outrageous parody of sophistic expository method (342a ff.), offering an even more perverse reading of Simonides than Protagoras'. At the end of it all he remarks that the sort of exercise they have been engaging in is not worth anything very much (347b–e).

These un-Socratic practices allow Socrates to outshine Protagoras and outmanoeuvre him. There lies the danger. The Socratic method is meant to be cooperative, not competitive, intent on truth, not victory. Competitive success is for the true Socrates no success at all. If he beats the sophist at his own game, he fails – it is the sophist's game, not his.

THE INTERLUDE ON PROCEDURE

The debate on procedure is occasioned by a breakdown in the elenchus which Socrates has been directing at Protagoras' views about the relation between the parts of virtue (329c–333e). Protagoras has had enough of the cross-questioning, and launches into a speech about the relativity of the beneficial, designed to show that the good is a diverse and complicated thing (333e–334c). Socrates requests shorter answers, affecting a bad memory; and after a little skirmishing Plato gives us the following revealing exchange (334e–335a):

> 'They do tell me', I said, 'that you are adept both as an exponent and as a teacher of the art of speaking either at length, if you choose, so that you never run dry, or briefly, so much so that no one could be more concise. So if you want to hold a discourse with me, please use the second mode – the brief one.'
>
> 'Socrates', he said, 'I have entered into a contest (*agon*) of *logoi* with many people in my time; and if I had done what you are telling me to do, discussing as my opponent told me to, I should have proved no better than the next man, and the name of Protagoras would not be celebrated throughout Greece.'

Socrates then argues that Protagoras should none the less accede to his request, pleads urgent business, and makes as if to leave.

Protagoras could scarcely have given a clearer articulation of a competitive conception of argument. His characterisation of discussion as a 'contest of *logoi*' and his related concern for his own standing as a sophist sum up the whole spirit of that part of the dialogue which takes place in the house of Callias. In case we have not got the message, Plato has Socrates go on to compare discussion between him and Protagoras to an unequal competition in a foot-race (335e–336a). Hardly less obvious, however, is Socrates' complicity in this competitive ideology. Presumably his real interest in brief answers ought to be that only so can an elenchus be conducted, and only by means of the elenchus can false pretensions to knowledge be stripped away, and only in this way can the soul be properly cared for. But he is made to treat the issue of brevity in Protagorean style, as a matter of what technique he can best cope with. This is itself gamesmanship, all of a piece with the tactics he uses here to get his way. Once again the sequel reinforces the point. Callias, Alcibiades and the other sophists join in an elaborate argument about the proper *rules* for discussion, all competing with each other to propound a more impressive suggestion, culminating in Hippias' idea of a chairman (as in a public meeting: 338a), wickedly glossed by Socrates as the proposal of an umpire (as in the games: 338b) – which he succeeds in defeating mostly by the grossly insincere argument that it would be impossible to find one wiser than Protagoras (338c). Everything Socrates says and does in this interlude on procedure will have confirmed in their interpretation readers inclined to construe Socrates' conduct of the elenchus (329c–333e) as competitive in motivation.

It has in fact often been felt that the elenchus in the *Protagoras* falls short of the disinterested ideal of cooperative enquiry it is officially meant to fulfil. This is mostly because some of the argumentation is palpably slick and shallow: for example several of the moves in the section on justice and holiness, 330c–331e; the final steps in the first argument on wisdom and courage, 349e–350c; and the equivalences asserted between the fine, the good and the pleasurable in the final argument on the same subject, 358b–360e. Partly it is because Socrates seems not to be content until he has forced Protagoras into explicit submission. Sympathy is evoked[10] by Protagoras' remark at the very end of the last elenchus (360e):

> 'You seem to me greedy for victory, Socrates, in this business of my being the answerer. Well, I will satisfy your desire . . .'

Of course, it is Plato who puts this dignified response in his mouth, just as earlier he furnishes him with *prima facie* reasonable objections to some of Socrates' slippery inferences (331b–c, 331d–332a, 350c–351b).

Sometimes dissatisfaction with Socrates' arguments has taken the form of a suggestion that Plato deploys deliberate fallacies in the *Protagoras*.[11] Scholarship has found it hard to evaluate the suggestion. What seems more promising is the idea that Plato has deliberately portrayed Socrates as more competitive than the cooperative ideal would lead one to expect, and that the style of his arguments in the house of Callias fits that picture. For it is characteristic of competitors (or at least of the paradigm ancient Greek competitors of *Iliad* XXIII) to score points off each other, and to take short cuts to achieve their objects. The short cuts in argument may or may not be defensible in the light of fuller and more thoughtful consideration: the point is that the circumstances of the competition make it tempting to *take* the short cut. I think it is significant that while Plato never in any dialogue presents a diagnosis of a fallacy (except ambiguity once, in *Euthydemus* 277d–278b: the *Euthydemus* is principally about sophistry, a quite different thing), a concern with alternative routes to the same philosophical goal, and particularly with short cuts and longer ways round, becomes thematic and indeed almost obsessive in dialogues like the *Phaedo, Republic, Parmenides* and *Theaetetus*.

We should distinguish between a competitive or eristic and an adversarial style of elenchus. Gilbert Ryle in *Plato's Progress* obliterated the difference, and actually defined the elenctic dialogues of Plato as eristic.[12] The mistake here was pointed out recently by Gregory Vlastos – who is himself responsible for something unhelpful, in building the notion of 'adversary argument' into his definition of elenchus.[13] He does not think that Socrates necessarily conceives of the interlocutors whose beliefs he examines as opponents, but is simply trying to capture the point that in an elenchus Socrates always argues *against* someone. Even that is too strong: young Hippocrates is the subject of probing, scarcely of counter-argument. It would probably be better to reserve 'adversarial' to describe the use of the elenchus against a stubborn and/or versatile interlocutor, with a strongly ingrained conceit of knowledge. Here the elenchus, always liable to be intimidating, may need to become aggressive – to attack an articulated or tenaciously held position, rather than just examine a sincere view. So long as the goal is the elimination of false belief, not victory, it will be adversarial without being competitive. The adversarial elenchus may for that end use reasoning which is from some points of view too slick by half (as, for instance, against Polus in the *Gorgias*), so short cuts are not an infallible sign of the competitive use of argument, even if that is what they are evidence of in the *Protagoras*.

THE ARGUMENT AGAINST THE MANY

From the perspective we have been adopting, and on the evidence reviewed so far, the *Protagoras* looks like a literary success but a philosophical failure. I do not mean to deny that Protagoras is portrayed as the subject of a successful elenchus, albeit an elenchus pursued more competitively than ideally it should be. It may be that by the end of the dialogue we are meant to suppose that Protagoras' conceit of knowledge has been punctured. Certainly he is made to revise his original position on the unity of the virtues (349d), and at 360e concedes, painfully but eventually with a little grace, that the argument he has just agreed to entails that wisdom and courage are the same. Nor does his reluctance to concede this show that the elenchus is somehow vitiated, whether by fallacy or otherwise. The unsettling of one's beliefs is intrinsically liable to be disconcerting.

But Protagoras, after all, is only a character in a fiction. What really matters for a piece of writing to be profitable as philosophy is its ability to engage the reader in the appropriate way: it is one of Plato's enduring achievements to have taught us that. Yet he so writes the conversation between Socrates and Protagoras as to make the reader continually aware of its properties as performance – brilliant, complicated, competitive performance. If philosophy involves immersion in the pursuit of argument for its own sake, the coruscating surface of the text and its focus on performance obstruct a properly philosophical response to the issues being presented. To put it another way, Socrates' conception of philosophy has not been recommended to us here strongly enough in its own terms: which, as the conversation with Hippocrates was designed to remind us, are as far removed as could be from preoccupation with performance. One might infer not only that the *Protagoras* is a philosophical failure but that Plato has constructed it exactly as such.

It would not be the only Platonic dialogue to have elicited this sort of diagnosis. *Republic* I is sometimes read as a failure of this kind. On this view, Socrates is not allowed to take the full measure of Thrasymachus' cynical position on justice, but is made to defeat it and advance his own conception of virtue by a sequence of slick and otherwise unsatisfactory arguments which persuade neither Thrasymachus nor the reader. Hence Plato's decision to make Glaucon and Adeimantus demand something better by way of response to Thrasymachus at the beginning of Book II. It is tempting once again to suppose that the failure is deliberate. Scholars have guessed that it effectively signals Plato's abandonment of the elenchus or at any rate the elenctic dialogue.[14] Perhaps he had come to the conclusion that if positive understanding of truth is ever to be attained, it will not be achieved by elenctic examination of the views of sophists, since they share too little in common with Platonic philosophy either in their sense of where truth is to be located or in the spirit in which they conduct discussion. Given an interpretation on these lines, the *Protagoras* and Book I of the *Republic* could be seen as similar demonstrations of the impossibility of fruitful dialogue between sophists and philosophers. Thrasymachus and Protagoras even sulk in the same style.

I think there are indeed in the *Protagoras* seeds of the apostasy from the elenchus which *Republic* I was to make final – but only seeds, or perhaps an embryo. For the *Protagoras* contains, as *Republic* I does not, an elenctic passage in the discussion with the sophists which manages to escape the twin perils of competitiveness and superficiality. In this passage, at least, the *Protagoras* attains the kind of philosophical success which I have argued is in general not achieved. It is as though Plato still sees in the elenctic dialogue a literary vehicle for philosophy capable of properly commanding the reader's philosophical attention and concern. The text I have in mind is the long argument from hedonistic premises to the impossibility of doing knowingly what one knows or believes to be against one's own best interests (351b–357e).

This is the one stretch of Socratic argument in the dialogue which in my experience as a reader of articles and commentaries and especially as a teacher is found wholly compelling and absorbing as philosophy. It is a sustained and theoretically ambitious piece of thinking, palpably careful and devoid of slick short cuts (even if it doesn't work). The issues raised, particularly regarding the truth of hedonism and the commensurability of values, no less than the way they are raised, succeed in challenging our deep-seated beliefs and prejudices.[15] There is, of course, interest in whether Plato is here representing Socrates and/or Protagoras as committed to hedonism, and indeed whether he is a hedonist himself at this stage in his philosophical development.[16] But – again in my experience – interpretative questions such as these concern readers (*qua* readers) much less than the philosophical problems themselves.

How does the intensely competitive framework and ethos of the debate in the house of Callias accommodate a passage such as this? In a word: by indirection. What Plato engineers is a conversation in which Protagoras is no longer cross-examined directly by Socrates, but is persuaded – partly no doubt by Socrates' explicit appeal a little earlier to a cooperative conception of enquiry (348c–349a) – to join with him in a cross-examination of popular views about pleasure and knowledge. The elenchus here is an elenchus of the many by Socrates and Protagoras together. In other words, Plato makes Socrates finally secure Protagoras' cooperation in the elenchus by the simple but ingenious device of coopting Protagoras to the same side as Socrates – or to what a competitor like Protagoras would see as the same side: the cross-examining side, and thereby, of course, the side any competitor would wish to be on, the side with the initiative. A similar device is employed for similar purposes in the *Hippias Major*.[17] The sophist Hippias is not a natural or cooperative respondent, so Plato again avoids direct cross-examination, and invents a fictitious interlocutor who is imagined by Socrates as putting awkward questions both to himself and to Hippias (286c ff.). Once again Socrates and a sophist are bound together in an artificial solidarity, this time not as questioners but as fellow examinees, and the dialogue can proceed uncompetitively, without the distracting intrusions of amour propre.

In the *Protagoras* the device is made plausible by the fact that Socrates and Protagoras, i.e. the historical Socrates and the historical Protagoras (at least as Plato seems to have understood them), are intellectuals who genuinely share a common premise which ordinary people do not: viz. the thesis that knowledge is something possessing supreme power and authority. Where they differ is in the degree of their perception of the consequences of that version of this thesis which is concerned with knowledge of good. Socrates saw that it leads directly to the paradox that no man does wrong willingly, and that all the virtues come to the same thing: wisdom or knowledge or understanding. Protagoras apparently did not draw these consequences. So in the passage of the *Protagoras* with which we are concerned, the character Protagoras has to be got to appreciate them carefully and slowly, in the right stages, and initially and most importantly by realising that even a hedonist must under cross-examination admit that knowledge cannot be undermined by pleasure. It is only in the later stages that Protagoras is made to realise that he, the examiner, is actually in the same boat as those he is cross-examining: outmanoeuvred again, one might say, by a superior competitor.

What matters for the philosophical vitality and force of the *Protagoras*, however, is that the substitution of indirect for direct elenchus permits Plato to write a substantial stretch of dialogue in which personalities and their competitive ambitions are forgotten by the reader – who can simply concentrate on some philosophy. We must add that this is not the note on which the dialogue ends. At 358a Plato reminds us again that we are in the house of Callias in the company of sophists, and thereafter the discussion resumes the style which is more generally characteristic of the *Protagoras*. Socrates reverts to a final direct elenchus, in which one or two argumentative corners are cut, and sums up with some further urbane sparring. The sense of bathos registered by readers of the last four pages of the work is itself testimony to what the dialogue with the many at 351–7 succeeds in achieving. In those pages the *Protagoras* becomes no longer an encounter between Socrates and Protagoras but an elenctic dialogue in the reader's own soul.[18]

NOTES

1 Griswold (1986) and Ferrari (1987).
2 Translations from the *Protagoras* in this essay are mostly borrowed or adapted from Hubbard and Karnofsky (1982). I should add that they are more interested in literary questions about the dialogue than is C. C. W. Taylor in the otherwise excellent Clarendon Plato edition (Taylor 1976).
3 For the notion of the paradigmatic employed here see further my 1986: 5–31, at pp. 22–5, and more generally Griffin 1980: ch. 1.
4 Benson 1990: 19–65, at pp. 44–64. 'Two possible exceptions': p. 63, n. 84.
5 This point of affinity between the *Protagoras* and the *Symposium*, together with that noted on p. 123, should be added to the list compiled by Kahn 1988: 98–9. Note also the stylistic affinity between the two dialogues detected by G. R. Ledger's computer – Ledger 1989: 155.
6 Some commentators think that Hippocrates remains important for the interpretation of important aspects of the debate between Socrates and Protagoras. For a moderate statement of this viewpoint see Stokes 1986: 203–6, 209–12, 309–10, 370–91. Incidentally, to the interesting question raised by Stokes (194), 'Why does Socrates tell Protagoras that Hippocrates wishes to become "famous in the city" (315b–c) – when Hippocrates has said nothing of the kind?', I answer: because being notable or reputed is what *Protagoras* most values and understands, as is evidenced by the prediction for Socrates' future (316e) already noted on p. 123 above.
7 See Kirk, Raven and Schofield 1983: no. 288, with discussion on pp. 243–4.
8 See, e.g., O'Brien 1967: ch. 2; Guthrie 1969: ch. X.
9 See Sprague 1972: 289–90 (the 'third proof'). See also Kerferd 1981: 131–3.
10 As Gregory Vlastos noted (p. xxv, n. 4) in what remains the best approach to the *Protagoras* available in the literature, his introduction to Martin Ostwald's 1956 revision of the Jowett translation (Indianapolis and New York: Liberal Arts Press).
11 The most thorough working out of this view is by Klosko 1979: 125–42; cf. his 1983: 363–74.
12 Ryle 1966: 119–20, 193.

13 Vlastos 1983a: 31, n. 14, 30.
14 Annas 1981: 56–7; Reeve 1988: ch. 1.
15 See Nussbaum 1986: ch. 4.
16 See Zeyl 1980: 250–9; subsequently debate on the issues appears to have largely exhausted itself.
17 See Woodruff 1982: 97–8; cf. 107–8.
18 Thus I make the ultimate philosophical aim and also the technique of the *Protagoras* something analogous to what Myles Burnyeat postulates – in a richer and more complex version – for Parts II and III of the *Theaetetus*. See his 1990.

5

SOCRATIC ETHICS[1]

C. C. W. Taylor

First a word in elucidation of my title. By 'Socratic Ethics' I intend, not 'the ethical theories of the historical Socrates' but 'the ethical theories of Plato's Socratic dialogues', and by 'Socratic dialogues' I refer to those dialogues, generally reckoned to be early, in which (a) there is no mention of the Theory of Forms, and (b) Socratic elenchus is a central or at least prominent feature of the discussion.[2] I do not, therefore, propose to grapple directly with the classical 'Socratic question', viz. the question of how much of the historical Socrates may be recovered from our literary sources. Rather, I shall be exploring the internal connection between certain items of Plato's presentation of Socratic ethics, on the one hand the attempt to reach definitions and on the other the two theses which have come to be labelled as 'the Socratic paradoxes', (i) that virtue is knowledge and (ii) that no one does wrong willingly or intentionally. Yet this enquiry, though not directly historical in intention, is not totally without historical interest, in that all those items are ascribed to Socrates by Aristotle. The two theses are attributed to him, directly or by implication, in the *Nicomachean Ethics*. At 1144b19–20 Aristotle says that Socrates thought that all the virtues were sorts (or perhaps instances) of *phronesis*, and a few lines later (29–30) that they were kinds (or instances) of knowledge, which I take to be in the context equivalent statements. Earlier (1116b4–5) he has attributed to Socrates an instance of this generalisation, viz. the thesis that courage is a kind (or instance) of knowledge. As regards the second thesis, Aristotle famously sets up his discussion of akrasia in part via the claim, on which Socrates used to insist, that 'no one acts contrary to what is best in the belief that he is doing so, but through error' (1145b26–7), which Gerasimos Santas[3] has shown to be the foundation of the doctrine that no one does wrong

137

willingly. In a well-known passage of *Metaphysics* A 6 Aristotle singles out the search for ethical definitions as central to Socrates' contribution to the development of philosophy: 'Socrates . . . was occupying himself with ethical matters, neglecting the world of nature as a whole but seeking the universal in ethical matters; he was the first to concentrate attention on definitions' (987b1–4). He repeats this information in *Metaphysics* M 4 1078b17ff. with some important additions (b27–32): 'there are two things which may justly be ascribed to Socrates, inductive arguments and general definitions, for both are concerned with the starting point of knowledge; Socrates did not, however, separate the universal or the definitions, but they [viz. Plato and his followers] did, calling them the Forms of things.'

Of course, we cannot simply take it for granted that Aristotle's evidence is independent of Plato. That the evidence for the Socratic denial of akrasia is derived from the dialogues is suggested by Aristotle's opening statement (1145b23–4) that 'it would be astonishing, as Socrates thought, if though knowledge were present something else overcame it and dragged it about like a slave', where the picturesque metaphor is a verbal echo of *Protagoras* 352c1–2. Nothing in the contexts of the other *Nicomachean Ethics* passages requires that they should be independent of Platonic texts. On the other hand, in the *Metaphysics* Aristotle is attempting to identify the contribution of the historical Socrates to the development of philosophy, and in particular to the development of Platonism, and he distinguishes Socrates from Plato by a criterion which is not derived from the Platonic dialogues, viz. that Socrates did not separate the Forms, whereas Plato did.[4] We are therefore justified in believing that not merely the Platonic but also the historical Socrates did seek ethical definitions, and that in his search for them he made use of inductive arguments (and also elenchus of his interlocutors).[5] Beyond that I do not think we can go far in reconstructing the views of the historical Socrates. It seems to me quite likely that he did maintain the Socratic paradoxes in some form or other.[6] On the question of what kind of definition he sought, we have virtually no information from any source other than Plato,[7] and are therefore systematically debarred from being able to determine how much is Plato and how much Socrates.

From now on, therefore, I shall have no more to say about the historical Socrates. I shall instead consider what Plato's Socrates is looking for when he looks for an ethical definition, and how

138

the search for definitions connects with the Socratic paradoxes. I shall suggest that while Plato falls short of presenting Socrates as possessing a single clear conception of definition, one paradigm of definition predominates. Further, that paradigm has an intimate connection with the paradoxes; more precisely, the demand for definition is satisfied via the development of a psychological theory in which the paradoxes have a central position. I shall be focussing primarily on the *Meno*, which, though probably one of the latest of the Socratic dialogues, and in its introduction of the theory of recollection transitional to the metaphysical dialogues of the middle period, is none the less Socratic by my criteria of the prominence of elenchus and the absence of Forms, and is of all the Socratic dialogues the richest in evidence for the Platonic/Socratic theory and practice of definition.

What is a Socratic definition a definition of? Not, in the first instance, of any of the items that might spring to the mind of the modern reader, such as a term, the meaning of a word, or a concept. Ideally, a Socratic definition answers the question 'What is . . . ?', where the blank is filled in by a word designating some quality or feature of agents, such as courage or excellence. So literally, what are to be defined are those qualities or features themselves, not anything standing for them, as words or perhaps concepts might be thought to do. But, of course, we cannot in general draw a sharp distinction between specifying what something is and defining or elucidating the concept of that thing. The concept of F (where 'F' is some general term) is what we understand or possess when we use the term 'F' with understanding, and in some cases saying what F is just is defining or elucidating the concept of F. Thus if I answer the question 'What is justice?' by saying that justice is giving everyone their due, I have thereby attempted (however inadequately) to elucidate the concept of justice, in that the answer is intended to make explicit what is standardly conveyed by our talk of justice. The ultimate authority for the correctness of that sort of definition is the competent speaker of the language in which the elucidation is expressed, and the ultimate test which that authority applies is conformity with his or her linguistic intuitions. In other cases, however, the question 'What is F?' is aimed to elicit, not an elucidation of the ordinary concept of F, but an account of the phenomenon couched in terms of the best available scientific theory. For example, 'light is a stream of photons' is not an elucidation of the ordinary concept of light, i.e. of what the standard speaker of

English understands by the word 'light'. It is an account of what light is, i.e. of what science has discovered light to be, and that account presupposes, but is not exhausted by, the grasp of the concept which is available to the competent but pre-theoretical speaker of the language. Hence the ultimate test of its adequacy is not its fit with that speaker's linguistic intuitions, but its explanatory power, empirical testability, or whatever else constitutes the test of a good scientific theory. The form of words 'What is . . . ?' may express the search for a definition of either kind (and in any case the distinction between the two is less sharp than the foregoing over-simplification has suggested[8]). Precisely what kind of search is afoot has to be determined by the context, which cannot be guaranteed to provide an unambiguous result.

We learn from the *Euthyphro* that a Socratic definition of a given quality should (a) specify what is common to all and only those things to which the name of the quality applies (5d), (b) specify that in virtue of which the name applies to them (i.e. give the nature of the quality, not merely a distinguishing mark of its presence) (6d, 11a), and (c) provide a criterion by reference to which disputed cases may be determined (6e). Requirements (a) and (b) are explicitly endorsed at *Meno* 72c, where Meno is invited to specify 'the single nature they [i.e. the various types of human excellence] all have in virtue of which (*di' ho*) they are excellences', and though the *Meno* has nothing to say about disputed cases of *arete*, we have no reason to suppose that the third requirement has been abandoned. These three requirements are satisfied alike by conceptual elucidations and by that kind of account which we have contrasted with those, and which we might call, traditionally, 'real definitions' or, perhaps more informatively, 'substantive scientific accounts'. But the specific context of the *Meno* in which Socrates is prompted to ask 'What is excellence?' suggests that elucidation of the ordinary concept is unlikely to be sufficient for the purpose of the dialogue. The context is provided by Meno's opening question (70a): 'Is excellence something which can be taught, or is it rather acquired by practice, or is it a natural endowment, or is it acquired in some other way?' That is to say, Meno wants to know how one may come to acquire excellence, i.e. how one can come to be an excellent or outstanding person, to which Socrates correctly replies (71b) that one cannot answer that question unless one first understands what excellence is.

Now, what kind of understanding of the nature of a quality is required if one is to know how to acquire that quality? Socrates generalises Meno's question, maintaining (cf. *Republic* I: 354b–c) that in general one cannot answer the question 'Is *x* F?' unless one can first answer the question 'What is *x*?' and glossing that requirement as analogous to the requirement that one should know who Meno is in order to know whether he is, for instance, handsome. The gloss is unhelpful: in order to know whether some predicate holds of an individual subject such as Meno one must indeed be able to individuate that subject, but the ability to individuate Meno does not require that one possess any uniquely individuating specification of Meno; one might, for instance, individuate Meno ostensively, just as 'that man over there'. The analogue in the case of a universal such as excellence seems to be no more than the minimal requirement to know what we are talking about when we use the word, a requirement which again does not presuppose the ability to give a verbal specification, but which might be satisfied by the ability reliably to recognise typical instances. But that minimal knowledge of what excellence is (which Socrates and Meno obviously have already, otherwise the conversation could not even start) is clearly no help at all when it comes to the question of how to acquire excellence.

An analogy with another evaluative predication may help to make the point clearer. Asking how to acquire excellence at tennis, I am told by Socrates that I must first know what excellence at tennis is, just as in order to know whether Meno is handsome I must first know who Meno is. But in that sense, i.e. that I must be able to identify Meno, of course I know what excellence at tennis is. Unless I could recognise it when I came across it, how could I ever raise the question of how to acquire *it*? So I need more than the bare ability to know what I am talking about. Perhaps, then, I need an elucidation of the concept. But now what counts as such an elucidation? A bare specification of the meaning of the expression 'excellence at tennis', for example 'ability to play tennis to a high standard', is plainly no help in guiding me towards the acquisition of excellence at tennis. For that I need some substantive knowledge of what excellence at tennis consists in, i.e. of what qualities go to make a first-class tennis player. There are at least two kinds of qualities which excellence at tennis may be said to consist in: first of all, since the game is composed of a variety of kinds of stroke, one might analyse excellence at tennis into the excellent performance of each of those kinds, having a good service, a good forehand, etc. That kind of analysis would be of some use to the novice, in so far as it articulates the undifferentiated goal of acquiring excellence at tennis into a number of subordinate goals. But it provides no guidance as to how each of the subordinate goals is to be pursued. For that, the general notion of excellence at tennis, and thereby the specific excellences constitutive of that excellence, excellent service, etc., have to be analysed via a specification of that complex of qualities which are *causally* necessary and sufficient for success at the game: for instance excellence in tennis is achieved via a complex of attributes such as hand–eye coordination, speed of reaction, stamina, tactical insight and motivation. That is to say, I need to have the rudiments of a theory of tennis, which *explains* excellence by identifying its causes and thereby indicating appropriate methods of acquiring it.

The practical orientation of the discussion in the *Meno* thus suggests that the account of excellence which is being sought ought to be an explanatory account of the type exemplified immediately above. Such an account would not only fulfil the requirements stated in the *Euthyphro*, but would give Meno the practical guidance he is looking for, as an elucidation of the ordinary concept of excellence would not. The text of the dialogue does, I believe, confirm that that type of account is predominant in Plato's mind, but the evidence is by no means unambiguous: indeed the complexities are such as to force us to acknowledge that the distinction between conceptual elucidation and explanatory theory emerges with less than total clarity.

Invited to say what excellence is, Meno first responds by the suggestion that there are various forms of human excellence, corresponding to certain primary social roles held by various kinds of person, the adult male, adult (married) woman, child, etc. (71e–72a). Socrates then poses his usual challenge to say what all these kinds of excellence have in common in virtue of which they all count as types of excellence (72a–d), and himself takes what is presumably the first step towards meeting this challenge by pointing out that excellence in each of Meno's primary social roles requires the possession of justice and self-control (73a–c). This looks like a move towards the first of our two patterns of analysis of the conception of excellence at tennis, in which a complex characteristic is decomposed into its constituents; completed to Socrates' satisfaction it would exhibit human excellence of each of Meno's primary types as consisting in the possession of the same set of specific excellences or virtues, justice, self-control, courage, wisdom and perhaps some others (cf. 74a, 88a; *Protagoras* 349b). But, as in our tennis example, the practical question of how to acquire excellence would still require a further account of each of those specific virtues, which would, it seems, have to be of the causally explanatory type. Socrates, however, is dissatisfied with this account for a quite different reason, viz. that it, like Meno's original suggestion, fails to meet the requirement to say what all the instances (in this case all the specific virtues) have in common (74a). *Prima facie* the application of that requirement to this case is extremely puzzling. Surely what the specific virtues have in common is precisely that they are all constituents of overall human excellence: what more could Socrates possibly expect by way of answer? It is as if, being told that hand–eye coordination and motivation are constituents of excellence at tennis, one were to ask what they have in common. Plainly, they need have nothing in common other than that both are required in order to excel at tennis. If (implausibly) it were to turn out that coordination and motivation are themselves manifestations of some further, common power or property, that would have to be discovered empirically, not guaranteed a priori by the fact of our counting both these attributes as constituents of excellence at tennis.

Socrates nevertheless presses his demand for a specification of what the specific virtues have in common, elucidating this demand by providing a model of the kind of specification he is looking for, a definition of shape (75b). This procedure is flawed, since the model is appropriate only if justice and self-control stand to overall human excellence as circularity and squareness stand to shape, but in fact they do not. Whereas specific shapes are all determinates of a common determinable, justice and self-control are not determinates of the determinable excellence, but constituents of excellence.[9] There is no determinable of which they are determinates. There is indeed a general concept of which they are instances, viz. 'constituent of overall human excellence', but Socrates and Meno have already agreed that that concept applies to justice and self-control, so giving that definition would not advance the discussion. But although Socrates has taken a wrong turning in looking for a general account of excellence analogous to his definition of shape, there is some interest in seeing what kind of definition the latter is. In fact Socrates gives two definitions of shape. The first, 'the only thing which always accompanies colour' (75b10–11), does not appear to satisfy the requirement that a definition should specify what the thing to be defined is, and not merely give a distinguishing mark. One does not say what a property is by pointing to another property of which it is the invariable accompaniment, any more than one explains what night is by saying that it is the only thing which invariably follows day. (In fact, since a number of properties, for example visibility, extension, size, luminosity, always accompany colour, the so-called 'definition' is true of nothing.) However, nothing in the text indicates that this account is recognised as failing to meet the standard requirements for a definition; indeed Socrates says (75b11–c1) that he would be content if Meno could define excellence in that way. Meno demurs indeed, describing the definition as 'silly', but for an altogether different reason, viz. that it would not be informative to someone who did not understand what colour is (75c). He states a requirement of the *informativeness* of any definition, viz. that it should not contain any term which is not understood by the person to whom the definition is given, but that requirement is not an objection to the *correctness* of this or any definition. In reply Socrates gives another definition of shape, having first made sure that Meno understands all the component terms, viz. 'shape is the limit of a solid' (76a7). This account of shape, as the external boundary or limit of a body, does appear to be an elucidation of the concept. And since that is given by Socrates as a model of the kind of definition of excellence he is looking for, we have to recognise a divergence between the kind of account suggested by the practical direction of the enquiry, viz. a causally explanatory account, and the preferred Socratic model. A similar situation occurs in the *Laches*, where the practically motivated search for a definition of courage is illustrated by a model definition of quickness as 'the power of doing many things in a short time' (192b1–2), which is also a conceptual elucidation.

The situation is complicated even further by Socrates' offer of yet another definition, this time (in deference to Meno's insistence) of colour. This is not a conceptual elucidation, but an explanatory account of colour in terms of a scientific theory, viz. the physiology of Empedocles: 'Colour is a flowing out [sc. from the coloured object] of shapes [i.e. physical particles of various shapes] symmetrical to vision [i.e. of such shapes and sizes as enable them to penetrate the channels in the eye] and perceptible' (76d4–5).[10] (The modern analogue would be an account of colour in terms of light waves of different lengths.) Here we have an example of just the kind of explanatory causal theory suggested by the practical motivation of the dialogue; were Socrates to say that this is the most satisfactory of the definitions he has offered, we should have a nice fit between the shape of the dialogue and the explicit witness of the text. In fact he says that it is inferior to the definition of shape (76e; presumably it is the second of the two definitions of shape that he refers to, but the text does not make that explicit). But he does not say why it is inferior. *Perhaps* Plato is aware of the distinction between conceptual elucidation and causally explanatory account, and regards the former as in general the preferred sort of definition. But Socrates does not say so, and the text suggests other possibilities. Socrates offers the definition of colour as one in the manner of Gorgias, which will therefore be familiar to Meno (76c),[11] and remarks on its 'high-flown' character, which he thinks pleases Meno (76e3–4). This suggests that Socrates may regard this definition as inferior to the other, not because causally explanatory accounts are as such inferior to conceptual elucidations, but because this particular account is couched in over-elaborate technical terminology. Perhaps, too, he thinks that it is simply false, but has merely picked on it to gratify Meno by citing something familiar. Given these hints, it would be rash to conclude that Socrates' preference for the definition of shape indicates a preference for one type of definition, conceptual elucidation, over another, a causally explanatory account. Indeed, the text thus far gives no indication that Plato is even aware of the distinction between the two types of definition.

Let me sum up the position so far. Socrates responds to Meno's practical question of how excellence is to be acquired by stating a minimal requirement for any enquiry, viz. that the object of the enquiry should be identified. But that requirement is already fulfilled from the outset. Socrates is in fact demanding the fulfilment of a stronger requirement, viz. to provide an account of excellence which will meet the standards set out in the *Euthyphro*. Those standards do not differentiate between a conceptual elucidation and a causally explanatory account, but the practical ends of the enquiry would be better served by the latter. In the course of the discussion Socrates gives samples of accounts: the first, which gives a distinguishing mark of the object 'defined' rather than specifying what the object is, fails to meet the *Euthyphro* standard, the second is a conceptual elucidation, the third a causally explanatory account. Socrates gives no sign of regarding the three as belonging to different kinds, but merely states that, for reasons unspecified, he prefers the second to the third. Thus far, then, the question 'What kind of definition is Socrates looking for in the *Meno*?' has no unambiguous answer. If such an answer is to be had, we must take into consideration the rest of the dialogue. That may seem unpromising, since in that portion of the dialogue nothing more is said about the methodology of definition, nor are any more examples given. The dialogue does, however, reach an answer, or rather answers, to the question 'What is excellence?' Excellence is first (87c–89a) argued to be knowledge, then another argument leads to the revision of that account in favour of the answer 'Excellence is true opinion' (99b–c), an account which is further qualified by a strong hint at 100a that the former answer gives the true account of genuine excellence, while the latter gives an account of what passes for excellence by ordinary standards. What kind of definition is represented by these answers?

What these answers share is a conception of excellence as a cognitive state, or more portentously, a grasp of truth. We are not concerned with the details of the distinction between knowledge and true opinion, but its essence is the firmness or reliability of the grasp; knowledge is a reliable (because systematic) grasp of the truth, true opinion is an unreliable (because unsystematic) grasp of truth. What sort of account of *excellence* is provided by the conception of it as a cognitive state? Note that Socrates and Meno are not discussing excellence in some theoretical sphere, such as excellence at mathematics; the paradigms of excellence in this final stage of the discussion are individuals such as Pericles who embody the same ideal of success in public and private affairs as Meno had assumed from the outset. That is to say, cognitive states are presented as giving an account of all-embracing social and political merit, of the state of the totally well-rounded, successful and admirable person (= man, by this stage of the discussion). In what sense is that person's admirable state a cognitive one? The sort of excellence in question is above all practical, manifested in action and a whole style of behaviour; it does not seem that specification of a cognitive state could give an account of *the manifestation of* excellence. That is to say, 'knowledge or true opinion' does not offer the same kind of account of excellence as 'having a good service, ground strokes and volley' does of excellence at tennis, since the latter account does precisely specify the kind of actions which manifest that excellence, whereas the former does not. Rather, it gives an account of *what is manifest in* excellent performance, as 'coordination, stamina, courtcraft, etc.' does of what is manifested in excellent tennis-playing. And as that account expresses, not an elucidation of the concept of excellent tennis-playing, but an empirical theory of the causes of the type of play which we count as excellent, so the cognitive account of overall human excellence expresses, not an elucidation of that concept, but a causally explanatory theory, what we may call the Cognitive Theory of Virtue. We find, then, that despite Socrates' expressed preference for the conceptual definition of shape over the causally explanatory account of colour, the account of excellence which he endorses in the concluding section of the dialogue is of a type represented, not by the former, but by the latter.

The aim of our enquiry into the nature of definition in the Socratic dialogues was the elucidation of the connection between definition and the Socratic paradoxes. That aim has now been achieved in part, since the first paradox, the thesis that virtue is knowledge, has now turned out to be the Cognitive Theory. But that elucidation lacks content without further exploration of just what the Cognitive Theory claims. That exploration will also, I hope, indicate the connection between the Cognitive Theory and the second paradox, the thesis that no one does wrong willingly.

The Cognitive Theory is a theory to the effect that overall success in human life is guaranteed by the possession of certain cognitive states. This theory in turn rests on a theory of the explanation of intentional action which combines to a remarkable degree a staggering audacity and simplicity with a high degree of plausibility. It states that provided that the agent has a conception of what is overall best for the agent, or (equivalently) what is maximally productive of *eudaimonia* (for the agent), that conception is sufficient to motivate action with a view to its own realisation. That is emphatically not to say that motivation does not require desire as well as belief. On the contrary, Socrates makes clear his view (77c1–2; 78b4–6) that everyone desires good things, which in context has to be interpreted as the strong thesis that the desire for good is an invariable motive. That desire is then conceived as a standing motive, which requires to be focussed in one direction or another via a conception of the overall good. Given that focus, desire is as it were locked on to the target which is picked out by the conception, without the possibility of interference by conflicting desires. Hence, given the standing desire, all that is required for correct conduct, i.e. for the

147

manifestations of excellence, is the correct focus. And that focus has to be a correct conception of the good for the agent, i.e. a correct conception of *eudaimonia*.

I have just stated the theory underlying the Cognitive Theory in a conditional form, viz. provided that the agent has a conception of what is overall good, that conception provides uniform motivation. That form allows the possibility that an agent might lack the conception of such a good altogether, and simply be motivated in a haphazard way by considerations of particular goods on each occasion of action. A stronger version of the theory would be the thesis that on every occasion every agent is motivated by his or her conception of what is best overall. That version has the disadvantages (a) of going beyond the letter of the relevant texts (*Meno* 77–8; *Protagoras* 358), and (b) of extreme implausibility. On the other hand, the weaker thesis has the disadvantage that it leaves the uniformity of motivation, given the conception of overall good, virtually unexplained. If agents are capable, lacking the conception of overall good, of being motivated towards different, and therefore potentially conflicting goods, what guarantees that the conception of overall good, once in place, will be sufficient to silence conflicting motivations? *Protagoras* 358c–d states that it is impossible (literally, 'not in human nature') to choose what you think bad (sc. for you) instead of what is good, but gives no argument or explanation. *Meno* 77e–78a gives an argument, but an unsound one: to want things which you think bad for you is to want to be harmed, and to want to be harmed is to want to be wretched and unfortunate, but no one wants to be wretched and unfortunate. (The first premise is false, because wanting does not cross envisaged causal connections: from the fact that I want x, and believe that x causes y, it does not follow that I want y.) Plato might perhaps rely on that argument, faced with the objection which I have just raised. I suspect, however, that the objection would not have occurred to him, because he may not have made the distinction between the desire for particular goods and desire for the good overall on which the objection depends. The argument of *Protagoras* 355c–d, leading to the conclusion that it would be absurd to describe someone as knowingly doing bad things (i.e. things bad for him) because he is overcome by the desire for goods, depends on failure to make that distinction. It is absurd to describe someone as abandoning the conception of the overall good because he is seduced by the attractions of the overall good, but not absurd to describe one as doing so because he is seduced by particular goods which are incompatible with the overall good (for example short-term pleasures which are believed to be harmful in the long run). It is therefore quite likely that Plato was not sensitive to the distinction; and with the distinction goes the distinction between the weaker and the stronger forms of the theory of motivation on which the Cognitive Theory rests. On the weaker form, motivation is (a) always towards some envisaged good, and (b) towards the envisaged overall good when the conception of that good is present. On the stronger form, motivation is always towards the envisaged overall good. On either form, excellence in human performance is guaranteed by possession, with greater or less reliability, of the correct conception of the good.

In turning to the second Socratic paradox I shall assume Santas' distinction between the self-interested paradox, 'No one acts intentionally against his or her overall interest', and the moral form, 'No one does intentionally what is morally wrong.' The former falls directly out of the theory of motivation which we have seen to underly the Cognitive Theory. The latter, as Santas demonstrates, follows from the former, together with the thesis, argued for in the *Gorgias*, that it is always in the agent's interest to do what is morally right. The agent must, of course, believe that it is in his or her interest to do what is morally right, but the correct conception of the good for the agent will guarantee that he or she has that belief. For the correct conception of the agent's good (see *Gorgias* 504a–d) is that it is a state of the personality organised in accordance with the requirements of virtue, analogous with bodily health (cf. *Crito* 47e). Given that conception, together with true beliefs as to what actions will realise it, the prudential thesis guarantees that the agent will be motivated to do those actions. Hence, by contraposition, if the agent is not thus motivated, he or she either lacks that conception or lacks those true beliefs. In either case, the agent's wrongdoing is due to error, and is therefore unintentional, which is what the moral paradox states.

The practical orientation of the initial enquiry in the *Meno*, then, suggests that the kind of account of excellence which is required is a causally explanatory account. That hypothesis is neither confirmed nor refuted by Socrates' model definitions, which are of diverse kinds, including both a causal account and a conceptual elucidation, without any clear recognition of the distinction between those kinds. On the other hand the alternative accounts of excellence which are finally arrived at are in fact causal accounts. Cognitive states explain how practical excellence is achieved, the explanation being embedded in a theory of motivation which also yields the Socratic paradoxes.

To guard against possible misunderstanding, I do not of course deny that the Socratic conception of excellence, as mentioned in the *Crito* and spelt out in the *Gorgias*, is revisionary. The 'Periclean' paradigm of excellence is assumed in the *Meno* only for the sake of argument, and in fact represents at best an approximation to real excellence. But that does not affect my central contention, that the relation of the cognitive grasp of the good to excellence itself is in the Socratic dialogues a causal one, the causal mechanism being that described in the theory of motivation which I have just sketched. In the authentic Socratic conception the good of which the excellent person has knowledge is itself a state of the personality, analogous to bodily health, in which the various impulses to action are harmonised under the direction of the agent's conception of the supreme good. But now the theory collapses into inconsistency. By the Cognitive Theory excellence is knowledge of how to achieve the good, while by the analogy with health excellence is the health of the soul and therefore the good itself which is to be achieved via knowledge. On the former account excellence should, like medicine, be valuable only instrumentally, whereas by the latter it is valuable intrinsically. Further, the theory of the *Gorgias* requires that the personality should be organised in such a way as to realise a prior conception of the good, whereas the only conception of the good envisaged in the Cognitive Theory is the conception of the state of the personality itself. The conception of the supreme good as the Form of the Good, developed in the middle dialogues, gives Plato at least the sketch-plan of an escape from this dilemma.

In the foregoing I have dealt largely, though not exclusively, with the *Meno*. The causal character of Socratic accounts of the virtues is also discernible in the *Protagoras*, where Socrates argues for the thesis that all the virtues are forms of knowledge, and is suggested by the *Laches* and the *Charmides*, where the respective discussions indicate, without definitively enunciating, accounts of courage as 'knowledge of what is fearful' (an account adopted at *Protagoras* 360d) and *sophrosyne* as 'knowledge of the good'.

In conclusion, all that I hope to have shown is that in the most extended treatment of Socratic definition, the definition sought and arrived at is not a conceptual elucidation, but a causally explanatory account, that that sort of definition is prominent in other Socratic dialogues, and that, given the theory of motivation presupposed in the particular definition which is given in the *Meno*, the connection between that definition and the Socratic paradoxes is both intimate and reasonably perspicuous. To repeat myself, I do not think that there is any indication that Plato made any explicit distinction between conceptual elucidation and causal account; the distinction which I have emphasised (and whose sharpness I may have exaggerated) emerges, not in Plato's theory, but in his dialectical practice.

NOTES

1 Some material from this chapter appears in my 'Platonic Ethics', in Everson (forthcoming).
2 The dialogues discussed in this chapter are *Charmides, Crito, Euthyphro, Gorgias, Laches, Meno* and *Protagoras*.
3 Santas 1964; Santas 1979.
4 As was argued long ago by Ross in his 1924: vol. 1, xxxiii–xiv.
5 In his *Memorabilia* Xenophon ascribes all three to Socrates. For definitions see I.1.16, III.9.4–9, IV.6, esp. sect. 1; inductive arguments and elenchus are pervasive features of Socrates' argumentative technique, as reported by Xenophon, e.g. II.3 (induction), III.6 (elenchus). I do not assume that Xenophon's portrait is historically more accurate than Plato's, but merely cite these passages as further evidence, probably independent of Plato, for Socrates' practice of argument.
6 At *Memorabilia* III.9.4, Xenophon's Socrates maintains that everyone does what seems to him to be most advantageous to him, a claim which leads to the first paradox, that no one does wrong willingly. (The claim is repeated at IV.6.6.) The second paradox, that virtue is knowledge, is maintained at III.9.5; 'he said that justice and all the rest of excellence is wisdom'. (For the explicit identification of wisdom with knowledge see IV.6.7.)
7 The passages from Xenophon cited in n. 5 above contain instances of both types of definition distinguished in the chapter, viz. conceptual elucidation and substantive account, without any sign of a distinction between the two. Nor do these passages provide any clear evidence of Xenophon's view of what the theoretical role of Socratic definition was. In general, Xenophon's examples of Socratic definition are so few, and his treatment of them so cursory, that it is unsafe to base any conclusions on them.
8 See Putnam 1975.
9 Determinates of a single determinable, such as specific shapes and specific colours, are mutually incompatible; constituents of a complex property are (a) mutually compatible, (b) such that every instance of the

complex property in fact instantiates some sub-set of the constituents. See Searle 1967.

10 Cf. Diels–Kranz 31 A 86 (Theophrastus) and 92 (Aetius).

11 Gorgias had reputedly been a student of Empedocles (Diogenes Laertius VIII.58: Diels–Kranz 82 A 3), and Meno had studied with Gorgias (71c).

6

THE LEGACY OF SOCRATES

P. J. FitzPatrick

A shorter form of this chapter was written for oral delivery. I have not tried to disguise the fact, but have added notes, which I hope may serve as guides through a variety of materials. I express my gratitude for the facilities provided by libraries in Durham and in London – above all by the Warburg Institute. The editorial help given me by my colleague Dr B. S. Gower is much appreciated. Some titles in works consulted were prolix: the bibliography abbreviates them.

INTRODUCTORY

In my contribution I have an impossible task. Twenty-four centuries separate us from Socrates, and it falls to me to evaluate what those centuries have made of him. And, clearly, that cannot be done in a way that will do justice to the topic: I shall have to over-simplify, to cut corners, and to make brutal omissions of important material. But I think the attempt is worth making. Not only can it teach us something, but its very incompleteness will show just how wide-ranging is the theme allotted to me.

I begin by asking you to look at two illustrations. Figure 1 is David's masterpiece, *The Death of Socrates*, exhibited by him in 1787; we shall see later that he has followed the account given in Plato's *Phaedo*, but with one remarkable addition. Figure 2 is Raphael's *The School of Athens*, a fresco painted for the Stanza della Segnatura in the Vatican, about 1510; its very familiarity may obscure what will turn out to be quite a complex structure and design.

Having noticed the two pictures, I practise the first of my brutal omissions. I pass over the whole theme of what was made of

Figure 6.1 The Death of Socrates, David, 1787.

Figure 6.2 The School of Athens, Raphael, c.1510.

Socrates by writers in the ancient world: the different versions in Plato and Xenophon; the very earliest presentation of him by Aristophanes; the multiplicity of anecdotes and judgements preserved by later Greek and Roman writers. This theme is notorious for the controversies it has aroused and is still arousing, and it demands a fuller treatment than it could receive as part of a wider survey.[1] I want to go rather to stages in the legacy of Socrates that are not so well known, and to see what they have to teach us.[2] And so I pass to the first stage I consider: what was made of Socrates by some of those Christian writers of the early centuries known as the 'Fathers of the Church'.

SOCRATES AND THE FATHERS[3]

About the year AD 160, when the philosophically-minded Marcus Aurelius was Emperor at Rome, two addresses were composed – one to him, and a second to the Senate – by Justin, a native of Palestine. Both were defences (*Apologiae*) of the new religion that was spreading through the cities of the Empire, and whose adherents were being accused of atheism because they would not take part in the worship of the official gods of the state. Justin appeals to the example of Socrates, in his second defence of his fellow Christians. Socrates faced a similar accusation, simply because he had rejected the fables to do with the gods of Olympus, banished from his ideal state the poets who sang of them, and taught that one creating God should be worshipped. Christ had been partly known by Socrates, for whatever has been taught or well said by philosophers has been reached by some sharing in the Word, the Word that is in all things and that spoke through the prophets (II *Apol.* 10; 6 PG 460–1). What contradictions there are among philosophers come from their imperfect grasp of unseen wisdom; whatever has been well said by them 'belongs to us Christians' (II *Apol.* 13; 6 PG 465).

I note here a point of logic that is fraught with consequences. If whatever has been well said belongs to the Christians, it follows that whatever does not belong to them cannot have been well said. Consequently, whatever pagans say must either be false (because not well said); or in some way borrowed (because well said). These consequences were not universally drawn, but they were drawn both readily and repeatedly. Socrates had claimed negative guidance by some inner voice, to which the name *daimonion* was usually given. The etymology was not happy for Christians, given

156

what they thought of demons, and Socrates was at times condemned for having a familiar spirit. He was also condemned for requesting at the hour of his death that a cock be sacrificed to Aesculapius, the god of healing.[4] On the other hand, things had been said by him and by other Greek philosophers that resembled things to be found in the Bible. For Justin, as we saw, those philosophers had some share in the wisdom of the Word. But for others, such philosophers must have taken the good things from the Old Testament – stolen them, as some put it.

The crudity of this pattern of reasoning should not obscure the real tension that prompted it, a tension that is already present in Justin. His claim that whatever has been well said belongs to the Christians could be taken in a 'widening' sense, a sense in which Christians can welcome good things found among the pagans; but it could be and often was taken in the 'narrowing' sense we have seen – whatever pagans have said well is at best borrowed. The tension was bound to be acute in the variety of judgements passed on Socrates, whose teaching and behaviour seemed to offer excellences that were independent of what the Fathers regarded as necessary for true goodness and eternal salvation. The tension expressed itself, we might say, in an unwillingness to acknowledge the *Diversity of Goods* – and this is a theme which we shall be meeting time and again.

Here and now, we can notice a recurrence of the theme by moving from Justin to the one whose writings were to have the most influence of all in the Western Church – St Augustine (†430). Augustine gives his views on Greek philosophy at the start of the eighth book of his *The City of God*, but they are derivative in more than one sense. He had little or no Greek, acquiring at most a small amount in his old age.[5] His acquaintance was with later writers in the Platonic tradition, not with Plato himself. His account there of the progress of Greek philosophy reads dismally like the summaries and surveys the Ancient World liked so much (*De civitate Dei* VIII.1–2; 41 PL 223–6), and elsewhere in the work he retails an anecdote to do with Socrates and Alcibiades while hesitating over the latter's name (XIV.8; 41 PL 413). His praise of Socrates and his account of his 'philosophical descent' from earlier thinkers are also in the eighth book (VIII. 2–3; 41 PL 226–7). On the one hand, he is ready to praise Socrates and to ascribe his condemnation to calumny, calumny prompted by rancour among those he had shown to lack the wisdom they claimed; indeed,

Augustine adds for good measure the tale that Socrates' accusers came to miserable ends. For Augustine, Plato is the writer who comes nearest to Christianity, and he speculated at one time whether Plato might have become acquainted with teachings of the Old Testament while in Egypt (VIII.9–11; 41 PL 235). It is when he considers the eternal salvation of pagans that the limited nature of his praise becomes clear. It would be wrong, he says, to claim that nobody outside Israel in the ages before Christ could belong to the heavenly Jerusalem – which sounds hopeful. Less hopeful is the way he continues: Job must be so admitted, even though not a Jew, because of the justice and piety expressed in his utterances. And others outside the chosen people may also have belonged to the heavenly Jerusalem – but nobody can so belong unless Christ has been revealed to him. Which, once more, brings us back to the Diversity of Goods.

SOCRATES AND THE MIDDLE AGES

When Augustine died in 430, the Vandals were besieging the city of Carthage, where he had been bishop. Within fifty years of his death the Roman Empire in the West had collapsed and it looked as if all knowledge of Socrates – and indeed all knowledge of the Ancient World – would perish with it. The story of what was saved, and of the revival of knowledge, has often been told. One way of grasping the pattern of loss and recovery in philosophical matters is to move forward for a moment as far as 1310, the year in which Dante composed the first part of his *Divina Commedia* – the *Inferno*, a journey through hell. In its fourth Canto he visits a 'Noble Castle' where dwell virtuous pagans – barred from heaven because they lack faith, though not otherwise tormented. But now the philosophical scene has greatly changed. For the authors we have seen so far, it is Socrates and Plato who claimed most attention, and it is the Platonic tradition that represented for them the philosophical thought nearest to their own beliefs. Things are very different for Dante. The central figure now is Aristotle, 'the master of those who know', who is 'seated amid the philosophical family' and honoured by all; Socrates and Plato are no more than 'those who stand nearest to him'. What had happened over the centuries to change things so much?

In the centuries following the collapse of the Roman Empire in the West (its last Emperor was deposed in 476), learning of all sorts disintegrated in many places. We owe to the monks above all the preservation of what did survive, and that this preservation of a pagan inheritance was at times reluctant and unplanned does not diminish our debt of gratitude.[6] Knowledge of Greek itself had already been declining – we saw that Augustine had very little, and in the next century the future Pope Gregory the Great was to spend years in Constantinople as envoy to the Eastern Roman Emperor without acquiring any. Inevitably, the disturbed years saw its extinction in most places, along with the loss of so much else. But not every place lost it totally. There were Greek-speaking immigrants to Rome, people who were at odds with the religious disturbances of the Eastern Empire. Greek continued to be used as a liturgical language in parts of Italy. Greek writings were available in some, but not many, places, and some people there, but not many, could read them. What was undoubtedly lost was the *range* of Greek writing, whether in the original or in translation. It was predictable that literature and history should disappear, but even the philosophical texts available were late and few. Moreover, the popularity of *florilegia* – collections of summaries and of extracts from authors – makes it difficult to tell just what earlier sources had been read *in extenso*. As time went on, it was in some passages of Cicero, and in writers of the later Roman Empire such as Macrobius († c. 420) and Martianus Capella (fl. c. 450), that philosophical speculations of the Greeks were available. The Platonic tradition itself underwent transformations, and elements from Stoicism and from Aristotle were integrated into various forms of what is known as 'Neo-Platonism'. Some writers in this (still largely pagan) tradition were read, such as Proclus († 485) and the author known as 'Dionysius the Areopagite' (c. 500). However, what Proclus wrote was ascribed to Aristotle, and Dionysius was erroneously supposed to have been a Christian – indeed, a disciple of St Paul.[7]

Of Plato himself, part of one dialogue (the *Timaeus*) had some circulation in Latin, while of Aristotle there survived early works on logic. Later on, Latin versions were made of other Platonic dialogues, but it was not until the fifteenth century that a translation of the complete text of Plato became available in Western Europe. For centuries, therefore, it was rather Plato as interpreted by the later Platonic tradition who was in any measure known; it was this tradition that had coloured the writings of Augustine; and Augustine's writings were to be more widely diffused in the

159

West than any book except the Latin Bible.[8] The character of
this 'mediated Plato', if I may so call it, can best be seen if we
go back for a moment to the illustration of Raphael's *School of
Athens*. Here I direct your attention to the *hands* of Socrates and
Plato: those of Socrates are marking off points in an argument;
Plato is simply pointing upwards, and he is not arguing at all. It
is this 'non-Socratic' side to Plato that we find in the Neo-Platonic
tradition. The tradition was systematic where Socrates had been
tentative, and expository where he had questioned. It taught a
theology of ascent to the divine, where he had professed ignorance.
And it was this side of the Platonic tradition that became an essential
part of what intellectual life there was in Western Europe over the
seven centuries that followed Augustine's death.

Then, in the later years of the twelfth century, things began to
change. Contact with the East became greater, and to the earlier and
limited inheritance from the philosophical past there began to be
added the massive corpus of Aristotle's writings, with commentaries
thereon by pagan, Moslem and Jewish writers.[9] Understandably,
the long and complex story of the reception of Aristotle into the
West involves the story of the tensions the reception produced
with the earlier pattern of thought. The new material was touched
with Neo-Platonic elements; and the older traditions in theology,
associated with names like Augustine and Anselm, were combined
in different ways. It is not surprising that the thirteenth century
saw fierce debate over the mixtures produced. For our purposes
here, it is enough to notice that the sheer *bulk* of the new material
– it ranged from logic to metaphysics, and from natural history to
theology and politics – overshadowed all else from Antiquity.[10]
But the arrival of the Aristotelian texts and commentaries did more
than give philosophy a new bulk and independence. It changed the
balance of learning in Europe, arresting the literary flowering of the
twelfth century and turning attention to more abstract studies. The
temperature dropped, we might say, and we can in consequence
expect little concern with the person of Socrates in the Middle
Ages. A writer like Aquinas knew of his death, and of some things
to do with his teaching.[11] Aquinas here had at his disposal some
works of Cicero, Augustine's *City of God*, and also that incurably
popular farrago of anecdotes, Valerius Maximus (first century AD),
but his main source of information was Aristotle, and there was
little personal detail to be found there. Indeed, the impersonality of
the figure of Socrates in the Middle Ages shows itself in the words

'Sor' and 'Sortes' used then as standard names in logical examples – they are simply abbreviations of the name 'Socrates', apparently not recognised for what it was.[12] Dante, as we saw, gives pride of place to Aristotle, and only attendant roles to Socrates and Plato. For anything more, we must go beyond the Middle Ages – and so into the next section.

SOCRATES AND THE RENAISSANCE[13]

I turn to consider what was made of Socrates when, towards the end of the fifteenth century, a Latin version of Plato by the Florentine Marsilio Ficino († 1499) became available in Western Europe.[14] My considerations will lead naturally to seeing something of how the Platonic dialogues themselves were then interpreted. Having done all that, I will resume the general theme in the next section, and look at the figure of Socrates in the sixteenth century – and in the intellectual turmoil of the seventeenth.

Ficino's translation of Plato was published in 1482; among his other writings was a commentary on the *Symposium* (1469), and (the man was a prodigy of industry) a translation of Plotinus (1492). But his version of Plato was preceded in 1463 by a translation of writings ascribed to the legendary Egyptian sage Hermes Trismegistus. To see the reason is to understand more of what was then made of Plato and Socrates.

We saw in the preceding section that the arrival of the Aristotelian writings in Western Europe led to disagreements over their use in theology. We also saw that Dante gave pride of place to Aristotle where a writer like Augustine had given it to Plato. And we noticed a speculation of Augustine: that Plato had become acquainted with the Mosaic revelation during his visit to Egypt. Such a speculation was not surprising, given what Augustine made of the theme I have called 'The Diversity of Goods'. He could find in the Platonic tradition traces of a doctrine of creation, in which visible things represent their maker; he could find the survival of the soul and the notion of its judgement; he could even find expressions like 'Father', 'Maker', and 'Soul of the World' that seemed to resonate with what Christian belief itself proclaimed. Aquinas, as we know, gave a place to Aristotle that Augustine did not, yet he still finds this speculation by Augustine plausible – see at all events his early work, *Commentary on the Sentences* Pars I, dist. 3, qu. 1, art. 4, ad 1. But neither Aquinas, nor any other Christian writer of the Middle

Ages known to me, makes any such speculation about Aristotle. There seemed to be no need for any: Aristotle was silent over creation, had only fragmentary and much-debated passages over the survival of the soul, and had no resemblances in his vocabulary to what was said of the Trinity by Christians. Aristotle's writings did indeed achieve a place in Western thought that Dante's picture fairly represents, but the deficiencies in them were not forgotten, and neither were the likenesses in Plato to Christianity. Then, as the text of all the Platonic dialogues became generally available, a reading that stressed the likenesses was encouraged by a miscellany of writings also becoming available. These were referred to in a general way as *prisca gentilium theologia*, or 'primitive theology of the pagans'; a common name now is 'the Ancient Theology'. They were ascribed to venerable or mythical figures of Antiquity, such as Hermes Trismegistus in Egypt, Pythagoras and Orpheus in Greece and Zoroaster among the Chaldeans.[15] They were believed to contain a revelation made by God to the pagans, and so were seen as a precious confirmation of the Bible. And they, like Plato and writers in the Platonic tradition, were read as teaching (even if imperfectly) Christian doctrines like the Trinity of God and the immortality of the soul. The seventeenth century eventually saw them placed historically – they are a hodge-podge of Neo-Platonism, Gnosticism, Christianity and magic, going back to the early centuries of our era.[16] That was yet to come when Ficino translated Hermes; for him and for many others, the Ancient Theology could reinforce the closeness of Plato to Christianity. But in doing so, it also reinforced the reading of Plato as transmitted in the tradition of Neo-Platonism, what I called in the preceding section 'the non-Socratic' side to Plato. I want to suggest that the implications of reading Plato in this way, and of accepting the Ancient Theology, can be perceived in a visual manner if we go back to Raphael's *School of Athens*.

Consider the wider structure of the design. There are two niches on the wall of the building, and in the niches are statues: on Plato's side is Apollo, the god of heavenly inspiration; on Aristotle's side is Athene, the patron of intellectual skills. Some of these skills – mathematical and physical – are being exercised on this side in the foreground, where Euclid is explaining a geometrical diagram, and two sages, Ptolemy and Zoroaster, are holding up respectively a terrestial globe and a celestial sphere. But above them, on a higher level, are philosophers, and among these one is conspicuous. Wrapped in a dark cloak, he stands alone and in silence, in a position occupied by nobody on the other, 'Platonic' side. He *points* towards the groups below him; he *gazes* towards the group on the other side in the foreground. This figure is Pythagoras, reputedly the teacher of Plato and the first to describe himself as a philosopher; Pythagoras, who placed the harmony of the world in mathematical proportion, and whose utterances concerning the number three were taken as adumbrations of the Trinity; Pythagoras, who saw wisdom as consummated in silence. It is Pythagoras, himself an 'Ancient Theologian', who is indicating the ultimate resolution of the tension at the heart of the picture. For there, Plato is pointing upwards; his right hand follows the upward thrust of the arch behind him. But Aristotle's right hand is extended, palm downwards; if the curve of the same arch were continued as a circle, it would pass through this hand. Where Plato indicates an ascent, Aristotle exhibits a recall to earth. It is the two gestures of Pythagoras that show how this tension may be resolved by incorporation into something of a higher order. He is *pointing* to studies conducted by the gentiles, studies represented by Ptolemy, Euclid and Zoroaster – who came respectively from Egypt, Greece and Chaldea, the three homes of the Ancient Theology. But if it is to all this that Pythagoras is *pointing*, his *gaze* directs us elsewhere – to a group on Plato's side.

If we look closely at that group, we shall notice that something Pythagorean is there too: a diagram that includes the 'Tetractys', the figure representing ten as the sum of the numbers one to four,

$$\bullet \quad \bullet \quad \bullet \quad \bullet$$
$$\bullet \quad \bullet \quad \bullet$$
$$\bullet \quad \bullet$$
$$\bullet$$

together with lines expressing musical intervals. This diagram is being presented before the seated figure writing in a large volume. His writing is in columns, it is not diagrammatic, and the volume itself is firmly bound in a way that contrasts with the loosely secured books carried by the figure on the extreme left. The volume is a Gospel and the seated figure is an Evangelist; the Pythagorean diagram is in a sense a message submitted to him from the other side; it is, we might say, the fruit of the Ancient Theology. Pythagoras himself is indicating by his gaze where that theology can lead us – to the Gospel, with its revelation of what was

163

but imperfectly grasped among the pagans. And notice how just the same culminative role of the Gospel is displayed in the two figures – one wearing a turban – who are devoutly attentive to what the Evangelist is writing. We have already seen that, when Aristotle's works came to Western Europe, Moslem and Jewish commentaries came with them. The two figures represent these two sources of human wisdom, which find their fulfilment in the revelation given in the Gospel. Nearby stands another Evangelist – see once again that the volume he holds is securely bound. And between the two, clad in a luminous white robe, stands a beautiful youth representing the Evangelist St John, whose Gospel opens with the declaration concerning the Word of God, the *Logos*, the light that enlighteneth everyone born into this world, be he or she Christian or not – that is to say, we are invited to see that the search for traces of the truth among the pagans is not impious. John carries no volume – his Gospel ends with a denial that any accumulation of books could contain what can be said of Christ, the Word made flesh. But John's *position* in the picture displays the power of the Gospel. In the seventh book of his *Confessions*, Augustine had written that he had found in 'Platonic' books some things John wrote about the Word, but not that the Word was made flesh (VII.9; 32 PL 740–1). Here, John stands directly beneath the line of the nearest arch, just as Plato's upraised hand lies along the line of the most distant. We are invited to see that it is in the Gospel that the strivings of Platonism, its tensions with Aristotle's teaching, the content of the Ancient Theology, and Moslem and Jewish speculation, affected by both Plato and Aristotle, all find solution and satisfaction. The circular movement of the picture is complete.[17]

The design is indeed noble, and so could seem the hope expressed in it.[18] But such a reading of Plato and the Ancient Theology raised difficulties – theological, philosophical and moral. Each kind affected what was made of Socrates.

The *theological* difficulties were partly a matter of the lack of fit between the Christian doctrine of the Trinity and what could be found in Plato or the other authors. Thus, Plato himself holds a copy of the *Timaeus*, and that dialogue does contain phrases and statements which could be taken as pointing to Christian belief. But the pointing was equivocal, in that the second and third members of the 'triad' were unduly subordinated to the first. And unease went deeper – did not the quest for seeking Christian belief outside the Scriptures compromise their uniqueness, and blur the line between

164

nature and grace? Some of Ficino's expressions – his version of Plato included a Preface and Introductions – would have given colour to the charge. His description, given in a letter, of Plato as 'Moses speaking Greek' could at least claim a long pedigree; it seems to have started with the Neo-Platonist Numenius and was cited by Clement of Alexandria, about AD 200 (*Stromat.* I.22; 8 PG 395). But in the same letter Ficino went further, and in a way that would have grated on some ears. Exhorting his friend to the study of Plato, he promises him mysteries too great for expression in a letter, and thinks they will make him exclaim 'It is good for us to be here; let us make three thousand tabernacles.' When Ficino printed his letters in 1495, unfriendly readers of this one would have recalled that St Peter used a similar phrase on witnessing the Transfiguration of Christ, but was content to suggest building only three of them. Another letter would have grated still more. The Latin version of Plato allowed all who wished to encounter the vivid pictures of Socrates to be had there. Ficino – in a way oddly similar to the more extravagant mode of medieval Bible-interpretation – rummages among the stories to produce analogies between Socrates and the story of Jesus. They include appearances before an unjust judge; prophecies fulfilled after death; an exhortation to virtue delivered in the evening, and going with a thanksgiving and drinking of a cup; the mention of a cock; and a price of thirty pieces – where Ficino sets the fee paid to Judas beside the thirty minae proposed by Socrates at his trial as an alternative penalty (*Apology* 38b). Ficino admits – disarmingly – that the analogies have aroused opposition.

The theological difficulties, we might say, bring us back to what I have called the theme of the Diversity of Goods. The diversity is proving as hard as ever to admit – how hard, interpretations like Ficino's bear witness. What Plato says must in some way be of a piece with a revelation already admitted – if it is not, then it must be condemned as a distortion of it. And if curious analogies can bring Socrates nearer to the figure of Jesus, then they can be drawn. But the *philosophical* difficulties went further than the theological. They lay in the fact that, while some of the dialogues might be taken to offer analogies to Christian belief, others seemed quite unconnected with such topics. The answer was thought to lie in a way of reading Plato that went back to earlier Neo-Platonists: Plato's text needed 'deciphering', for its surface content concealed high mysteries.[19] A famous example was his dialogue *Parmenides*: the logical cut-and-thrust of it had been taken by the Neo-Platonist

Proclus († 485) as enshrining teachings to do with a mystery that lay beyond Being itself. Ficino followed Proclus here, despite the opposition of his nephew Pico della Mirandola († 1495), who collaborated in the translation of Plotinus. Pico's plea for a straightforward reading of the *Parmenides* went unheeded, such was the authority of Ficino and of the tradition with which he aligned himself. In short, the philosophical difficulties in a 'christianising' reading of Plato demanded that Socrates be seen as propounding in a concealed way high mysteries, mysteries to do with the soul's ascent to God, and with the divine nature. This is an obviously awkward reading of Socrates, and the awkwardness can best be put in terms already used in the preceding section: the hands of Socrates are indicating argument, the hand of Plato is not, and the proposed reading amounts to ignoring the difference. In fact, now that we have seen more of the structure of *The School of Athens*, we can add that Socrates does not fit at all well into the 'circular movement' I have invited readers to discern in Raphael's fresco: he has his back to Plato as he argues away, and is paying no attention whatsoever to the Evangelists below him.

The *moral* difficulties were greatest of all, for they called into question this whole project of reconciliation and cumulation in the Gospel. There was an uncomfortable element, both in the Ancient Theologians and in the Platonic tradition, of magical practices involving the cult of beings intermediate between God and man – *daemones*, in fact. The discomfort was all the greater because Augustine was known to have denounced in the *City of God* writings such as those of Hermes Trismegistus (*De civitate Dei* VIII.23f.; 10 PL 247–9); to have spoken slightingly of a Chaldean (that would be Zoroaster) who tried to purify his soul by practising the cult (X.10; 10 PL 288); and to have extended his denunciation to the Platonic tradition itself. For he had, while commending the great Neo-Platonist Plotinus, denounced the magical and idolatrous practices recommended by his disciple Porphyry (X.2,9f.; 10 PL 279–80, 286f.). Now that the texts themselves of these writers were available, and not just Augustine's reports, some defensive moves were possible. But the texts called for a measure of violence if they were to be assets rather than liabilities. The *daimonion* of Socrates could be seen as a divine admonition, but it could also be seen as an embarrassment. The whole Platonic setting of Socrates, in fact, was called into question, not just by the imperfections in Plato's supposed adumbrations of the Trinity, but by texts like the discourse of Diotima in the *Symposium*, with its account of *daemones* as intermediaries (202d), or the part of the *Epinomis* that talks of intermediate beings and of their cult of heaven (986). Christian belief, so some thought during the Renaissance, had received a powerful confirmation from these 'neutral' sources. For others, the material was a mixed blessing. I go on to note, very briefly, something of the two attitudes.

The brutality of the over-simplifications I am having to practise must not make us forget the complexity of the attitudes. Ficino's we have already sampled, but other texts of his are more cautious; even in the Introduction to his translation of Plotinus (where he speaks of him as *theios*, 'divine', and as very near Christianity), he is careful to prescind from the question of his salvation. Conversely, the rigidly Thomistic Antoninus, the Dominican Bishop of Florence who made Ficino read a work of Aquinas before beginning his translations, is quite prepared to discern the doctrine of the Trinity in Hermes Trismegistus.[20] The complexities seem embodied in the hopes of the French Neo-Platonist, Symphorien Champier († 1539). He wanted to exhibit substantial identity between Plato and Aristotle; he was anxious to dissociate Plato from Hermes Trismegistus; he gave to one of his books a mouthful of a title, claiming that the work offered 'compelling vindications of Christianity, drawn from poetic and philosophical writings among the pagans'. Also in the sixteenth century, it had been possible for the Vatican Librarian, Agostino Steuco, to hold that there was but one wisdom, knowable to all, be they Christian or pagan, a 'perennial philosophy' handed down over the centuries.[21] Now, things were changing, as the sixteenth century brought with it the Reformation and the Council of Trent. The medieval employment of Aristotle had been a target for some attacks of the Reformers – it was natural that the scholastic heritage should be defended by their opponents, and Trent itself used terminology found in Aquinas, in its decree on the Eucharist. Back in the thirteenth century, Aquinas had given a welcome to the use of Aristotelian concepts in theology that some of his contemporaries had not. Now, in the harsher climate of the Counter-Reformation, the favour he had shown Aristotle was made into a model for general imitation. Indeed, it became a credit to Aristotle that his speculations did *not* include the approaches to Christian belief seen in Plato and the Ancient Theologians. His defects were simply negative and could – it was believed – be simply remedied. He offered no deceptive analogies, but a copious set of terms and distinctions that could be put to use anywhere. Dante's placing of Aristotle turned out to be a vote on the winning side.

It is strange, then, that an effort in the other direction was made as late as the pontificate of Gregory XIV (1590–1). Francesco Patrizi (†1597) addressed to him a plea for a sound philosophy in the Church to combat the disorders of Christendom, and submitted that the philosophy should be Plato's, as interpreted in the Neo-Platonist tradition.[22] To favour this philosophy would be to return to the mind of the Fathers, who never mentioned Aristotle without denouncing him. The shift in allegiance was due, he goes on, to pressure exercised four hundred years ago by Aristotelians upon 'scholastic theologians' – *scholastici theologi*; see how the medieval synthesis has receded into the past. Patrizi's effort was, of course, made in vain; but that it should have been made at all is of interest. Of interest too is that, one year after the appearance of Patrizi's book, another and very different work should have been published on philosophy in the Church. The author was Giambattista Crispo, and the title shows the drift of what he wrote: *On the Need for Caution in Reading Pagan Philosophers*.[23] Crispo's work is not concerned with vindicating Aristotle against attractive but ambiguous resemblances in Plato to orthodox belief. Rather, it contends that all ancient philosophical thought, whether it be from Socrates, Plato or Aristotle, is a mixed blessing to the Church. We have come a long way from the confidence of the medieval synthesis of Christian theology with philosophical concepts of other origins. What lay ahead, the next section will try to show.

SOCRATES INTO THE SEVENTEENTH CENTURY

We associate the sixteenth and seventeenth centuries with exploration and disagreement. A recovery of Classical texts went with the Renaissance, and a wish to recover the original texts of Scripture was among the causes of the Reformation and its divisions. The voyages to new lands in the sixteenth century find analogies in the advances made in the sciences during the seventeenth. And it was this century which saw the beginnings of a more coherent understanding of the past, whether in the growing exactness of scholarship exercised upon the materials recovered in the Renaissance, or in the first attempts to apply critical techniques in biblical settings.[24] I want to trace the effect of this increased understanding in what was made of the figure of Socrates, but it is proper to notice first a shift of opinion concerning two matters mentioned in the previous section. The first is that, with the growth of critical methods, belief began to die out in the authenticity of the 'Ancient Theology' – those texts which had once seemed of such prophetic significance. The second is that a demand was made for an exegesis of Plato that would respect his text for its own structure and content, instead of taking it as the starting-point for decipherment and allegory. I have already noticed the resemblance between allegorical interpretations practised by Neo-Platonists and the styles of exegesis so popular in the Middle Ages; there is a corresponding resemblance between changes proposed in reading Plato and the changes in biblical exegesis associated with the Reformers.[25]

The figure of Socrates himself became more 'palpable', now that more material was available. Not only was Plato available (in Ficino's version of 1482, and in the original from 1513), but the accounts of Socrates by Plato's contemporary Xenophon, in his *Memorabilia*, and the gossipy life by 'Diogenes Laertius' (c. AD 220) were also put into Latin.[26] Diogenes had preserved the story that Socrates had been twice married, with the alternative version that he had the two wives simultaneously. Given this – and given the tales told of his wife Xanthippe in the sources – it was natural that his domestic life should provide themes for composition. A comic opera in 1680 portrayed him as a bigamist; the popular novelist Mme de Villedieu devoted to him in 1671 one instalment of her *Les Amours des grands hommes*, a work that soon received an English translation.[27] A third portrayal of the sage as a bigamist is by the Dutch painter Caesar van Everdingen († 1678) – the picture (at Strasburg) is not only pleasing, but embodies with some wit several anecdotes to be found in Diogenes Laertius. The two wives, apparently identical twins, are exuberantly Flemish and symmetrically displayed. One (this will be Xanthippe) is pouring water on to Socrates, while the other looks on approvingly. But the philosopher remains unmoved, partly because he seems half-drunk, and partly because he is gazing at a beautiful youth, whose identity can be discerned if we look carefully at the dog that accompanies him – the collar has inscribed upon it 'Alcibiades'.

Something of a very different order is to be found in Erasmus († 1536), who cast into the form of a letter to his friend John Colet († 1519) a comparison between the figures of Socrates in his cell and Christ in the Garden of Gethsemane. Erasmus epitomised for many the project of humanism that would do justice both to pagan

Antiquity and to the Christian revelation. His comparison between Socrates and Christ is of a piece with such a humanism, and with a belief that the past needs examining on its own terms, and by whatever critical means we have. It is a pity that the prolixity of the essay should obscure the range and sensitivity of the analysis offered in it. The general drift of what Erasmus writes is that Christ's beginning to grow sorrowful and to be sad, in contrast with the calm exhibited by Socrates, has not of itself any moral significance, but is a matter of difference between two temperaments (Erasmus 1704). The implications of this, and of what else Erasmus wrote in the essay, will occupy us later; they go far beyond what anyone else was to grasp at the time.

But that time is associated, not only with progress in physical and historical knowledge, but with sanguinary disputes in religion and with outbreaks of witch-burning. It was natural therefore that the *daimonion* or tutelary sign of Socrates should prove an embarrassment. Some sought to reduce it to manageable proportions. In his *Essais* (1580–8), Montaigne professes his antipathy to the *démonneries* and seeks at one point to interpret the *daimonion* as no more than exercises by Socrates of a sub-rational but valuable sagacity. Predictably he says he has found and used a similar gift in himself – indeed, we shall see that he professes to find in Socrates something like his own professions of ignorance and scepticism.[28] But arguments about the nature of the mysterious sign persisted throughout this period, as we can see if we examine two doctoral theses of the later seventeenth century. In one (Gerold 1658), defended at Strasburg, the candidate praises the merits of Socrates, and even has Aristophanes' anti-Socratic comedy *The Clouds* subsidised by the philosopher's enemies. But he also claims that there is a whiff of the *daimonion* in the proposal (*Republic* V.457c) for a community of wives. The conclusion he reaches is that nothing more was present than a native shrewdness which had been cultivated philosophically. A more expansive judgement was passed in another thesis (Sjliestrom 1686), defended at Stockholm. The candidate admits that there have been disagreements over the *daimonion*, submits that there are both good and evil tutelary spirits, concedes that in some cases we have no more than exercises of good sense by Socrates, but holds that in other cases we have to do with a genuine inspiration from God.[29]

This points to the fact that the greater knowledge possessed of Socrates, together with a greater awareness of the complexity and distinctiveness of the past, was sharpening the question concerning what was to be said of his eternal salvation – indeed, the life and death of the sage seemed to embody a challenge to the inherited opinions about paganism that we have already met. Religious controversies in the sixteenth and seventeenth centuries laid stress upon the need for divine grace through Christ, and older attitudes were still maintained. But they were sometimes maintained in a way that went with other characteristics of seventeenth-century thought, and so provided a contrast with earlier expressions. For a medieval writer like Aquinas, virtuous pagans were not excluded from heaven because they lacked virtues, but because their virtuous conduct was not ordered by divine grace towards the ultimate end to which that grace calls us. But for Malebranche, who gave in 1674 a classic account of the philosophy of Descartes, the exclusion had a different explanation. Without the habit of the love of God – bestowed by his grace and the sacraments – we persist in self-love; so Socrates, even in the act by which he heroically accepts death, still retains self-love as an inward habit and cannot be saved. Notice here how Malebranche's account, by exchanging talk of final causality for talk of inward habit, illustrates the ultimately sceptical dualism of the philosophical tradition to which he belonged: a gulf is fixed between observable actions and the content of the soul. Malebranche is associated with what is called 'Occasionalism' – the theory that what seems like causality is really only an *occasion* for God to exercise his almighty power. Occasionalism takes on theological consequences when faced with the challenge of Socrates' behaviour and death: his actions are evacuated of what seems their natural content; he was really held by self-love all the time.[30]

But newer verdicts also began to be heard. A work published in 1642 by La Mothe le Vayer († 1672) opened heaven to virtuous pagans by invoking the justice of God that bestows recompense. It was indeed condemned by the Sorbonne; but for all that, the author was later appointed, and by the pious Queen-Mother, tutor to the Duke of Orleans and then tutor to the Duke's brother, the boy-king Louis XIV. Indeed, according to one report, the condemnation itself was engineered by the author himself in order to boost the book's flagging sales.[31] There were other manifestations of the wish to open salvation to virtuous pagans, and they too can be seen as so many responses to the challenge made by the figure of Socrates.[32] But I now turn to another topic: Socrates' attitude to investigations into the physical world. It will lead us to see something more of the change then occurring, and in terms of two judgements passed on Socrates.

The two judgements are those of Montaigne († 1592) in his *Essais* (1580f.) and of Bayle († 1706) in his *Dictionnaire* (1697). A century and more separates the two, both of whom were acquainted with the ancient sources for what Socrates thought of physical investigations – Xenophon in his *Memorabilia*, Plato in the *Phaedo*. Both of them are associated with scepticism. But the settings and force of their scepticisms are very different, and the difference exhibits the change I have in mind.

According to the *Memorabilia*, Socrates recommended that astronomical studies should be limited to what was of practical value, while strongly dissuading pupils from further investigation, offering the philosopher Anaxagoras as an example of the madness which can go with attempts to scrutinise the devices of the gods, matters which they have not wished to make manifest (IV.7.4–7). Montaigne approves, and uses terms that recall some opinions held about Socrates among the Fathers. For Montaigne, it is not for us to pass judgement on 'the heaven' – so I translate his *le ciel*, which has the same ambiguity. Nor is this the only resemblance to patristic thought in the *Essais*, for he excludes pagans from salvation with a firmness that would have delighted Augustine himself: Socrates and Cato are virtuous in vain because they lack grace. For all that, the resemblances turn out not to be deep, while what does lie deep brings out the distinctiveness of Montaigne's scepticism. For him, ignorance and unconcern for physical investigations are 'a soft pillow', and we should rather strive to know ourselves – a topic which the whole drift of the *Essays* presents as endless, endlessly entertaining, and conducive to a general suspension of judgement. The sceptical turn is also given to what he writes of the lack of grace in Socrates and Cato, for he draws an analogy between their position and the position of arguments in favour of Christianity. Just as Socrates is virtuous in vain because he lacks grace, so arguments for Christianity need grace if they are to be effective; without grace they lack solidarity and firmness. So what looked like a call to reflection and an insistence on the salvific power of grace turns out to be an invitation to muse upon one's own oddities and to doubt all conclusions drawn from arguments, including arguments in favour of religion. Whatever may be thought of Montaigne's position, his commendation of Socrates here is part of a scepticism that is essentially *generic*. What we shall now find in

Bayle is also sceptical, but the scepticism has become *specific*. The change will show itself in what Bayle writes about Socrates, and it is a symptom of the many changes that had occurred in the century separating the two judgements.[33]

Between Montaigne and Bayle lie the cessation of wars of religion, and a growing sense of the futility of the arguments used in religious controversy; progress in mathematical and physical science, and the promise of more to come; the growth of greater freedom in printing; the beginnings of historical criticism; and its application to the mixed inheritance of beliefs and legends, sacred and profane, from earlier days. Over those years, Montaigne's general disregard for questions to do with the physical world had in effect been answered by the achievements of those who had actually put such questions and tried to answer them. His analyses of the human spirit remained and remain classic, but it was no longer possible to take seriously a scepticism bound up with so uncritical an accumulation of tall stories from ancient authors like Pliny the Elder. Bayle, in other words, was writing at a time when critical and sceptical views had to be more than a recital of quaint anecdotes and a general dismissal of interest in the physical world: the power of investigation into that world had become manifest, and the need for discrimination and scrutiny in our attitude to inherited beliefs had become just as plain. His contemporary Van Dale († 1708) had impugned the very existence of genuine oracles among the ancients, and Bayle himself exhibits a critical detachment towards the claims made earlier for them (we have come a long way from the Neo-Platonism of the Renaissance!). It is in this spirit that he examines the opinion ascribed to Socrates in Plato's *Phaedo* (97c). Once again, Socrates is referring to Anaxagoras. He narrates the disappointment he felt as a young man on reading the treatise published by him. He had heard that it gave a place to *nous* or mind in the ordering of the visible world; he hoped therefore to find in it an explanation of the purpose of all things in that world; but he found that the place given to *nous* was no more than preliminary, because the treatise itself was couched in mechanical terms. Bayle will have none of this complaint. Anaxagoras was under no obligation to offer explanations in terms of final causality. Indeed, the explanations he did offer were all the better for not appealing to the ordering function of *nous*, for that would be no better than the medieval scholastics' invocation of God when unable to offer any other reason. Final causality can be legitimately sought, but to seek it for the visible world as a whole is

173

to go beyond what human intelligence can achieve.[34] Bayle's attitude to Socrates is not only different from Montaigne's; he is able to adopt it because he writes in the setting of what had been achieved in the interval by a mechanical and mathematical investigation of the world. Investigations of this sort were to be the paradigm of success for the century that was to follow.

SOCRATES IN THE EIGHTEENTH CENTURY

In the *Spectator* for 9 July 1711, we are shown Sir Roger de Coverley at Sunday worship, surrounded by his tenantry. The motto prefixed by Addison to this urbane essay is taken from 'Pythagoras' – that is, from the *Carmina aurea* once erroneously ascribed to him. We have here what must be one of the last appeals made in England to the 'Ancient Theology'; but we also have what can serve as a text for much that was to follow. The motto commands the reader to 'honour first the immortal gods as is established by the law', and the scene in Sir Roger's parish church follows, as one way of doing so. One way. That there will be others is taken for granted in many of Addison's contributions, and he admits in an essay of the same year that many of his readers are 'unreasonably disposed to give a fairer reading to a Pagan Philosopher than to a Christian writer' (3 November 1711). The general pattern here will be familiar to readers. The eighteenth century was witnessing, not only changes in political and social structures, but the successful application and development of the mathematical and physical techniques which had been devised in the century before. The clarity and decidability of topics like these set them apart from the interminable brawlings about religion by which the preceding century had been disfigured. The moral was not hard to draw. A worship of the 'immortal gods' was proper and should be directed by us to the Author of all things. But that direction was dictated by reason; theological disputes and religious fanaticism were dictated by superstition and fostered by priests. Socrates, with his calm resignation and confession of ignorance in the face of death, was taken as a pattern for what rational religion – 'Deism', whether or not the name was acknowledged – ought to be.[35] A rational religion was attractive because it seemed of a piece with so much else that was rational.

Partial the picture may have been, but it was undoubtedly popular. Even some who defended Christian belief accepted it. One of them, in a work published in the 1730s, describes Socrates as 'The best Deist on record, excepting Job'. Socrates shows himself open to further instruction, and exhibits belief in future rewards and punishments; as such, he can be counted as having implicit faith in Christ. It is 'the modern Deist' who insolently rejects that faith (Smith 1740: 89).[36] The real trouble surely lay not so much in insolent rejection as in a presentation of religious belief that made its specifically biblical elements into an appendage – an appendage to be spoken of with respect but kept strictly within bounds. The story of Socrates could be narrated in a way that embodied such a presentation, and the very popular biography of him by Cooper is a classic example (it appeared in 1749, and by 1771 had reached its fourth edition): Socrates protested against the Athenian gods because 'False Religion is always a Bane to Morality'; his fate shows how such religion can inflame and blind the eyes of the understanding. Similar sentiments are found in France, where Voltaire put the last hours of Socrates into a play with a similar lesson, in 1759. Anytus (his accuser) is now a priest, annoyed at those who, like Socrates, do not pay for sacrifices but worship God by living virtuously – for good measure, Anytus is given a toady called 'Nonoti', after Nonotte, one of Voltaire's pet hates.[37] Perhaps the most extreme example of this treatment of religion is the deistic liturgy published by John Toland in 1720. Readers are invited to follow reason rather than custom, to leave the mob and join in a Symposium or 'Socratic Sodality'. There are invocations ('may Philosophy flourish'), a Collect (for freedom from superstition) and a Litany (where Socrates' name leads all the rest). Toland, be it said, came from Ulster.

Even by polemical standards there was more to be said than all this, and we shall see in due course how authors said it. But first we must notice the general principles of historical method discernible in what was being written about Socrates, for his figure serves yet again to indicate what changes of thought were occurring. A thesis presented in 1735 at the University of Leipzig on the character of Socrates makes the important admission that we must not judge one age by the standards of another (Ibbeken 1735). Several writers stress the need for critical discernment among the texts we do possess, if we are to reach Socrates himself. One was Brucker, whose *History of Philosophy* (1714f.) is the first of its kind in our sense; another is Mosheim, who, in 1733, translated into Latin the *True Intellectual System of the Universe* by Ralph Cudworth, a seventeenth-century Neo-Platonist at Cambridge. Brucker's *History* and Mosheim's *Notes to Cudworth* alike insist on distinguishing Plato and Socrates from later developments. Still further distinctions were demanded by Stapfer in 1786, who points to the difficulty of extracting what is genuinely Socratic from texts like those of Plato and Xenophon: the 'Socratic problem' has arrived.

But still more had arrived – the growth of awareness as to what was involved in trying to understand the past. Mauvillon († 1794; a friend of Mirabeau) published in 1777 an anonymous essay on the *daimonion* of Socrates. He sets the accounts of it beside the accounts of miracles in the Gospels, and claims that, since the religions of Socrates and Jesus contradict one another, both accounts cannot be true. He concludes that accepting the truth of a religion on the grounds of the truth of its miracles is something incomplete – it needs complementing by accepting the truth of the miracles on the grounds of the truth of the religion. For all the crudity of the argument, we can surely see it as an anticipation of what the next century was to call 'the hermeneutical circle'. And indeed another author anticipates the whole hermeneutical enterprise: this is the Abbé Garnier († 1805) in an essay of 1761 (reprinted in Montuori 1981a). Garnier acknowledges the heterogeneity of what is found in Plato's text, and acknowledges also the simplicity of the method of discernment proposed by Brucker – that we should accept as authentically Socratic only what is common to both Plato and Xenophon. But he goes on to put questions about conservation and alteration that are strikingly modern, however we judge his answers. Conservation in philosophy is not the same as conservation in a legal system, where an order of magistrates interprets. Philosophy is concerned with conviction, and what matters for conservation there is that the true principles of a master should not be betrayed; the force and joy in what we read helps to serve as a measure of what has been conserved. Xenophon's accounts of Socrates may give us the principles of morality, but it is in Plato alone that he lives, breathes and inspires us.

The attempt to estimate what had been conserved meant that, although the matter of Socrates' salvation was still raised, attention was given less to questions of nature and grace, and more to a study of the limitations of Socrates as an individual. We find then that the homosexual imagery found in Plato's dialogues was sufficiently embarrassing for the obvious inference to be dismissed without comment in the *Encyclopédie* (vol. XV, 1765; s.v. 'Socratique'). The *Gentleman's Magazine* for December 1786 also dismisses the charge of pederasty, but goes on to remind its English readers that in a country of 'more genial climate', 'the affections are stronger, and will express themselves in warmer terms than such as are usual with us of Northern Latitude'. But, a good deal earlier in the century, more thorough examinations had been made of Socrates' character and behaviour, sources had been examined, and verdicts reached. The first I have found is Mentz and Sommer 1716, in which the two joint authors claim that Socrates was deficient both as a husband and a father. Xanthippe was right to warn him of Alcibiades; he should have corrected her shrewishness; he did not give her the love and faithfulness that was her due; his refusal to accept fees meant that his household was poor; those who would admit him to heaven should recall the condemnation by St Paul (I Tim. v.8) of 'any who provide not for his own, and especially for those of his own house'. In another item – it is a disputation from 1735 – the very fortitude of Socrates in the face of death is unfavourably judged by one of the parties (Ibbeken 1735). After noticing that Socrates has been the object of both calumny and adulation, the proponent follows Seneca in distinguishing bravery (*fortitudo*) from bravado (*audacia*). Socrates should have accepted exile as a penalty; or sought help in the making of a proper defence; or taken the opportunity offered to escape. He ended by laying violent hands on himself; he provoked his accusers and judges alike to anger; he neglected his duties to his wife and children, and on the evening of his death behaved coldly to Xanthippe when she was weeping. The conclusion is that his bravery was at best imperfect, while the moral for us is that human nature is weak and needs grace and revelation.

All those works considered Socrates in his personal life, but others examined his conduct as a citizen. Montuori 1981a has reprinted two items from the eighteenth century which defended his condemnation. Both attacks appeared about the same time, and were independent of each other. The first was by Fréret in 1736, the second by Dresig or Dresigius in 1738. As we shall see, the general drift of both was the same.[38]

For Fréret († 1749), the charge of impiety was only a mask for a political accusation. The democratic party in Athens, restored in 403 BC after the downfall of the oligarchical Thirty, feared that Sparta might support an anti-democratic revolution. Socrates was known to ridicule popular government; Critias, the most extreme among the Thirty, had been a pupil of his; another pupil had been Alcibiades, the brilliant but unscrupulous soldier who had changed sides during the Peloponnesian War. A direct denunciation on political grounds was impossible, as an amnesty had been declared. But knowledge of the real reason persisted at Athens, and fifty-four years after Socrates' condemnation, the orator Aeschines could remind an Athenian jury that 'Socrates the sophist' had been executed because he was responsible for the education of Critias. So much for Fréret; Dresigius treats the charge of impiety in the same fashion, and adds that Socrates' conduct under the rule of the Thirty was not for the most part one of resistance – if it had been, they would have killed him. For Dresigius, the accusation of impiety would be sure to win popular support; and it could be supported by what Socrates had said – and said to the young – about their inherited myths, in his attacks upon poetry.

Both Fréret and Dresigius exhibit a good acquaintance with the ancient sources. To evaluate their charges lies beyond the scope of what I write here, but it may be of interest to notice that different 'political' verdicts were reached by others. For Rousseau, in his contribution on political economy to the *Encyclopédie*, Socrates is to be set below Cato of Utica precisely because his teachings were *not* political, but essentially private and philosophical, while Cato spent himself in defending the state, freedom and the law (vol. V, 1755; s.v. 'Economie politique'). By 1795, the French Revolution had led to war and to the invasion of Holland by the French. Luzac, the out-going Rector of the University of Leyden, offered Socrates in that year to his fellow citizens as an example of one who, instead of taking refuge in exile, stayed on amid disorder to offer advice to his fellow citizens, and who, while obeying the laws, would not commit injustice at a tyrant's behest. Dresigius and Luzac embody the different answers put to the dilemma: to stay or not to stay? It is a dilemma we shall meet again, when we come to what our own century has made of Socrates.

Some eighteenth-century writers were, it is true, content to repeat older positions without modification. One was Voltaire's bête-noire Nonotte, in his *Dictionnaire antiphilosophique* (1771; s.v. 'Payens'). Another combined the rigidity of the past with a delightful modernisation of the imagery he employed. We saw earlier how Malebranche the Cartesian wrote of the self-love that lies in the heart untouched by grace. Bernholdus in 1711 uses a *mechanical* analogy for the same purposes – the automata at Nuremberg perform all manner of activities, but without any intrinsic planning or intention of their own; a similar defect lies in Socrates and other pagans.[39]

178

I now turn to two themes that were characteristic of the later eighteenth century: one is the debate over Marmontel's novel *Bélisaire*, and the other is the making of comparisons between Socrates and Jesus.

It is not easy for us to understand the popularity of *Bélisaire* (1767) or the scandal it caused among some of the pious. It is a rather dull 'historical' novel about Belisarius († 565), the great general of the Eastern Roman Empire. But it went through edition after edition; the English translation was still being reprinted in the 1830s; it was translated into a variety of languages – Catherine the Great and her ladies-in-waiting even put it into Russian.[40] Perhaps its popularity was due to the offending fifteenth chapter, where the old general, now blind (the novel follows this untrustworthy variant of the story), expresses a hope that he will meet the great pagans in heaven, stresses the loving kindness of God, and reminds those who would use the sword in the cause of religion that their opponents have swords as well. The book appeared with the approval of the Censor (a position occupied at the time by the soft pornographer Crébillon *fils*), but aroused the wrath of the theologians of the Sorbonne, who protested alike at its opening heaven to pagans and at its denying to the Church the power of the sword to enforce decisions. But things had changed since the days of La Mothe le Vayer, and the whole affair blew over when Louis XV (a monarch one does not readily associate with theology) forbade the Sorbonne to persist in its course.[41]

The comparison between Socrates and Jesus is yet another example of how differences in attitudes to the philosopher can represent changes in how people think and feel. I contrast two attitudes: that of Diderot and other contributors to the *Encyclopédie*, and that of Rousseau. As we might expect, Diderot shows himself as very much a man of the eighteenth century, while Rousseau points towards what still lay in the future. For Diderot in his article 'Socratique' (vol. XV, 1765; 261f.) Socrates is a pattern of virtue and a martyr for belief in the unity of God; his benevolence resembles that of the Supreme Being; a prayer is addressed to him, confessing unworthiness and asking for assistance; and at his death his disciples 'divided his garment among them'. Another echo of the Gospel – this time concerning the burial of Jesus – is found in the article by Jaucourt, 'Ornemens funèbres': Apollodorus brings a precious robe to Socrates in the condemned cell, for him to wear in death – the action of Joseph of Arimathea is clearly suggested to the reader (vol. XI, 1765; 657).[42] With Rousseau, things are very different. The comparison is made in the discourse on religion put into the mouth of the 'Vicaire Savoyard', in the fourth book of *Emile* (1762), Rousseau's work on education. Here, as elsewhere in the discourse, what matters is the appeal to the heart made by the pattern of a life. Rousseau aligns himself with those Fathers of the Church who saw a prophecy of Christ in what Plato writes in the *Republic* of the sufferings of the just man; the death of Socrates is calm, and he dies surrounded by friends; Jesus dies in torments, mocked and cursed by the people. In one we have the life and death of a sage, but in the other the life and death of a God.[43]

Rousseau's comparison between the two deaths leads us to consider something that I have so far kept in the background – what the eighteenth century made of elements in Socrates that did not fit well into its pattern of rationality. To consider these will bring us to the writer who – in this matter as in so much else – wrote in terms that were to be taken up in the century that was to follow. The writer is Johann Georg Hamann († 1788), a fellow citizen of Kant in Königsberg; but first for the things about Socrates that made the eighteenth century uneasy – as indeed Hamann himself did.

One, obviously, was the *daimonion*. The occasional voice was raised against those who reduced it to no more than native sagacity – Herbst 1720 makes this protest – but reduction can be found in Cooper, as in many others. Voltaire was just as uneasy – it is no accident that, for all his admiration of Socrates, he also mentions him in his *Dictionnaire philosophique* s.v. 'Charlatan'. There he asks whether there was not something of the sort in the *daimonion*, and suggests that Socrates would have fared better if he had lived a century earlier. Another embarrassment was the hope expressed of immortality and the sacrifice to Aesculapius. Voltaire announces in a foot-note to his play that he has simply cut out much from the dialogue; Mosheim suggests that the request for the sacrifice was due to the clouding of Socrates' mind by the hemlock; for Cooper, Socrates spoke in religious terms before his death by way of condescension to the idolatrous ignorance of the Athenians. A third awkwardness was Socrates' talk of knowing nothing, and it was ascribed to irony – by one, in the course of an attack on Bayle's scepticism, to 'an elegant and modest exaggeration'. Once more, Rousseau shows himself to be out of tune with what his contemporaries took for granted – as early as 1749, in his discourse on the Sciences and Arts, he commends the severity of Socrates towards poets and artists, and sees him as despising our 'vaines sciences' and our piling up of books. But it is in Hamann that we find the greatest dissent from what has gone before, and another reading of Socratic ignorance. To Hamann I now turn.

For Hamann, we must take seriously what Socrates says of his own ignorance. He is not an eighteenth-century thinker indulging in irony. But neither is he a Christian. Nor can he be taken as a rational alternative to Christianity. Rather, he is a forerunner of it. He is essentially *incomplete*: his seeking to know himself and his confession of ignorance represent an urge within him that carries him beyond the intellect to faith. He is a genius, and so escapes the rules of his time. He cannot be 'reduced' in the way Cooper and others seek to reduce him. And Hamann relates what he is claiming about Socrates to his own view of human existence. Neither reductive rationalism nor romantic feelings are enough (he takes Newton and Rousseau as the respective types of these attitudes) – we must respond to reality with all our being.[44]

SOCRATES IN THE NINETEENTH CENTURY

I begin by seeing what encyclopaedias in our own country had to say of Socrates. His conduct is commended in the *Encyclopaedia Britannica*, where it is said that the *daimonion* is irreducible to unbiased reason, and the command to make a sacrifice to Aesculapius probably due to a wish to 'refute a calumny' which might injure his friends (vol. XIX, 1815, s.v. 'Socrates'); the calumny is presumably atheism. Socrates is commended also in the article 'Sophists'; the pernicious influence of the sophists on the youth is said to have been exposed by him. For the *Encyclopaedia Metropolitana*, the *daimonion* is no more than eminence in right judgement, and Socrates' language about it is ironic. As for the sacrifice, Mosheim's explanation is adopted – the poison had begun to work. These harsher judgements may be due to the clerical editorship of the enterprise; certainly the failure of Socrates to produce a reform in Greek morals is said to point to our need for a Saviour (vol. X, 1845).[45]

It is when we pass to the *Penny Cyclopaedia* (1833f.) that we find a treatment of something more than the personal qualities and circumstances of Socrates. He is commended for his stand in 406 BC after the battle of Arginusae, when he refused to let the generals be condemned without a trial. But he did not leave Athens when the Thirty ruled from 404 to 403 BC, and his sympathies seem to have been with the moderate oligarchs like Theramenes; his refusal to obey the Thirty's command to arrest Leon was due to kindness of heart rather than to political disagreement. Socrates was not a good citizen, because he could not bring his mind to accept public opinion, whereas laws in a democracy are made by the majority (vol. XXII, 1842, s.v. 'Socrates').[46] It is this matter of political rectitude that we shall now meet in another source of the time.

Five years earlier, a notorious work by Forchhammer had developed this theme of *incivisme*. Both charges made against Socrates, it claimed, were justified. In one sense he deserves our praise, for the gods in whom he refused to believe were not worthy of belief; others swore as he did the oath of reverence to them, and then accommodated what they had sworn to their own persuasions, but Socrates would not. Yet in another sense, he was a bad citizen (*Staatsverbrecher*) by refusing belief – he cannot be excused on the grounds that he would have accepted a higher faith, because hypotheses of the sort mean nothing in politics: whatever God allows to happen is the best. Socrates' personal *daimonion* was no substitute for the ancient divinities embodied in springs and other natural forms; it was to those gods that the state attributed its past achievements. The other charge – that of corrupting the youth – was just as well founded. The example of Alcibiades shows as much, and Critias, the most extreme oligarch, was also a disciple of Socrates. The Thirty did not molest him, nor did he offer Leon any positive help. The book caused much indignation: the historian Bishop Thirlwall wrote against it, and the Bishop's attack received approval in Grote's *History of Greece*.[47]

The year after Forchhammer's book, 1838, Brouwer pointed to the gap between what was claimed in it and what Socrates actually did – served as a good soldier, sought justice when assigned public office, and offered sacrifice. But he then makes a remark which shows again what we have seen so often – that the figure of Socrates serves as a measure of change. Brouwer wrote at a time when inherited religious belief was being questioned (Strauss' *Leben Jesu* had appeared in 1835). The Athenians' treatment of the oath they had taken, he writes, resembles the mental reservations with which people nowadays quieten their consciences in religious matters. Why should we impose upon Socrates a burden of literal fulfilment in a way worthy of the Council of Trent? And religion is also involved in what another writer has to say of Socrates' political attitudes. Twenty years after the publication of Forchhammer's book, Lasaulx objected to its extreme conclusions, while agreeing that no speaking against the monarchy would be allowed in Vienna or in Berlin – obviously the spectre of 1848 had not yet been exorcised by 1857. But Lasaulx, after making this political observation, turns to religion. He elaborates parallels between Socrates and Jesus in a way that recalls the Neo-Platonists (he does in fact cite both Ficino and Champier). Both had an attraction for those who met them; both taught and lived the truth; the touch of both was seen as invigorating (the Platonic analogue is *Theages* 130d); both were willing to converse with women of doubtful repute; the 'heart-burning' of a listener found in the story of the walk to Emmaus in the Gospels is also found in Plato's *Symposium* (215e); both taught that it is better to suffer wrong than to inflict it; and the friendships with the Beloved Disciple and with Alcibiades form another parallel. Lasaulx' own essay contained an admission that he knew the analogies would anger; his prophecy received prompt fulfilment in the angry Lindenbaur (1859), where at all events the irreducibility of grace to nature is once more stressed.[48] But some English examples can fill out what was felt about the relationship; and some of them, in ways that can still call for a response.

The year after Lasaulx' essay, Edward Goulburn addressed the YMCA on Socrates (Goulburn 1858). He reminds his audience that Athens was essentially an 'oral' community ('no reading rooms or Mechanics' Institutes for the lower classes'), and he lays stress upon the sincerity with which Socrates used his mode of cross-questioning and believed in an 'oracular voice'. He concedes that the effect of Socrates' questioning may have been to puzzle his listeners over right and wrong, but he finds the great lack in Socrates' character to be a love of sarcasm and a lack of sympathy. The endurance of Socrates is that of 'self-sufficient resolve' rather than of loving submission to God; which is what distinguishes his death from that of Jesus. It is worth recalling that Forchhammer himself brought yet another charge, and of a piece with this – that Socrates lacked love. We have already met something of the sort in Erasmus, in some of the eighteenth-century 'theses', and in Rousseau's *Emile*. We might call it the 'Socratic Chill'. We meet it more than once.

We find it, for example, in Matthew Arnold's distinction between 'Hebraism' and 'Hellenism' – between the ideals of the Bible and

183

those of the civilisation we inherit from Athens. When he drew the distinction (in his *Culture and Anarchy*), Arnold quoted a saying of Carlyle, that 'Socrates is terribly at ease in Zion'; and he observed that Hebraism is preoccupied with the impossibility of being at ease there. I hope it is not fanciful to fill out Arnold's distinction with yet another example of how the figure of Socrates marks change: this time the example touches a novel with Arnold's own father in it, the great liberal churchman and headmaster of Rugby. Thomas Hughes' *Tom Brown's Schooldays* (1857) has its hero pull himself together under the good influences of Arthur, a companion assigned him by Dr Arnold; he works at his Latin and Greek, and ends as captain of the Eleven. But the book's sequel, *Tom Brown at Oxford* (1861), is more sombre. Tom, guilty at his own conduct, turns to the last book he read at Rugby – Plato's *Apology*. He finds that Socrates' talk of the *daimonion* speaks to his condition, but wonders where the voice is to whom he can submit. And he is then reminded by a sterner companion that St Paul would have spoken to his condition too, but with the advantage that we, unlike Socrates, know the source of the voice, and the urgency of the demands it makes. As for Arthur, we read elsewhere that he is reading Moral Sciences at Cambridge; and that Tom writes him a letter suggesting that his time could be better spent. We are not at all at ease in Zion.

Lasaulx, Goulburn and Hughes have this much in common: they see a resemblance between Socrates and Christianity, but they deny an identity between them. They can be complemented by two farcical examples, which respectively deny the resemblance and assert the identity. The first, Highton (1873), is directed against the liberal Dean of Westminster, Arthur Stanley (prize-pupil of Dr Arnold – and, I understand, the original of 'Arthur'). We read there that Stanley, on the very day he had been appointed Select Preacher at Oxford, addressed a Working Men's Institute on Socrates, and spoke of him in terms that set him up as a rival to 'the heroes and martyrs of Christianity and Protestantism'. In fact Socrates' death was almost suicide, his morals were debased, he was frivolously superstitious (the cock sacrificed to Aesculapius), and he dealt with a familiar spirit. Schools and universities already offer the filthy pages of the classical poets to their students; is the pollution to extend to our mechanics' and workmen's institutes? But if Highton goes one way, a small and anonymous Russian work goes the other (Anonymous 1886). It imitates the studied simplicity of the style Tolstoy was using in the 1880s for his religious stories,

184

and narrates the story of Socrates accordingly. The sage comes to accept monotheism and to reject idolatry. He is denounced by the rich and idolatrous for proclaiming his beliefs, and dies a martyr. An illustration shows him holding the cup of hemlock like a liturgical vessel, and his request about Aesculapius has become 'My brethren, I die; do ye bless God.'[49]

The *daimonion* has been mentioned in passing by more than one nineteenth-century author so far, but there are two more works concerned with it that deserve a mention. One is Orlov (1897), which gives a balanced view of the accusations against Socrates, offers four hypotheses about the *daimonion* (an 'angel guardian'; the voice of conscience; hallucination; a wish to mystify), and says, disarmingly, that the reader is not likely to invent an explanation odder than some suggested already.[50] The other text I have in mind is by Archbishop (later Cardinal) Manning, and prints a paper read by him in January 1872 to the Royal Institute, 'The Daemon of Socrates'. He favours the view that it was an unanalysed act of judgement. Socrates ascribed to divine guidance what was the normal activity of his own intellectual and moral state; but a special providence may well have attended on him. And for good measure he mentions the Aristotelian *phronesis*, a power of sight which can discern with intuitive rapidity what is right or expedient in practice.[51]

Two themes have recurred in the texts we have seen so far. One is the relationship between Socrates and Athens – we might call it the Individual and Society. To the other theme I have already given a name – the Chill of Socrates: it has been associated with what was said of his relationship to Christianity. The two themes direct us to three dominant figures of the nineteenth century who are powerful in the twentieth: Hegel, Kierkegaard and Nietzsche. I have left them till now so that they can link this section with the next and final part of my chapter, in which we reach our own time.

Hegel is associated with the thesis that Socrates was justly condemned. By this time his opinion will not seem as unusual to us as it is sometimes claimed to be, but it does need to be put into the setting of Hegel's philosophy. He sees human thought and society as passing through successive stages, each taking up what has preceded (sometimes not without violence), and all part of a progress that cannot be reversed: Renaissance Neo-Platonism is no more than a mummy for Hegel. We cannot go back to the Athens that Socrates disturbed, for we have eaten of the fruit of knowledge he gave us. We can now appreciate him; the Athenians could not, and were right to condemn him. Just as Socrates embodies the shift from physical investigations to reflection on human thought and action, so he also embodies the shift to an individualistic appraisal of conduct. Athens up to then had an inherited code of behaviour, unreflectively practised – what Hegel calls *Sittlichkeit*. Socrates taught individuals to examine this code and to question it, and to find in their own reflective conscience how they should live – and this Hegel calls *Moralität*. Conflict was inevitable and tragic. The heroism of Socrates does not diminish the intolerable nature of what he said: his *daimonion*, in its privacy and absoluteness, is irreconcilable with the inherited oracles and gods of Athens. No people (*Volk*) can allow the tribunal of conscience, for there is no higher reason (*Vernunft*) than what the state declares to be right.[52]

We can see in all this one source of what Forchhammer wrote, and we can see all too much of what our own century has taken up. Nietzsche's estimate of what Socrates did to Athens resembles Hegel's, but he incorporates it into other claims that he makes. Here as elsewhere Nietzsche is not always self-consistent, but the general thrust of some of his contentions is plain enough. Socrates is the despiser of instinct, the jeering rationalist, the pessimist who is tired of life. His dialectic embodies the shift from the instinctive, healthy life of archaic Greece to the harsh daylight of queries and doubtings that are indeed a sickness; Euripides is seen by Nietzsche as performing a similar office for Greek drama. Socrates' use of irony shows his lowness of origin; irony needs to be used with finesse and restraint, if pupils are to receive benefit. Dialectic for Socrates is almost a revenge by one who is low and ugly; his requesting a sacrifice to Aesculapius, the god of healing, shows him as the pessimist who thinks death is a cure for life's sickness.[53]

Kierkegaard had read Hamann when he wrote his dissertation on irony 'with constant reference to Socrates'. Like Hamann, Kierkegaard sees Socrates as essentially incomplete and as pointing to Christianity by his very incompleteness. The irony he practises in his claims to ignorance serves to destroy the self-assurance of his listeners, and frees them from the captivity of what they wrongly take as satisfactory. But the 'nothingness' of Socrates is not as deep as the 'nothingness' that goes with Christianity. For Socrates, the sophists were wrong to say that excellence (*arete*) could be taught; it had to be extracted from the pupil, who had to be taught to know himself. For Christianity, salvation does not so come: it is something from without. Kierkegaard sees what he calls *anguish* as leading us away from a rationally ordered view of life where beauty and availability are what count, and bringing home to us our radical instability and our need for faith. Tom Brown, we might say, has passed from Rugby to Oxford.[54]

Hegel, Nietzsche and Kierkegaard all wrote at times as if they had our century in mind rather than their own, and it is a testimony to the perennial force in the figure of Socrates that each should have made him an object of study ('I constantly fight with him because he is so close to me', Nietzsche once claimed). I end this section by noticing two other sources that can also speak to us in our own century.

One is from the biblical scholar F. C. Baur. Edward Zeller the Platonic scholar was his son-in-law, and in 1876 edited his posthumous work on Socrates and Christ. Baur, who had used Hegelian categories on the Bible, uses them here too. Socrates, as Hegel put it, is the culmination of the individual, of subjectivity. For him, Man stands at the centre, and Baur claims that it was for Christianity to pass from self-knowledge to conviction of sin. But Christianity presupposes Plato, because Plato goes further than Socrates; he advances from the individual to the state. Allowing for all differences, Plato's state is a moral community similar in kind to the Christian Church. Baur's claim, whether viewed as philosophy or as religion, may make us uneasy; I set beside it a claim made by the Russian thinker Solovyov in 1898, in his book on Plato.[55] Plato's philosophical journey terminates in the state described in the *Laws*, and the society described in the *Laws* is a direct renunciation of Socrates; it is now with Anytus and Meletus that Plato takes his stand, the men whose accusation led to the trial and the hemlock for his old master. Once more, as we pass into our own century, Socrates will not leave us alone.

SOCRATES IN OUR OWN TIME

Socrates denounced for an excessive rationalism and for an insufficient regard for instinct; Socrates condemned as an offender against the state; Socrates found fault with for seeking within himself a salvation that must come from without: we have indeed reached our own century, and I have reached the final section of my chapter. In it I want first to give a few glimpses – only a few – of how Socrates has been regarded in our own part of the Cave, to speak in terms of Plato's great parable. And then I want to draw together some things we have seen on our journey, and to draw some morals from them. So first for the glimpses. Some are no more than ludicrous. Thus the *Great Soviet Encyclopaedia* (Russian edition of 1937) describes Socrates as sympathising with the oligarchical, slave-owning class. Well and good; but I did not expect to find that, twenty-three years later, the treatment of Socrates in a standard Russian history of philosophy would transcribe quite so much of the article as it does.[56] But other glimpses are less amusing, have more to teach us, and deserve a longer treatment.

The waters came flooding in very quickly after 1933 in Germany. The volume for 1935 of the *Rheinisches Museum*, the esteemed periodical for Classical learning, not only announced the resignation 'for reasons of health' of the editor Friedrich Marx, but announced it with effect from the end of the preceding volume. What had happened in the interval seems obvious enough, for Marx was a Jew – it is something that the notice about him at least set down his labours and faith in building up the journal after the First World War. I spoke a moment ago of 'our part of the Cave', so it is fitting here to see what was made of the image, and about that time, by two fellow countrymen of Marx. One, D. Roser, using a style more mystical than intelligible, distinguished in 1936 between upbringing (*Erziehung*, associated with Socrates) and leadership (*Führung*, associated with Plato). Present circumstances demand that a teacher be a leader (*Führer*) for youth and people; *Führung* calls for violence, just as the released prisoner in the Cave is compelled to turn around to the fire and then forcibly dragged up to the daylight; it is not through Classical studies that we shall arrive at what Plato meant, but by an ordering of our lives according to his spirit, and only thus can Plato be our *Führer* (Roser 1936). I turn to another use of the Cave, made by Heidegger in a seminar of 1931–2 (Heidegger 1988). He who, like the returned prisoner in Plato, would set others free must face the fact of his own death. Philosophy is powerless against the prevailing sense of 'obviousness' in the Cave; the honours bestowed there include praise and reputation and all the other things that can captivate and put an end to the philosopher. Nor can he escape by ironic detachment – that only makes him an accessory to his own poisoning. Rather, he must accept his incapacity to share in the prisoners' game of guessing at the shadows; he must fasten on one or two and seek to release them by his strenuous activity; and in moments of decision he must in his loneliness stand his ground.

Heidegger's own conduct makes this text an obvious if unkind choice. But it is a choice which also enables me to mention someone who did behave in the way Heidegger said a philosopher should. In 1938, there was published in the *Proceedings of the Prussian Academy of Sciences* an article devoted to Hegel's judgement on Socrates. After rehearsing the view, the author turns to criticism of it. Family, laws and society can survive only if they are supported and developed by what Hegel associates with Socrates – subjective consciousness. The individual's conscience is indispensable for the realm of ethics, and must stand its ground and do battle. But while doing so, it must accept that, being bound to a simple individual, it will be bruised and will perish. And the author uses Hegel's own words: if a higher life is to be manifested in the world, then the world's heart must first be broken (Spranger 1938). The author was Eduard Spranger, a wise and courageous man; let his name close the series of names we have met in following the posthumous fortunes of Socrates over twenty-four centuries.[57]

It has had to be a long journey: the early Christian writers, with their polemic against Socrates' fellow pagans; the Middle Ages, with the dominance of Aristotle leaving Socrates little more than a name; the recovery of Plato and of other ancient texts at the Renaissance, and the growth in critical appraisal of them into the seventeenth century, with new questions put about Socrates; the cool rationalism of the eighteenth century, accommodating Socrates to a deistic view of religion but feeling uneasy at things in him that did not square with its own preferences, and the same century growing more aware of just what is involved in making sense of the past; and the nineteenth century, with its philosophical exaltation of the state, its doubts over religion, and its seeing in Socrates a figure that cannot be ignored. After so long a journey, what response are we ourselves to make to Socrates, in a century which has been acting out so direly what philosophers were debating a century or more ago as they argued over the man? At the start of my chapter, I warned you that I should have to make brutal over-simplifications, and the warning is peculiarly appropriate with respect to the morals I shall now try to draw. I have allotted labels to them, some of which I have used earlier. They are: the Diversity of Goods, the Diversity of Temperatures, the One and the Many, Within and

189

Without, the Survival of the Word. To these I add a refrain from Vergil – 'non omnia possumus omnes' (more or less, 'We cannot all do everything'); and a final picture – the Marketplace. All these are linked, and they intertwine with each other as I come to this, the conclusion of my chapter.

What I call 'the Diversity of Goods' we met in the section to do with the Fathers, with their varied and discordant claims that all things well said belong to the Christians; that Plato had been acquainted with the Mosaic revelation; that Plato and Socrates and all the rest were deceivers; that Socrates perished for refusing to worship false gods; that Socrates had a familiar spirit. We met the theme again in the Renaissance Neo-Platonists, for they read Plato (and the Ancient Theology) as prophetic of Christianity, as needing only a suitably allegorical reading for the prophecy to be made plain. And we met it in the enduring debate about the salvation of pagans, down to the condemnation of *Bélisaire* for its plea in their favour, or Highton's denunciation of Stanley for his praise of Socrates. All these – and much else – rest on an initial decision to exclude a certain level of *diversity* in good things: a refusal to acknowledge that there may be good things which are simply different in kind from and irreducible to some other good things – things which our own upbringing encourages us to make the basis of everything else. It is a tribute to Socrates (and incidentally a tribute to the coherence of the picture that we form from the reports of Plato and Xenophon) that he has proved so resistant to so many well-meant attempts at homogenisation. Plato is not so resistant. He could, as we saw, be incorporated into Raphael's pictorial reconciliation of the tensions within the ancient wisdom, by means of the Christian tradition. He is majestic in Raphael's fresco, with his silent gesture; but he is silent. In the same picture, Socrates persists in his arguings and questionings. He obstinately remains himself.

The self he does remain has been found cold by more than one author – which brings me to what I have called 'the Diversity of Temperatures', just as I wrote earlier of 'the Chill of Socrates'. Whatever we think of the Fathers, Christianity was able to speak to the condition of the masses in a way that the tradition associated with Socrates could not. And things in what we have seen since can show why. The perceptive comments of Erasmus on the Agony in the Garden show how the figure of Christ can reach the heart in a way that is different from the way in which the figure of Socrates can reach it. All this is true, but the difference is just as true – we have here yet another example of the Diversity of Goods. Comparisons between Socrates and Jesus fail, not because of artificiality or irreverence, but for a deeper reason: what could be the common measure of the two that would not omit things we want to retain from each? Rousseau's contrast in *Emile* between the two deaths is a deserved rebuke to eighteenth-century elegance. But Socrates still does represent a willingness to question, to argue, and to confess ignorance – qualities essential if we are to live as we should, but qualities for which we shall look in vain in the Gospels.

We cannot all do everything, *non omnia possumus omnes*: that is the melancholy fact of the matter. It is no accident that dramatists and poets have tried to warm the figure of Socrates a little – even Mme de Villedieu's giving him a female disciple is an instance of something persistently and justifiably felt. The tales told of Xanthippe's shrewishness may be no more than the kind of ludicrous gossip that attaches itself to the private life of the illustrious. It is the parting between her and Socrates in the *Phaedo* (60a) that appals, with its presentation of the pair as having very little to say goodbye about. Socrates' habits of questioning and debating provide an example that we desperately need – but they had to be paid for. And there are testimonies from the Ancient World which indicate why.

'Paederast, drunkard, violent' – so (according to some sources) exclaimed a physiognomist visiting Athens, when introduced to Socrates. Socrates checked the indignation of his disciples – 'I am all these things: but I control myself.'[58] I complement the anecdote with three pictures. Figure 3 shows the face of the statue of Socrates in the British Museum. From this I have had figures 4 and 5 prepared; they exhibit likenesses made up respectively of the right and left sides of his face. The contrast is startling.[59] Perhaps the physiognomist saw something like that – if he did, Socrates may well have had to pay a high price for the detachment and self-sufficiency he notoriously possessed. And I support my conjecture with another testimony, this time a passage near the start of the *Phaedo* (60e). One of his friends, who has come to be with his master when he dies, asks about some poems he is said to have been writing. Socrates explains that earlier in his life he had often been commanded in a dream to 'make music (*mousike*) and work at it'. *Mousike* is a wide term, covering all literary as well as musical creation, and Socrates says that he had taken his own pursuit of abstract argument – *philosophia* – to be the best *mousike*. But he now feels that it is safer, before his departure, to obey the dream by making *mousike* in the usual sense. And so he first composed a hymn to Apollo, whose feast it was. Then, knowing that a poet should make up tales (*mythoi*) rather than speeches (*logoi*), but not having the skill to compose tales, he versified some of Aesop's fables. And there I see the lesson, for these were animal tales, tales about the birds and beasts of the field. Socrates was right to think that poets deal in *mythoi* rather than *logoi*, so cannot his venture into poetic composition be taken as an acknowledgement that *logoi* are not always enough? If so, cannot we take the venture as also an acknowledgement that coolness is not always enough either? The birds and the beasts in the *mythoi* show that Socrates cannot do without warm-blooded things any more than we can – was not his repeated dream telling him as much?

If it was, he would not have been altogether surprised at its message. Throughout our journey we have seen that there is a side to him distinct from the pattern of argument and detachment. It is the side that embarrassed the eighteenth century: the claim to know nothing, the sacrifice to Aesculapius, and obviously the talk about the *daimonion*. But there are other things as well which show this side to Socrates. In all Athens, what could seem more alien to him in 'temperature' than the frenzied dancing and music of the Corybantes as they worshipped? And yet it is to them that he goes for an image, when declining the offer of a chance to escape from prison. He seems, he says, to hear the laws of Athens demanding that he stay and pay the penalty – just as the Corybantes hear things; he can hear nothing else (*Crito* 54d). Just so, when the long conversation about immortality is over in the *Phaedo* (114d), he says that we should repeatedly intone (*epadein*) such things, in order to produce conviction in ourselves. Once more, there is this side to Socrates too, and there has to be. Just as there has to be in all of us.

I turn to the theme I have called 'the One and the Many'. We found in Hegel and in Forchhammer a contrast between the individual's conscience and the state's decisions and customs. With that contrast we today have become all too familiar, and it would have been easy to find still more examples of it from sources in our own century. We need to recall that the contrast is perennial, and that it too can be seen as an example of the Diversity of Goods: if it is true that no man is an island, it is also true that no state forms only one person. Not that the contrast is confined to state

Figure 6.3 Head of statuette of Socrates from the British Museum.
(All rights reserved, The British Museum, London.)

Figure 6.4 Likeness made up of right side of Socrates' face.
(All rights reserved, The British Museum, London.)

Figure 6.5 Likeness made up of left side of Socrates' face.
(All rights reserved, The British Museum, London.)

and individual, for the history of religion provides classic examples of it. We saw that Baur offers a cheerful picture of Christianity as presupposing the step made by Plato beyond Socrates – the step from the individual to the state; Solovyov can remind us that Plato's own journey took him to proposing a state in which Socrates would not have survived. Baur still more cheerfully insists that Christianity, unlike Plato, allows a subjective freedom; we are entitled to ask how long Socrates would have survived in the Christian Church. There is indeed a Diversity of Temperaments, and the Chill of Socrates can disconcert; but higher temperatures have to be paid for at higher prices.

And so to the theme I have called 'Within and Without'. Socrates' claim to know nothing was, time and again at Athens, a prelude to the discomfiture of a fellow citizen who believed himself to know something. The discomfiture would often be witnessed by young men, who were glad to watch the exposure of their elders. 'It is not lacking in pleasure' is the description Socrates gives in the *Apology* (33c), and the comment repels by its complacent chill. But the avowal of ignorance has been praised as a refusal to meddle with what is above us. We saw this in Montaigne, and similar things are found in the Fathers. Indeed, this view of the matter could be supported by an appeal to the way in which Socrates deprecated investigation into the physical world. I have already submitted that Montaigne's posture of universal scepticism is, even if entertaining, too generic to be substantial. I now suggest that the discipline of observing natural phenomena would have served as a corrective to Socrates and his followers. It would have lessened the destructive effects of his interrogations and arguments, by making them a part of a wider pattern of enquiries. The opinion was put forward in ancient times (Aquinas followed it) that Socrates betook himself to moral philosophy because he despaired of attaining certainty through the senses. To the extent that this is true, it does not represent the best of motives for studying ethics; Socrates would have done better to give the senses a chance and to see what could be attained by them. The suggestion is not the anachronism it looks, for others were then making intelligent guesses at the causes of things. And the investigation would have been eminently Socratic, given the respect he always shows for the skills of craftsmen. We need, if I may so speak, a Without as well as a Within. As it was, there were followers of Socrates who (like the vast majority of human beings) could not share in the austere restraint of his avowal of ignorance. If their certainty over some things had been loosened by his questions, they would find certainty elsewhere, if only the certainty of self-aggrandisement. We are back to the Diversity of Temperatures: it was a matter of who was listening when Socrates put his questions, a matter of who heard him or overheard his words.

Which brings us to the various senses of my last theme – the Survival of the Word. First, in the sense just mentioned: the hearers of what is spoken matter as well as the speaker. And with what Socrates said, the hearers mattered all too much. Whatever we think of the justice of accusations made against him, the making of them was surely not surprising. Wise men concerned with the individual's betterment are not usually far-sighted in political and social matters. Jesus was not, either – the Sermon on the Mount is no more a recipe for the running of society than was the communism of the first Christians. Once more, *non omnia possumus omnes*: it is as simple and as sad as that. But not just sad, because talk in terms of running society can never be enough – that way lie Forchhammer, and Hegel, and so much else we know so much about. The One and the Many, as Spranger reminded us, cannot easily co-exist; it is no accident that neither Socrates nor Jesus died a natural death.

But there are other senses to this theme of the Survival of the Word. First, the sheer, material persistence of evidence, and here we can be both disconcerted and saddened by the *fragmentary randomness* of what has come down to us from the Ancient World – the endless debates over the evidence concerning Socrates are proof of that. But there is also the human side to survival, and our journey has shown us how real it is. If there is the permanent temptation to homogenise what we do not know with what we do, so there is the permanent need to let what we have recovered from the past put its questions to us in the present and be questioned by us in return – a need, that is, if we think that what we are trying to understand still lives for us. This tension between what we might call understanding and confrontation is inevitable, and makes our stance inevitably awkward, for we are not wholly of·the past or of the present in what we are trying to do. And I submit that the awkwardness of our stance is complemented here by the unique awkwardness of the unique figure of Socrates – persistent, exasperating, imperturbable; undercutting what he had said with claims to ignorance, persevering even unto death in that questioning he had practised in the Athenian *agora* or marketplace.

And the Marketplace is the image we can bear away with us. It is essentially *draughty*: a meeting place for the diverse, a place for exchanges, a spot for conversations as we go on our different journeys. We must accept the Diversity of Goods in the marketplace: making Socrates a prophet of Jesus makes as much and as little sense as making Jesus a prophet of Socrates. We need Socrates for his own sake – his questionings, his solitary obstinacy, his courage. There will be complaints we shall want to make about him, and I have made some of mine, and there is more to what we need than what Socrates can give us. But beyond any question we do need what he does give; and twenty-four centuries on, we need it as much as ever.

And so we come back to where we started, to David's great picture of the death of Socrates (see Figure 1).[60] When David was planning the work, he sought advice from a classically minded friend, a priest called Adry. His friend gave him the information he wanted, but suggested that he add to the picture the figure of Plato. Now, as we know from Plato himself (*Phaedo* 69b), he was ill at the time and not present – presumably Adry was working on the hagiographical principle that, if certain events narrated in the lives of saints never occurred, then (I quote Newman) they ought to have occurred.[61] But David's reaction was, while putting in Plato, to depict him as an old man. There he sits apart, at the foot of the bed; he is the one figure in all the group who reacts to the death of Socrates, not by a gesture of grief, but by silence and recollection. And, to show that the figure is indeed Plato, David has put beneath his chair what Plato employed to make the scene still unforgettable after nearly 2,400 years: he has shown there scrolls, ink and pens. The painter's genius has turned the proposal for a pious fable into an embodiment of our understanding of the past. In that sense Plato must be there, for it is Plato who has woven the golden web of words in which we come to read the story of Socrates, to think about his questions, and to watch him as he comes to die. And just as Plato must be there in the picture, so he must, I submit, be also in the conclusion of what I have to say, which is his story of the death of his master. Many will know the passage at the end of the *Phaedo*; bear with me as I abbreviate it a little and recall it for those who do not. This book would not be complete without it.

The man has presented Socrates with the cup of hemlock, and Socrates puts a question to him:

'What would you say to my pouring out a libation to the gods from this drink?'

'Socrates', the man answered, 'we prepare just what we think will be sufficient.'

'I understand', said Socrates, 'but it is lawful and fitting that I should at least utter a prayer to the gods, that my passing over may be fortunate. Thus I do pray; and so be it.' Then he put the cup to his lips, and very cheerfully and calmly drained it off. At this we could no longer restrain ourselves. I covered my face and wept – not for Socrates himself, but for my own loss of such a man for my friend. He exhorted us not to give way so; in our shame we ceased from weeping. He walked for a while, then said his legs felt heavy, and lay down. The man showed us how he was gradually growing cold and said that when it reached the heart he would be gone. As it drew near he uncovered his face and spoke these last words: 'Crito, we owe a cock to Aesculapius. Pay it, and do not neglect the matter.'

'It shall be done', said Crito. 'But have you anything else to say?' There was no answer. A little time later, he gave a movement. The man uncovered his face and his gaze was fixed. Crito, seeing this, closed his mouth and eyes.

Such was the death of our friend, a man whom we might call, of all we then knew, the best, and the wisest, and the most just.

NOTES

1 The ancient testimonies concerning Socrates have been assembled by J. Ferguson in translation, but with references to the original texts, in his admirable work (1970).

2 Two Socratic bibliographies are Patzer 1985 and Navia and Katz 1988. The British Library's catalogues give much material under 'Socrates'. I regret that I have not been able to consult Herbert Spiegelberg's work on this subject.

3 It is customary to add to locations of passages from the Fathers the numbers of the volume and column in the two lengthy series *Patrologia Graeca* and *Patrologia Latina*, edited in the last century (1857f.; 1844f.) by the Abbé J.–P. Migne. I cite the two series as 'PG' and 'PL' respectively, with volume-number preceding and column-number following. I naturally give references also by book and chapter; these apply to all editions. The whole question of the relation between the Fathers and Greek thought (especially Platonism) is a vast topic. One of the best accounts is still Arnou 1933. Another account, serviceable

both for its text and its bibliography, is Gilson 1955 – its title is rather misleading, for the book goes further back than the Middle Ages.

4 Justin also writes of the *daimones*, whom he believes to have been begotten by fallen angels (II *Apol.* 5; 6 PG 452). They are evil, and persecute good people like Socrates (II *Apol.* 7; 6 PG 456). Justin does not explain how he keeps Socrates' own talk of his *daimonion* apart from this – he makes the casting out of the fables and poets an attack upon the *daimones* by Socrates (II *Apol.* 10; 6 PG 461). It is to the horrible Tertullian († c. 225) in his *Liber Apologeticus* that we owe the accusations that Socrates' *daimonion* was some kind of familiar spirit, inciting to evil (22; I PL 405); that his last request for a sacrifice to Aesculapius was a gesture of human respect to the Athenians; that his constancy in the face of death was affected indifference, not faith in a discovered truth; and that the charge that he 'corrupted the youth' was a proof of his unchastity (46; I PL 509).

5 There are references in Brown 1967: 36.

6 The survival of writings from the Ancient World into the Middle Ages has been surveyed in many works. Marrou 1938–49 is a classic account; as its title suggests, it lays stress upon the part played by Augustine as a link between earlier and later times. Gilson 1955 is again useful, both for its text and its bibliography. More recent, and containing a remarkable amount of information for its size, is Haran 1985. Bolgar 1973 is only one of the several valued contributions made by this author to the topic. I add two observations. The first is that writings by Cicero to do with rhetoric, and later text-books concerning it, preserved information about ancient philosophy (Halm 1863, since reprinted, conveniently assembles texts). For the part played by such things, and for much else, see Curtius 1953. My second observation is very simple, but is sometimes forgotten: the very concept of 'survival' needs treating by us with some caution, for we think in terms of easily reproducible material. Survival in those days had a *local* quality that it now lacks.

7 The fate of Greek in the West as far as the sixth century can be followed in Courcelle 1969. Noble 1985 is a short but illuminating study of its later fortunes in Rome itself, until the ninth century. Gregory the Great's *Moralia* could be put into Greek there in the 740s, for the immigrants' use (poor immigrants!); Greek books could be sent to Gaul, at the request of Pepin († 768) – their content was entirely religious. The Irishman Eriugena († c. 875) translated Dionysius the Areopagite when in Gaul, from a text provided in 827 by the Eastern Emperor. He seems to have known nothing of Plato's text at first hand. For all this, and much else, see O'Meara 1988.

8 The translation in which Augustine read Plotinus was made by the fourth-century Neo-Platonist Marius Victorinus, who eventually became a Christian. Boethius, whose Platonic *Consolation of Philosophy*, written in the face of death, has secured an unrivalled succession of translators into English, planned to render all Plato and Aristotle into Latin. He got no further than portions of Aristotle's logic, while also translating a commentary on one of them by the Neo-Platonist

Porphyry. Details are in Wallis 1972. This is a rich source of information about the whole Neo-Platonic tradition, from its origins in the Academy down to the suppression by the Emperor Justinian in 527 of the school at Athens; his final chapter gives a survey of the further endurance of the tradition.

9 Klibansky 1939 among many others traces the later fortunes of ancient philosophy, and how texts of Plato and Aristotle were translated and studied among Moslems and Jews. I learn from Bergmann 1936 that some Jewish thinkers held that Plato had derived his teaching from Moses; that Socrates was an ascetic who lived in a barrel; and that Aristotle was a Jew. The development of the Platonic and Aristotelian traditions there is also considered by Klibansky; it can naturally be followed as well in all general works. The most enduring consequence was that, when the corpus of Aristotle's works reached Western Europe towards the end of the twelfth century, the arrival brought Neo-Platonic elements with it.

10 The arrival of Aristotle's works in the West – the works of a pagan, accompanied by commentaries from other pagans, or from Moslems and Jews – is surely the greatest culture-shock that Europe has ever undergone. The complexity and diversity of reactions to the arrival are given a masterly survey in van Steenberghen 1966, which draws on many earlier writings of his. As I read him, I take the sheer bulk of the material that arrived to have altered, not so much the balance within existing disciplines, as the notion of what disciplines were available. Philosophical speculation (and we must never forget that the word had a far wider connotation then than it has now) acquired a 'massiveness' and independence, because of the quantity and range of the material on which it could now be exercised. Earlier, the only texts of Aristotle available for exposition at the University of Paris, in its Faculty of Arts, were parts of his logic. Things were different now, and by the 1220s these quasi-Aristotelian speculations there had begun to affect the teaching of theology.

11 Aquinas had no Greek, but encouraged his fellow Dominican William of Moerbeke to make closer translations of Aristotle than some then in circulation. William produced word-for-word renderings; it is a tribute to Aquinas that he made such good sense of so odd a result. Deman 1940 collects and surveys texts to do with what Aquinas writes of Socrates.

12 Details in Nelson 1948; further details in Maravall 1957.

13 The whole topic of Renaissance philosophy has recently been given extensive and scholarly treatment in a volume of the Cambridge histories of philosophy (Schmitt, Skinner and Kessler 1988); the book is a fitting conclusion to the labours of C. B. Schmitt, to whose investigations into this period so much is owed.

14 Ficino was supported by Cosmo de' Medici, who took advantage of the presence of scholarly Greeks at the Council of Florence (1439–45) to encourage the study of the language and of its written remains. A volume of essays edited by O'Meara (1982) deals with the tensions between religious belief and philosophical speculation among

Neo-Platonists at that time. Tigerstedt 1974 deals with the endurance of this tradition of interpreting Plato.

15 For 'the Ancient Theology' we have interesting and informative essays in Walker 1972 – indeed, the term 'Ancient Theology' is of his devising. He gives details and references to do with the very complicated story of the origin of the texts, the use made of them, and the varied estimates of their authenticity. Our own time has seen the publication of a critical text of Hermes Trismegistus (1945f.) by Festugière, who deals with the content and literary fate of this strange material in his 1950–3, a mine of information.

16 The magical element in the Platonic tradition and in the Ancient Theology is a vast theme. Dodds 1951 has an Appendix devoted to these practices in late Antiquity – 'theurgy', to use a term going back to the second century of our era. His later work, Dodds 1965, analyses and reflects upon the growth of the practices between Marcus Aurelius and Constantine – an age in which religious beliefs laid stress upon the transitory nature of material things, the gap between the human and the divine, and the quest for powers and intermediaries by which the gap might be bridged. The account in Bevan 1920 is brief and very readable.

17 I have taken the main constituents of this interpretation – the gestures of Pythagoras, the presentation made to the Evangelist and the figures round him – from Gutman 1941. But that it should be the Ancient Theology that is finding completion in the Gospel is a contribution of my own, as is the symmetry of John's figure with Plato's raised hand. I add at once that this interpretation differs from those offered by others, including Dussler, and also Gombrich and Wind, authors to whom so much is owed in the field of iconography. Gombrich 1972: 98 takes the figure I see as a seated Evangelist as a 'writing sage'. Wind 1968: 54, n. 4 takes as Pythagoras the figure painted in the style of Michelangelo, seated in the foreground by a block; the figure was not in Raphael's original design, as may be seen from the reproduction of the cartoon in Cuzin 1985: 118–19. I am not persuaded that the matter is closed, for Wind adds something that – or so I think – tells in my favour. He mentions a Latin poem by one of Raphael's sitters, the Venetian scholar Andrea Navagero (the portrait can be seen in Jones and Penny 1983: 164). The poem is on an image of Pythagoras, and Wind suggests that phrases in it may have been inspired by the Pythagoras of Raphael's fresco. I have traced the poem, which is most conveniently available in Perosa and Sparrow 1979: 231–2, and I translate some lines from it: 'He is certainly meditating on something worthy, such gravity is in his face, so hath he quite retreated into himself with his great heart; he could utter the high themes of his mind – but, bound by his ancient vow, he is silent.' I like Wind's suggestion (though his text might have been more explicit here; the object in Navagero's poem was a piece of sculpture). But I submit that the figure I see as Pythagoras in the fresco fits Navagero's words better. Wind's figure is not really silent; just as Gombrich's is busy writing, and having what he writes looked at and copied, so Wind's is seated at a marble block, on which he is

drawing a diagram. Mine, as we have seen, does nothing but point and gaze.

18 Gombrich examines the fresco in one of the essays in his 1972 – I have, needless to say, learnt very much from it, nor (even if I had the competence) should I want to dispute the account he gives. His first objection to the theme of 'presentation' in what Gutman writes takes up what has been objected earlier – that the interpretation sets together Christian and pagan imagery. To this I have two responses, the first of which I draw from Gombrich's own essay. The decoration of the Stanza della Segnatura, he insists, has to be interpreted as a whole, from the ceiling downwards, and to treat any one wall in isolation is to miss the point. I wholly agree – but if the room is to be taken as a whole, then the imagery of this whole includes not only the Christian Eucharist, but the philosophers of Greece, and Apollo and the poets on Parnassus. To blame an interpretation of *The School of Athens* for making it set together Christian and pagan imagery is hardly fair; they are set together by the room itself. My second reply develops the first: to read as I do the 'Ancient Theology' into the fresco is to accept such a setting of them together – not in any sense that would have Raphael put paganism on a level with Christianity, but in the sense that some pieces of pagan wisdom are displayed as finding their fulfilment in the Gospel.

But Gombrich also raises a wider objection. He points to the variety of interpretations the fresco has received, gives salutary warnings against pressing iconographic investigations to absurdity, and shows by illustrations that Raphael was glad to use motifs and elements from earlier paintings. He rightly insists that he would above all have sought decorum and splendour in depicting such a scene; his aim would not have been to produce a *catalogue raisonné* of Greek philosophy. And, once more, I agree; but, again once more, I go to Gombrich himself for a further reply. He describes the detailed demands for 'significance' that could be made then by patrons, and the programmes which were drawn up for the symbolic presentation by painters of this or that meaning, printing one at pp. 23ff. Of course we possess no such programme for Raphael's fresco, but there seems an ambiguity in what Gombrich and others have written about identifying figures in it. Are identifications rejected because we lack information, or because the whole notion makes no sense? Identifications have been made for various figures elsewhere on the walls; why should not some 'programme' or other have been given to Raphael, whatever degree of fidelity to it he may have observed? Nor does the fact, rightly stressed by Gombrich, that he incorporated earlier motifs mean that he attached no significance to them. Once more, I am wholly in agreement with Gombrich's insistence that it is a *picture* we have, with all the needs of a picture for balance and colour. It is a matter of degree – of how detailed an exegesis can be attempted. For me, the general 'sweep' of the fresco can combine both splendour and a lesson. I add that Cuzin 1985 gives a good reproduction of the fresco; that the Vatican Museum provides a poster which, being bigger, is even better; but that for the detail on what is being 'presented' to the Evangelist, we must still go to the drawings in Springer 1883 – a work which is a mine of information about interpretations of the fresco.

19 Such a treatment of Plato, here and elsewhere, raises wider issues. To read Plato's text as in some way cloaking mysteries, and so as needing deciphering, is to muffle the delicacy, tautness and wealth of the language he actually used. Such, at all events, is my own diagnosis; and, having made it, I have to add that I find Renaissance Neo-Platonism virtually unreadable.

20 Details of this work are in Walker 1972.

21 To this day, frescos in the exhibition-gallery of the Library exhibit founders of alphabets. The founders include Adam, Christ, the Emperor Claudius and Hercules.

22 Patrizi's final plea for a philosophy based on Plato for the Church (Patrizi 1593) is of a piece with other writings of his – translations of the 'Chaldean Oracles', supposedly by Zoroaster; of the *Elements of Theology* of Proclus; and of Hermes Trismegistus.

23 The work is notable for one image: Plato was captured by the Christian Church in its victory over paganism; but, kept a prisoner, he did grievous damage to the camp of his enemies. Which brings us back to the views of some acquaintances of Ficino, a century earlier (details once more in Walker 1972).

24 The growth of Classical scholarship, and its chequered career in an age of war and strife, is described – with much material to do with the links between that scholarship and the religious movements of the time – in Pfeiffer 1978.

25 Walker 1972 is again useful for the topic of how belief dwindled in the 'Ancient Theology'. Of the demand for an exegesis of Plato that would not allegorise, Leibniz himself provides an example. He had read – just as he had read everything else – the Renaissance Neo-Platonists, and called for something more simple and solid than elaborations of Plato's more 'hyperbolic' ideas. Writing to Simon Foucher in 1686, he says that Plato himself had endeavoured to give exact definitions, and that we should endeavour to imitate them (Gerhardt 1875–90: vol. 1, 380).

26 The earliest modern life of Socrates was composed as far back as 1440 by Manetti; it relies largely upon Diogenes Laertius, and has been edited in our own time by Montuori 1981a.

27 The comic opera (first performed in Prague of all places) was called *The Madness of Socrates with his Two Wives*. The romantic novelette by Mme de Villedieu is of no intrinsic value, but shows Socrates to have been a figure her readers would know. It makes him have a female pupil; who loves Alcibiades; and so on.

28 The reduction of the *daimonion* to instinctive sagacity comes at the end of the eleventh essay of the first book, 'On Prognostications'; and the most prominent place of all is given to his unease at talk of *démonneries* – it comes at the very end of the final essay (Montaigne 1930: vol. 1, 73; vol. 3, 479). Schuhl 1956 is devoted to the place of Socrates in Montaigne's writings.

29 Gerold shows a fair acquaintance with Classical and patristic literature

on the point, and also cites the Epicurean Gassendi, then recently deceased, but gives no reference. Sjliestrom cites ancient authorities – but it is significant, given the milder interpretation, that he shows familiarity as well with Ficino.

30 The reference to what Malebranche writes of Socrates' salvation is to the fourth chapter of his *Traité de morale* (1684: vol. 11, 55–6); the passage in Aquinas with which I contrast it comes in his *Summa theologiae*, 1/2.65.2.

31 The tale of his securing a condemnation for commercial purposes I take from a note pencilled into the British Library's copy. I cannot pronounce on its historical value – the book was certainly denounced by the grace-obsessed theologian Antoine Arnauld († 1694), but then he was by nature a great denouncer.

32 Milder opinions had been expressed in the preceding century. Zwingli († 1531), the Swiss reformer, expressed them (his heaven incorporates Hercules and Theseus). So did – more tentatively, and yet reproved – Roman Catholics like Vivès († 1540; tutor to Bloody Mary) and Payva d'Andrada († 1578; a preacher at the Council of Trent). Erasmus is associated with 'Saint Socrates, pray for us!', but as Marcel 1951 points out, the invocation has a tentative setting and is part of a dialogue.

33 Montaigne's *Essais* are divided into three books. The *locus classicus* for his scepticism is the long twelfth essay in the second book, where he reflects upon a work of Christian apologetic by Raimond Sebond: his pronouncement on Socrates and Cato (and the analogy with religious argument) is near the start of it, and his siding with Socrates about astronomy is about two-thirds of the way through. The final essay of the last book, 'On experience', contains his preference for ignorance and a concentration upon the infinite theme of 'know thyself': these come about a fifth of the way through.

34 Bayle's distinctive opinions are usually in the 'Notes' to articles. What he has to say of Socrates and Anaxagoras and about oracles is to be found in Note R to the article 'Anaxagore' and Note A to 'Agesipolis' and Note E to 'Amphiarus'. Bayle was a born journalist, and to read him on authors I have mentioned in this section ('La Mothe le Vayer' is particularly amusing) is to see what awaits us in the century to come.

35 The Everyman edition of the *Spectator* has a useful index, which gives an idea of how prominent a place Socrates had in the mind of a writer like Addison – even the invocation by Erasmus we met earlier appears, in the number for 3 November 1711.

36 When Smith writes that Socrates shows himself open to instruction, he is referring to the *Second Alcibiades*, a dialogue on worship that is now regarded as not by Plato; references to it are not uncommon in the eighteenth century.

37 Voltaire's *Socrate* is destitute of any literary merit except for one remark given to Xanthippe – it can serve to show Voltaire's mixed feelings about his hero. She makes it when Socrates declares the soul to be immortal because we are now thinking and so shall think for ever: 'I don't understand. I am now wiping my nose – am I to wipe that for ever?'

38 Fréret was better known than Dresigius: it seems that, confined for some time to the Bastille, he devoted himself to Bayle's *Dictionnaire* and emerged a convinced sceptic. His learned writings were a quarry for others, but I have not found any reference to this work on Socrates.

39 He cannot be thinking of the moving figures on the great clock at Nuremberg: he seems to have seen a whole 'town' of such things. His essay was already rare when it was reprinted in the edition I have used, as its Preface states.

40 Catherine the Great undertook the ninth chapter of the Russian translation. I have found one addition made by her, to a list of things that tyrants have on their minds in their countries: 'the partiality of its laws' ('po pristrastiyu eya zakonov').

41 For the trouble at Paris over *Bélisaire*, see Renwick 1967. The novel led to controversy in Germany also, where Eberhard († 1809) wrote in a liberal sense concerning pagans in 1770. He was reproved – on the grounds of contradicting Christian teaching – by none other than Lessing. But in 1774 Lessing published the famous fragments of the rationalistic work by Reimarus on the Gospels, and with notorious consequences. So•I think I am entitled to entertain the hypothesis that his reproof of Eberhard was Socratically ironic.

42 The figure of Socrates for Diderot was of central importance, and the biography by Wilson 1972 gives several examples – including Diderot's having used a seal depicting Socrates as a signet-ring. Diderot's own imprisonment in Vincennes, and his abjuration of errors there, would have made the relationship all the more poignant. His later quarrel with Rousseau will explain why, in the article 'Socratique', he makes one of his disciples the gloomy Timon, who abandons mankind and takes to the woods; this is said to be Rousseau, with his attack on civilisation.

43 We can set what Rousseau writes of Socrates and Jesus in *Emile* beside his advice given, in a letter of 15 January 1769, to a correspondent inclined to atheism. Similar distinctions are drawn there, but this time the suggestion is made that Jesus stands at a disadvantage to Socrates because of their respective chroniclers – what would we make of them if Plato and the Evangelists had changed places (*Correspondence* XXXVII: 13f.)?

44 'Hamann does not have a style; he is one' – that is one pronouncement by Hegel with which all can agree. O'Flaherty's edition of Hamann's *Socratic Memorabilia* is therefore all the more valuable – it has the original text, an English translation *en regard*, and very helpful notes and references. One 'rationalist' with whom Hamann engaged in polemic was Moses Mendelssohn, the liberal Jewish thinker – it is worth recording that while Mendelssohn, in his *Jerusalem*, had taken his account of Socrates from Cooper, Hamann dismissed that work as 'a school-exercise'. Hamann's part in the controversy can be followed in his *Golgotha und Schlebimini*. If 'followed' be the verb.

45 The *Encyclopaedia Metropolitana*, to judge by its editorial board and its name, had links with the newly established King's College in London.

It is arranged by a rational division of topics rather than alphabetically, which makes it excessively hard to use. I understand that it was the brain-child of Coleridge in the first place.

46 The *Penny Cyclopaedia* is notable for the excellence of its articles on mathematics; these are by De Morgan, who is said to have furnished up to one-sixth of the total bulk. Its line is not always consistent: 'Philosophy' gets little praise, 'Plato' a good deal.

47 Forchhammer's style as well as his thesis may have annoyed – it is rollicking and not reverent. He refers to a recent disaster to which noble youths have been led by the anti-social example of Socrates – as he was writing in Kiel in 1837, this must refer to the disturbances that followed the accession to the throne of Hanover of Ernest, Queen Victoria's wickedest uncle.

48 Lasaulx wrote on a variety of Classical topics, and can be encountered in Burckhardt's foot-notes. Lindenbaur, a parish priest, does not help his cause by claiming that all the leading Classical scholars of every nation were loyal adherents of the Church, and that the early Christian leaders had brought more or less all the fruit of Classical civilisation into the order of Christianity (Lindenbaur 1859: vii).

49 The cover advertises other works of piety. Given the pamphlet's dishonesty, it is good to see that one of them is *Fabiola*, Cardinal Wiseman's tawdry and disingenuous novelette about early Christians in Rome.

50 The cover of Orlov's book shows that G. H. Lewes' *History of Philosophy* was available in Russian, and that Grote too had been translated. Plato apparently had not been; presumably he would be read in French or German.

51 Manning associates his own view of the *daimonion* with that of the Balliol Classical scholar James Riddell, editor of Plato's *Apology*. He does not mention the resemblance of all this to what Newman had written about drawing conclusions in concrete matters. (The *Grammar of Assent* had appeared in 1870.)

52 Hegel writes of Socrates in various places, but the most accessible are in his *Lectures on the History of Philosophy*. His general principles can be found in the introductory portion; his specific treatment of Socrates later, in the second chapter of Part I. I notice at this point a Russian prize-essay on Socrates, written in an Hegelian manner. The author was A. Velikanov, gold-medallist in 1842 at the Lycée Richelieu in Odessa. It states the conflict, but it goes on to say that Athens after the Peloponnesian War was sinking 'into anarchy and despotism', and that 'when any government is on the verge of collapse, virtue and morality will be degraded'. How the Censor let these sentences by I cannot think – the ruthless autocrat Nicholas I then reigned. I have looked in vain for 'Velikanov' in Russian works of reference; he cannot have survived long.

53 Nietzsche writes of Socrates in many places; Sandvoss 1966 gives a useful collection of the texts, with lucid and sensible comment. The early work *On the Birth of Tragedy* (splendidly translated and elucidated in 1981 by Silk and Stern) is one *locus*; another is the late

work, *Twilight of the Idols*, which has an essay on 'The problem of Socrates'.

54 Of commentaries on Kierkegaard, I found Burnier 1943 a luminously helpful piece of critical sympathy.

55 I also notice here that Solovyov was responsible for philosophical articles in the enormous *Russian Encyclopaedia* (1890f.). The article on Socrates there by Radlov records the interesting suggestion made by a Russian contemporary that Socrates can be seen as a social reformer.

56 The passage can be found in Yovchuk *et al.* 1960: 58, a work also remarkable for its division of philosophy into two main periods, pre-Marxist and Marxist.

57 The story of Eduard Spranger is worth recalling (he has an entry in the *Encyclopaedia of Philosophy*). He was Professor of Paedagogy at Berlin and resigned when the Nazis came to power. He was persuaded by his friends to stay on and to do what he could (one thinks of Luzac on Socrates). In 1944 he was arrested but was released at the intercession of the Japanese Ambassador – he had lectured in Tokyo before the war. In 1945 the Allied Powers made him Rector of the University of Berlin, but he found academic life under communism just as uncongenial, and eventually moved to the University of Tübingen for the rest of his career.

58 There are several sources for the physiognomist's remark, varying slightly among themselves. The most easily accessible are in Cicero's *Tusculan Disputations* (IV.37) and Cassian's *Conferences* (XIII.5.3); all can be found in Ferguson 1970. It is worth noticing here that Socrates' ugliness was linked by Nietzsche with the other things he said about him in *Twilight of the Idols*. However, Nietzsche does not give the reply made by Socrates about self-control.

59 I have compared the right and left sides of other images of Socrates in, for instance, Richter 1965. None yielded the contrast that the British Museum's statue yields: could this speak in favour of what the Museum has?

60 For David's painting, Salmon 1962 and Brookner 1974 are useful and informative.

61 The remark can be found in Newman's 'Sermon on the Theory of Developments in Religious Doctrine'. He qualifies his words with 'If I may so speak'. Not all will agree that he may.

REFERENCES

Anonymous (1886) *Socrates* (in Russian), Moscow: Sytin.

Adam, J. (1897) *Platonis Apologia Socratis*, 2nd edn, Cambridge: Cambridge University Press.

Adkins, A. W. H. (1960) *Merit and Responsibility: a study in Greek values*, Oxford: Clarendon Press.

Allen, R. E. (1980) *Socrates and Legal Obligation*, Minneapolis: University of Minnesota Press.

Amandry, P. (1950) *La Mantique apollinienne à Delphes*, Paris: Bibliothèque des Ecoles Françaises d'Athènes et de Rome.

Annas, J. (1981) *An Introduction to Plato's Republic*, Oxford: Oxford University Press.

Armleder, P. (1966) 'Death in Plato's *Apology*', *Classical Bulletin* 42: 46.

Arnim, H. von. (1923) *Xenophons Memorabilien und Apologie des Sokrates*, Copenhagen: Royal Danish Academy of Science.

Arnou, R. (1933) 'Platonisme des Pères', in *Dictionnaire de théologie catholique*, vol. XII, cols. 2258–395, Paris: Letouzey & Ané.

Baur, F. C. (1876) 'Das Christliche des Platonismus, oder Sokrates und Christus', in *Drei Abhandlungen zur Geschichte der Alten Philosophie und ihres Verhältnisses zum Christentum*, ed. E. Zeller, Leipzig: Fué's Verlag.

Benson, H. (1990) 'The priority of definition and the Socratic elenchus', *Oxford Studies in Ancient Philosophy* 8: 19–45.

Bergmann, J. (1936) 'Sokrates in der jüdischen Literatur', *Monatsschrift für Geschichte und Wissenschaft des Judentums* 80: 3–13.

Bernholdus, B. (1731) *De probitate Socratis sive modica sive nulla* (1711). Reprinted in F. J. Beyschlagius, *Sylloge variorum opusculorum*, vol. ii, item iv, Halae Suevorum: Mayer.

Bevan, E. (1920) *Hellenism and Christianity*, New York: George H. Doran.

Bolgar, R. R. (1973) *The Classical Heritage and its Beneficiaries*, Cambridge: Cambridge University Press.

Bostock, D. (1990) 'The interpretation of Plato's *Crito*', *Phronesis* 35: 1–20.

Brickhouse, T. C. and Smith, N. D. (1989) *Socrates on Trial*, Oxford: Clarendon Press.

Brookner, A. (1974) 'Jacques-Louis David: a personal interpretation', *Proceedings of the British Academy* 60: 155–71.

Brouwer, P. van L. (1838) *Apologia Socratis contra ... calumniam ... Forchhammeri*, Groningen: Van Boekeren.

Brown, P. (1967) *Augustine of Hippo*, London: Faber & Faber.

Brucker, J. (1767) *Historia critica philosophiae*, Lipsiae: Weidmann & Reich.

Burnet, J. (1924) *Plato's Euthyphro, Apology of Socrates and Crito*, Oxford: Oxford University Press.

Burnier, A. (1943) 'La Pensée de Kierkegaard', *Revue de théologie et de philosophie*, n.s. 311 101–13.

Burnyeat, M. (1990) *The Theaetetus of Plato*, Indianapolis: Hackett.

Calvert, B. (1987) 'Plato's *Crito* and Richard Kraut' in S. Panagiotou (ed.), *Justice, Law and Method in Plato and Aristotle*, Edmonton: Academic Publishing and Printing, 17–33.

Cameron, A. (1940) 'An epigram of the fifth century B.C.', *Harvard Theological Review* 33: 97–130.

Champier, S. (1516) *Symphonia Platonis cum Aristotele*, Parrhisiis: a Iodoco Badio.

Cooper, J. G. (1749) *The Life of Socrates* (4th edn 1771), London: J. Dodsley.

Coulter, James (1964) 'The relation of the *Apology of Socrates* to Gorgias' *Defence of Palamedes* and Plato's defence of Gorgianic rhetoric', *Harvard Studies in Classical Philology* 68: 269–303.

Courcelle, P. (1949) *Late Latin Writers and their Greek Sources* (Eng. tr. 1969), Cambridge, Massachusetts: Harvard University Press.

Crispus, J. B. (1594) *De ethnicis philosophis caute legendis*, Romae: Zanetti.

Curtius, E. R. (1973) *European Literature and the Latin Middle Ages*, London: Routledge & Kegan Paul.

Cuzin, J.-P. (1985) *Raphael: his life and works*, London: Alpine Fine Art Collections.

Deman, T. (1940) 'Socrate dans l'œuvre de saint Thomas d'Aquin', *Revue des sciences philosophiques et théologiques* 29: 177–205.

——(1942) *Le Témoignage d'Aristote sur Socrate*, Paris: Les Belles Lettres.

Dodds, E. R. (1951) *The Greeks and the Irrational*, Berkeley: University of California Press.

——(1965) *Pagan and Christian in an Age of Anxiety*, Cambridge: Cambridge University Press.

Dover, K. J. (1974) *Greek Popular Morality in the Time of Plato and Aristotle*, Oxford: Basil Blackwell.

Eberhard, A. (1772) *Neue Apologie des Socrates ...*, Berlin & Stettin: F. Nicolai.

Ehrenberg, V. (1973) *From Solon to Socrates*, 2nd edn, London: Methuen.

Encyclopaedia – Britannica (1815f.) *Encyclopaedia Britannica*, Edinburgh: Edinburgh University Press.

Encyclopaedia – Encyclopédie (1751f.) *Encyclopédie ou dictionnaire raisonné. Mis en ordre par M. Diderot . . . M. D'Alembert*, Paris: Briasson & c.

Encyclopaedia – Metropolitan (1845) *Encyclopaedia metropolitana*, vol. X: *History and Biography*; vol. 2. London: B. Fellowes & c.

Encyclopaedia – Penny (1833f.) *Penny Cyclopaedia, published by the Society for diffusion of useful knowledge*, London: Knight.

Encyclopaedia – Russian (1890f.) *Encyclopaedic Dictionary* (in Russian), St Petersburg: Brokgaus & Efron.

Encyclopaedia – Soviet (1937) *Great Soviet Encyclopaedia* (in Russian), Moscow: Gossudarstvenii Nauchnii Institut.

Erasmus, D. (1704) 'Disputatiuncula de taedio et tristitia Jesu . . .', in his vol. V, cols. 1265–92 of *Erasmi Opera*, Lugduni Batuvorum: Van der Aa.

Everson, S. (ed.) (forthcoming) *Companions to Ancient Thought 4: Ethics*, Cambridge: Cambridge University Press.

Ferguson, J. (1970) *Socrates: A Source Book*, London: Macmillan.

Ferrari, G. R. F. (1987) *Listening to the Cicadas*, Cambridge: Cambridge University Press.

Festugière, A. J. (1950–3) *La Révélation d'Hermès Trismégiste*, Paris: J. Gabalda.

Fontenrose, J. (1978) *The Delphic Oracle*, Berkeley: University of California Press.

Forchhammer, P. W. (1837) *Die Athener und Sokrates*, Berlin: Nicolaische Buchhandlung.

Gerhardt, C. I. (ed.) (1875–90) *G. W. Leibniz: die Philosophischen Schriften*, 7 vols., Berlin.

Gerold, J. J. (1658) *Socrates quem examini sistet*, Argentinae: J. Pickel.

Gill, C. (1973) 'The death of Socrates', *Classical Quarterly* 23: 25–9.

Gilson, E. (1955) *History of Christian Philosophy in the Middle Ages*, London: Sheed & Ward.

Gladigow, B. (1965) *Sophia und Kosmos*, Hildesheim: Olms.

Gombrich, E. H. J. (1972) *Symbolic Images: studies in the art of the Renaissance*, London: Phaidon.

Gomperz, T. (1905) *Greek Thinkers*, vol. 2, tr. G. G. Berry, London: Murray.

Goulburn, E. M. (1858) *Socrates: a lecture delivered to the Young Men's Christian Association in Exeter Hall*, London: Rivingtons.

Griffin, J. (1980) *Homer on Life and Death*, Oxford: Clarendon Press.

Griswold, C. (1986) *Self-knowledge in Plato's Phaedrus*, New Haven & London: Yale University Press.

Grote, G. (1865) *Plato, and the Other Companions of Socrates*, London: John Murray.

Guthrie, W. K. C. (1969) *A History of Greek Philosophy*, vol. 3, Cambridge: Cambridge University Press.

——(1971) *The Sophists*, Cambridge: Cambridge University Press. First published as Part I of *A History of Greek Philosophy*, vol. 3.

Gutman, H. B. (1941) 'The medieval content of Raphael's "School of Athens"', *Journal of the History of Ideas* 2: 120–9.

Hackforth, R. (1933) *The Composition of Plato's Apology*, Cambridge: Cambridge University Press.

Halm, C. (1863) *Rhetores latini minores*, Lipsiae: Teubner.

Hamann, J. G. (1967) *Hamann's 'Socratic memorabilia' [with] a translation and commentary by J. C. O'Flaherty*, Baltimore: Johns Hopkins Press.

Haran, M. (1985) *Medieval Thought from Antiquity to the Thirteenth Century*, London: Macmillan.

Harrison, A. R. W. (1968–71) *The Law of Athens*, 2 vols, Oxford: Clarendon Press.

Hegel, G. W. F. (1971) *Vorlesungen über die Geschichte der Philosophie*, in his *Werke*, vol. 18, Frankfurt am Main: Suhrkamp.

Heidegger, M. (1988) *Zu Platons Hohlengleichnis und Theätet*, in *Gesamtausgabe*, vol. 34, Frankfurt: Klostermann.

Herbst, J. (1720) *De Socratis daemonio*, Lipsiae: Litteris schedianis.

Hermes Trismegistus (1945f.) *Corpus Hermeticum*, Collection Budé, Paris: Les Belles Lettres.

Herzog, R. (1922) 'Das Delphische Orakel als ethischer Preisrichter', in Horneffer 1922: 149–70.

Highton, H. (1873) *Dean Stanley and Saint Socrates: the ethics of the philosopher and the philosophy of the divine*, London: Elliot Stock.

Horneffer, E. (1922) *Der junge Platon I: Sokrates und die Apologie*, Giessen: A. Töpelmann.

Hubbard, B. A. F. and Karnofsky, E. S. (1982) *Plato's Protagoras: a Socratic commentary*, London: Duckworth.

Ibbeken, G. C. (1735) *De Socrate mortem minus fortiter subeunte . . . disputabunt . . . et respondens D. G. Langreuter*, Lipsiae: I. C. Langenheimii.

Jones, R. and Penny, N. (1983) *Raphael*, New Haven: Yale University Press.

Jordan, W. (1990) *Ancient Concepts of Philosophy*, London: Routledge.

Kahn, C. (1988) 'On the relative dates of the *Gorgias* and the *Protagoras*', *Oxford Studies in Ancient Philosophy* 6: 69–102.

Kerferd, G. B. (1981) *The Sophistic Movement*, Cambridge: Cambridge University Press.

Kierkegaard, S. *The Concept of Irony, with constant reference to Socrates* (tr. L. M. Capel), London: Collins.

Kirk, G. S., Raven, J. E. and Schofield, M. (1983) *The Presocratic Philosophers*, 2nd edn, Cambridge: Cambridge University Press.

Klibansky, R. (1939) *The Continuity of the Platonic Tradition in the Middle Ages*, London: Warburg Institute.

Klosko, G. (1979) 'Towards a consistent interpretation of the *Protagoras*', *Archiv für Geschichte der Philosophie* 61: 125–42.

——(1983) 'Criteria of fallacy and sophistry for use in the analysis of Platonic dialogues', *Classical Quarterly* 33: 363–74.

Kraut, R. (1984) *Socrates and the State*, Princeton: Princeton University Press.

Kristeller, O. (1943) *The Philosophy of Marsilio Ficino*, Columbia Studies in Philosophy, New York: Columbia University Press.

——(1944) 'The scholastic background of Marsilius Ficino', *Traditio* 2: 259–318.

Lacey, A. R. (1971) 'Our knowledge of Socrates', in G. Vlastos (ed.), *The Philosophy of Socrates*, New York: Doubleday.

Lasaulx, E. von (1857) *Des Sokrates Leben, Lehre, und Tod nach den Zeugnissen der Alten dargestellt*, München: J. G. Cotta.

Latte, K. (1940) 'The coming of the Pythia', *Harvard Theological Review* 33: 9–18.

Ledger, G. R. (1989) *Re-counting Plato*, Oxford: Clarendon Press.

Lindenbaur, A. (1859) *Apologie des Christenthums gegen Uebergriffe der Philologie und Philosophie, oder des Sokrates Leben, Lehre und Tod . . .*, Augsburg: Kleinle.

Lloyd-Jones, P. H. J. (1971) *The Justice of Zeus*, Berkeley: University of California Press.

Lobeck, C. A. (1829) *Aglaophamus*, n.p.: Regiomontii Prussorum.

Luzac, J. (1796) *Oratio de Socrate cive*, Lugduni Batavorum: Hontzkoop.

MacDowell, D. M. (1978) *The Law in Classical Athens*, London: Thames & Hudson.

Malebranche, N. (1966) *Traité de morale* (1684), in *Œuvres de Malebranche*, vol. XI, 55–6.

Malkin, I. (1987) *Religion and Colonization in Ancient Greece*, Leyden: Brill.

Manetti, J. (1974) *Vita Socratis*, prima edizione . . . a cura di Mario Montuori, Firenze: Sansoni.

Manning, H. E. (1872) *The Daemonion of Socrates . . .*, London: Longman, Green.

Maravall, J. (1957) 'La estimación de Sócrate en la edad media española', *Revista de archivos, bibliotecas y museos* 63: 5–68.

Marcel, R. (1951) '"Saint" Socrate, patron de l'humanisme', *Revue Internationale de Philosophie* 5: 135–43.

Marmontel, J. F. (1785) *Bélisaire* (in Russian), Moscow: Novikoff.

——(1825) *Bélisaire*, London: Low.

Marrou, H. I. (1938–49) *Saint Augustin et la fin de la culture antique*, Paris: Bibliothèque des Écoles Françaises d'Athènes et de Rome, 145.

[Mauvillon, E.] (1777) 'Vom Genius des Sokrates', *Deutsches Museum* January–June 1777: 481–510.

Mentz, M. F. and Sommer, F. W. (1716) *Socrates nec officiosus maritus nec laudandus paterfamilias . . . exhibitus . . .*, Lipsiae: Titius.

Meyer, Thomas (1962) *Platons Apologie*, Stuttgart: Kohlhammer.

Migne, J.-P. (1844–90) *Patrologiae cursus completus . . . ser. Latina*, 221 vols. Paris.

——(1857–66) *Patrologiae cursus completus . . . ser. Graeca*, 162 vols. Paris.

Mikalson, J. D. (1983) *Athenian Popular Religion*, Chapel Hill: University of North Carolina Press.

Montaigne, M. de (c. 1930?) *Essais*, 3 vols. Paris: Nelson.

Montuori, M. (1981a) *De Socrate juste damnato: the rise of the Socratic problem in the eighteenth century*, London Studies in Classical Philology 7, Amsterdam: J. Gieben.

213

——(1981b) *Socrates: physiology of a myth*, tr. J M P. Langdale and M. Langdale, Amsterdam: J. Gieben.

Mosheim, J. (1733) *Systema intellectuale hujus universi* (Translation of R. Cudworth's *True Intellectual System of the Universe*, with notes), Lugduni Batavorum: Luchtmans.

Navin, L.E. and Katz, E. L. (1988) *Socrates: an annotated bibliography*, New York: Garland.

Nehamas, A. (1975–6) 'Confusing universals and particulars in Plato's early dialogues', *Review of Metaphysics* 29: 288–306.

Nelson, A. (1948) 'Über den Ursprung des lateinischen Terminus *Sortes, Sor*', *Eranos* 46: 161–4.

Noble, F. X. (1985) 'The declining knowledge of Greek in eighth and ninth century Papal Rome', *Byzantische Zeitschrift* 68: 56–62.

Nussbaum, M. (1980) 'Aristophanes and Socrates on learning practical wisdom', *Yale Classical Studies* 26: 43–97.

——(1986) *The Fragility of Goodness*, Cambridge: Cambridge University Press.

O'Brien, M. J. (1967) *The Socratic Paradoxes and the Greek Mind*, Chapel Hill: University of North Carolina Press.

O'Meara, D. J. (ed.) (1982) *Neo-Platonism and Christian Thought*, Norfolk, Virginia: International Society for Platonic Studies.

O'Meara, J. J. (1988) *Eriugena*, Oxford: Clarendon Press.

Orlov, E. N. (1897) *Socrates: his life and philosophical activity* (in Russian), St Petersburg: Obshchestvennaya Pol'zya.

Ostwald, M. (tr.) (1956) *Plato's Protagoras*, with introduction by G. Vlastos, New York: Bobbs-Merrill.

Owen, A. S. (1939) *Euripides: Ion*, Oxford: Clarendon Press.

Panagiotou, S. (1987a) 'Justified disobedience in the *Crito*?' in S. Panagiotou (ed.), *Justice, Law and Method in Plato and Aristotle*, Edmonton: Academic Publishing and Printing, 35–50.

——(1987b) 'Socrates' "defiance" in the *Apology*', *Apeiron* 20: 39–61.

Parke, H. W. (1967) *Greek Oracles*, London: Hutchinson.

Parke, H. W. and Wormell, D. E. W. (1956) *The Delphic Oracle*, 2 vols., Oxford: Basil Blackwell.

Patrizi, F. (1593) *Nova de universis philosophia*, Venetiis: R. Meiettus.

Patzer, A. (1985) *Bibliographica Socratica: die wissenschaftliche Literatur . . . von den Anfängen bis auf die neueste Zeit . . .*, Freiburg: Karl Alber.

Perosa, A. and Sparrow, J. (eds) (1979) *Renaissance Latin Verse: An Anthology*, London: Duckworth.

Pfeiffer, R. (1978) *History of Classical Scholarship from 1300 to 1850*, Oxford: Clarendon Press.

Putnam, H. (1975) 'The meaning of "meaning"', in his *Mind, Language and Reality: Philosophical Papers*, vol. 2, Cambridge: Cambridge University Press, 215–71.

Reeve, C. D. C. (1988) *Philosopher-Kings*, Princeton: Princeton University Press.

——(1989) *Socrates in the Apology*, Indianapolis: Hackett.

Renwick, J. (1967) 'Reconstruction and interpretation of the Belisarius affair', *Studies on Voltaire and the Eighteenth Century* 52: 171–222.

Rhodes, P. J. (1985) *What Alcibiades Did or What Happened to Him: an inaugural lecture*, Durham: University of Durham.

——(1986) *The Greek City States: a source book*, London: Croom Helm.

Richter, G. (1965) *Portraits of Greeks*, London: Phaidon.

Roser, D. (1936) *Erziehung und Führung. Versuch über Sokrates und Platon*, Stuttgart: Kohlhammer.

Ross, W. D. (1924) 'Socrates, Plato, and the Platonists', in his *Aristotle's Metaphysics*, 2 vols., Oxford: Clarendon Press, vol. 1, xxxiii-lxxvi.

Rousseau, J. J. (1762) *Emile: ou de l'Éducation*, Amsterdam: J. Néaulme.

——(1980) *Correspondance complète*, vol. 37, Oxford: Voltaire Foundation.

Ryle, G. (1966) *Plato's Progress*, Cambridge: Cambridge University Press.

Salmon, A. (1962) 'Le "Socrate" de David et le "Phédon" de Platon', *Revue belge de philosophie et de l'histoire* 40: 90–111.

Sandvoss, E. (1966) *Sokrates und Nietzsche*, Leiden: Brill.

Santas, G. X. (1964) 'The Socratic paradoxes', *Philosophical Review* 73: 147–64.

——(1979) *Socrates: philosophy in Plato's early dialogues*, London: Routledge.

Schmitt, C. B. (1966) 'Perennial philosophy: from Steuco to Leibniz', *Journal of the History of Ideas* 27: 505–32.

Schmitt, C. B., Skinner, Q. and Kessler, E. (eds) (1988) *The Cambridge History of Renaissance Philosophy*, Cambridge: Cambridge University Press.

Schofield, M. (1986) '*Euboulia* in the *Iliad*', *Classical Quarterly* 36: 5–31.

Schuhl, P. M. (1956) 'Montaigne et Socrate', *France–Grèce* 15.

Searle, J. (1967) 'Determinables and determinates', in P. Edwards (ed.), *The Encyclopedia of Philosophy*, London & New York: Macmillan, vol. 1, 357–9.

Silk, M. S. and Stern, J. P. (1981) *Nietzsche on Tragedy*, Cambridge: Cambridge University Press.

Sjliestrom, L. (1686) *Socrates philosophus . . . quod publico examini sistet . . .*, Holmiae: Eberdts.

Smith, E. (1740) *The Cure of Deism: in answer to 'Christianity as old as the creation'*, 3rd edn, London: J. Wyat.

Solovyov, V. (1853) *The Drama of Plato's Life*, 1935 reprint of Eng. tr. (1890), London: Nott.

Sprague, R. K. (ed.) (1972) *The Older Sophists*, Columbia, SC: University of South Carolina Press.

Spranger, E. (1938) 'Hegel über Sokrates', *Sitzungsberichte der preussischen Akademie der Wissenschaften: Philosophisch-historische Klasse*, 284–96.

Springer, A. (1883) 'Raffael's "Schule von Athen"', *Die gräphischen Künste* 5: 53–106.

Stahl, J. M. (1907) *Syntax des griechischen Verbums*, Heidelberg: Winter.

Stapfer, E. (1786) *De philosophia Socratis*, Bernae: ex officina typographica Illustr. Reipublicae.

Steenberghen, F. van (1966) *La Philosophie au XIIIe siècle*, Louvain: Publications Universitaires.

Stokes, M. C. (1971) *One and Many in Presocratic Philosophy*, Washington & Cambridge, MA: Center for Hellenic Studies.

——(1986) *Plato's Socratic Conversations*, London: Athlone Press.

Stone, I. F. (1988) *The Trial of Socrates*, London: Jonathan Cape.

Taylor, A. E. (1917) 'Plato's biography of Socrates', *Proceedings of the British Academy*, 93–132.

——(1933) *Socrates: the man and his thought*, London: Peter Davies.

——(1937) *Plato: the man and his work*, 4th edn, London: Methuen.

Taylor, C. C. W. (1976) *Plato: Protagoras*, Oxford: Clarendon Press.

Tigerstedt, E. N. (1974) *The Decline and Fall of the Neo-Platonic Interpretation of Plato*, Societas Scientiarum Fennica, commentationes.

Toole, H. (1973–4) Ἡ ἱστορικότης τῆς Πλατωνικῆς Ἀπολογίας', Ἐπιστημονικὴ Ἐπετηρὶς τῆς φιλοσοφικῆς Σχολῆς τοῦ Πανεπιστημίου Ἀθηνῶν 24: 383–96.

Velikanov, A. (1842) *Concerning the Reform Brought by Socrates into Philosophy* (in Russian), Odessa: V. Gorodskoi Tipografii.

Vlastos, G. (ed.) (1971) *The Philosophy of Socrates*, New York: Doubleday.

——(1983a) 'The Socratic elenchus', *Oxford Studies in Ancient Philosophy* 1: 27–58.

——(1983b) 'The historical Socrates and Athenian democracy', *Political Theory* 11: 495–516.

——(1985) 'Socrates' disavowal of knowledge', *Philosophical Quarterly* 35: 1–31.

——(1991) *Socrates: ironist and moral philosopher*, Cambridge: Cambridge University Press.

Walker, D. P. (1972) *The Ancient Theology*, London: Duckworth.

Wallis, R. T. (1972) *Neo-Platonism*, London: Duckworth.

Wilamowitz-Moellendorf, U. von (1920) *Platon*, vol. 2, 2nd edn, Berlin: Weidmann.

——(1931–2) *Der Glaube der Hellenen*, 2 vols., Berlin: Weidmann.

Wilson, A. M. (1972) *Diderot*, Oxford: Oxford University Press.

Wind, E. (1968) *Pagan Mysteries in the Renaissance*, 2nd edn, London: Faber & Faber.

Woodbury, L. (1973) 'Socrates and the daughter of Aristides', *Phoenix* 27: 7–25.

Woodruff, P. (1982) *Plato: Hippias Major*, Oxford: Oxford University Press.

Woozley, A. D. (1979) *Law and Obedience: the arguments of Plato's Crito*, London: Duckworth.

Yovchuk, M. T. et al. (1960) *Short Sketch of the History of Philosophy* (in Russian), Moscow: Izdatel'stvo Sotsial'no-ekonomicheskoi Literaturi.

Zeyl, D. (1980) 'Socrates and hedonism', *Phronesis* 25: 250–9.

INDEX LOCORUM

GENERAL INDEX

228